To Mother –
Mother's Day,

Gordon & Sharon

Six Came Flying

SIX CAME

New York

FLYING

Marquis MacSwiney
          of *Mashanaglass*

1972

ALFRED · A · KNOPF

TO MY WIFE

AND

TO ALL WHO LOVE

THE WILD ONES

Contents

*16 pages of photographs
will be found following page 114.*

Acknowledgments

Thanks are due to the United States Department of the Interior, Fish and Wildlife Service, for permission to reproduce Winston E. Banko's photograph of two cruising trumpeter swans; to David B. Marshall, Regional Refuge Biologist of the same Department, in Oregon, for sharpening my appreciation of the natural world around me and of the true values of conservation; to Dr. Janet Kear of the Wildfowl Trust, Slimbridge, Glos., England, for her constant guidance on many points and for her unfailing patience; to H. M. Swan Keeper, Mr. F. J. Turk, for information concerning the Thames mute swans; to Dr. P. J. K. Burton, the Natural History Museum, South Kensington, for reconstructing the bones of the wing from which the sketch on p. 174 was made; to Charles Harvard Gibbs-Smith of the Victoria and Albert Museum, for his enthusiasm and encouragement from the start, and for reading and correcting the proofs; to Antony Burton-Brown of the *Reader's Digest,* without whose guidance, expertise and help this book would not have been possible in its present form; to my daughter, who spent long and often uncomfortable hours getting the photographs that I wanted, and lastly, to the swans, Hans and Leda, who have brought great joy into my life.

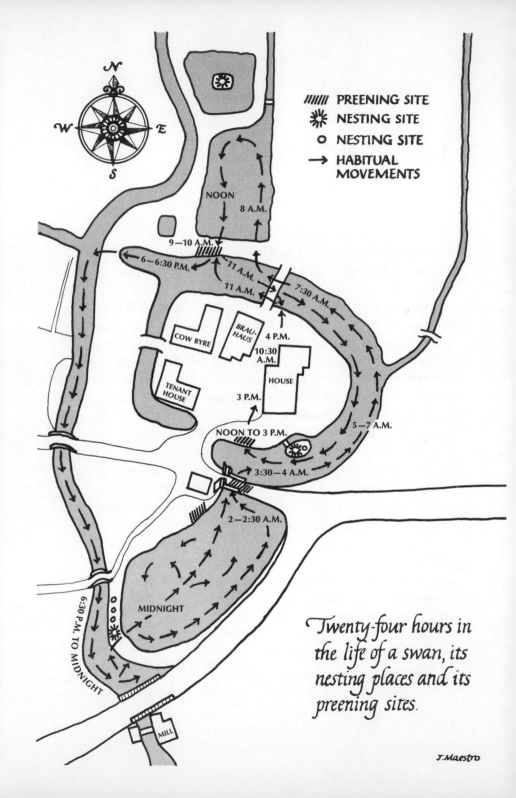

Twenty-four hours in the life of a swan, its nesting places and its preening sites.

Six Came Flying

The Swans Return

"WHAT IS IT, KATJA? WHAT IS IT, GIRL?" I SCREWED UP my eyes against the evening sun. Katja was trained as a gundog; she normally never gives tongue. But now, tense and quivering, she was sitting bolt upright by my side. I strained to see, following the direction of her gaze over the gardens, but my eyes and ears were no match for hers.

"Come on girl. Let's walk."

For the first time in her adult life, the word "walk" failed. The black labrador sat rooted to the ground while I stared at her dumbly. When she uttered another strange, sharp cry, half yelp, half bark, a thought flashed through my mind. It was February, the right time of year for the swans to come back. It *could* be the swans, far away in the distance. It could even be Hans and Leda, "our" swans, returning from their winter abroad, although I hardly dared hope. A little patience and I would soon know.

The domesticated pheasants, geese and ducks had been

3

fed, watered and tucked up for the night, safe against predators. Having finished our evening rounds, we had cut
across the main courtyard in front of the house, across the
moat, to begin our walk along the half-mile perimeter
track that skirted the park. A cock pheasant had got up
under my feet, protesting angrily at this monstrous inva-
sion of his privacy. Not a flicker from the dog. I had lingered a moment despite the raw wind blowing straight
across the flat plains of northern Germany from the frozen
wastes of Russia. It was the Humbold hour, peculiar to
our part of North Rhine Westphalia, that hour before
sunset when every detail stands out in relief in the crystal
air. The scene was familiar enough, with the great sweep
of meadow, dotted with huge, solitary copper beeches, the
small baroque chapel by the edge of the wood on my left,
the orchards and garden to my right. But in this curious,
romantic light, every twig stood out, etched against the
broad slashes of gold and pink in the sky. I had never seen
the park so transformed.

Then I heard it, in the far, far distance, and my heart
began to pound. Ckwich–whick–ckwich–whick, growing
steadily louder as I strained to see; the rhythmic, powerful,
unmistakable sound of swans in flight. My heart began to
pound harder. For five months I had been waiting for this
moment. Of course it could easily be another pair, but I
brushed the thought away impatiently. It *must* be Hans
and Leda.

Then I saw them coming straight toward us out of the
westering sun, low over the horizon. Like two chameleons,
they had borrowed the gold and the pink from the sky, so
that only part of their half-shadowed undersides remained
pure white. They approached majestically over the great
naked beeches; they were flying close together, the big cob

4

a little ahead of his pen, about a hundred feet up, their long necks stretched out ahead of their boat-shaped bodies. Hans and Leda? There was only one sure test, the test that had never failed.

"Oy—oy—oy," I called, using the old warwhoop that Hans knew so well. "Whoop—whoop—whoop—whoop." My voice broke the stillness of the enchanted moment, and I looked up anxiously as they passed overhead. To my joy, the big cob seemed to falter, to hesitate for a split second when he heard the warwhoop. Then he looked down.

The moment the cob looked down, I knew that it was Hans. I took to my heels, and sprinted the fifty-odd yards back to the house screaming at the top of my voice.

"The swans are back!" I shouted. "Hans and Leda! Coming in over the fishpond!" Without waiting for any reaction from the family, I dashed through the side door, into the corridor leading off the old kitchen. By the time I reached the foodstore, I was trembling with excitement, and fumbled clumsily for a few precious seconds with the lock. Grabbing a pannikin of maize from the bin, I rushed out again, and looked anxiously over the moat toward the fishpond.

"They must have landed by now!" I muttered anxiously to Katja, sitting patiently by my side. Various ducks, Canada geese and snow geese were idling about on the thick ice. Not a swan to be seen. According to my calculations, they should have made a great swinging half-circle over the fields behind the house before facing up into the wind, like aircraft banking for a final approach, and coming in to land on the fishpond. My spirits were sinking rapidly. After all, why should they come back? Why should they land? They were wild swans, free to come and go as they pleased. Yet ours was a very special relationship, which must be rare: as amateurs, we had managed to make real and personal friends of our feral swans, yet succeeded in preserving their natural independence and their free way of life. Five months before, in early autumn, they had grabbed their freedom in the way that we had both hoped and feared. They had vanished at dawn, heading for some river or swan colony we knew not where. Throughout the long, cold winter I had wearied the family like the Ancient Mariner, convinced that they would come back again: a conviction that blossoms afresh each year after their annual departure.

Then I saw them. Two pairs of black beady eyes, peeping suspiciously over the dike between the fishpond and the moat, followed by low long periscope necks. After pausing at the top for a short rest, they took a few shuffling steps, waggling their tails, and slithered clumsily down the near-side bank, landing with a bellyflop on the hard ice. Telling Katja to sit and stay, I began to call them softly, rattling the maize, using the gentle, coaxing call that I always used when offering food. They quickened their pace, slapping their big webbed feet on the ice, skidding like a couple of inexperienced skaters.

As I watched them marching toward me, lifting their heads up and down in greeting, I felt all my doubts drain away, replaced by a flood of thankful relief. As soon as they waddled into the courtyard, I moved quietly across to their feeding table, a manhole cover by the corner of the house, raised about four inches off the ground. Squatting on my heels beside it, I poured out a generous offering of maize, continuing to call softly.

"Come on, you two nitwits. Come and get it!"

Old habits die hard. When he was about twenty-five yards away, Hans began to flap his huge wings vigorously.

Ignoring the dog, he came straight for me, head down, neck outstretched into the attack. I raised an eyebrow as he slammed on the brakes two feet away from where I was crouching, and came unceremoniously to a halt. As though furious at my refusal to budge, he aimed a short, sharp stab at my sleeve with his beak.

"Stop it, Hans! Stop showing off!"

Honor satisfied, Hans and Leda attacked the maize. I watched them affectionately, noting with pleasure how both seemed in fine shape. We were together again. The year had begun at last.

We Acquire Some Ducks

TWELVE YEARS BEFORE, I HAD WALKED DOWN THE STEPS from the only surviving chapel of the ruined cathedral at Münster, with my wife Thaddäa on my arm.

As we walked down those few steps together, with the shell of the huge church behind us, we had to pause for a moment while friends and the press took their photographs. FASHION MAN WEDS read the caption that subsequently appeared below the picture in a London evening newspaper. It never occurred to the fashion man that he would ever become involved with swans, of that I am quite certain. At that moment he was absorbed in the scene about him, particularly in a little girl, his newly acquired daughter.

Walburga, a tall child for her eleven years, was blonde and had the fresh complexion that goes with it. In fact she was rather a tomboy, and I often used to ask her if *maybe perhaps* she wasn't a little boy in disguise. I knew from photographs that she greatly resembled her father, whom she had never seen, and who, for that matter, never saw her. He had been killed in Russia, on the eve of returning home to see his two-month-old daughter for the first time. As I looked at her in her red knitted cap, her gray coat and gaiters, I knew that acquiring me as a new father must be a disturbing experience, even though we had long since decided that we approved of each other.

I caught her eye several times during the luncheon that followed, and she grinned at me impishly. Wedding breakfasts are not the custom in Germany as they are in England and Ireland, but since she was hungrily tucking away the food, I felt no cause to worry. What was to happen had long been planned. She would go to stay with my new wife's brother and his family in Frankfurt, and go from there to a German boarding school. It would be hard for her in the beginning, leaving home for the first time, leaving the big old manor house with its spacious grounds, woods and farmland. It was her inheritance from her father, in which her mother had a life interest, the home where she had always lived, and to which she would eventually return.

As my new brother-in-law stressed in his speech, I was taking my wife back with me to England. Our families knew and approved, but this was less popular locally. When I went to buy Thaddäa (pronounced Taddeya) some flowers, the good lady in the shop told me quite seriously that the local people would not forgive me in a hurry. I was taking away the beautiful Baroness, *their* beautiful Baroness, from the Schloss. Nor was the florist the only one who had misgivings. The cook asked my wife if she really knew what she was doing.

"Foreigners are foreigners," she said in a worried tone, frowning heavily. "They're not the same as we are. Some don't even use knives and forks!" My wife assured her that yes, she knew quite well what she was doing and told her that she herself had taught me to use a knife and fork. But the cook was not consoled and went away shaking her head, muttering that she was sorry to hear it.

When my wife had moved into my minuscule bachelor flat in the West End of London, she settled down quickly. But there is an immense difference between living in a London flat, and living in a sizable house ringed by a moat full of water, with a private park and garden at your disposal, and with old and beautiful trees forming the backdrop. She never admitted it, but I think that she missed the tender greens of spring and the changing colors of autumn. No city park has the power to bring home these changes in the seasons in quite the same way. I know that she missed her roses too, because whenever she could she would go to Regent's Park, to the rose gardens in the inner circle there.

Those were happy days, and I was happier than I had ever been before. I had everything that I had ever wanted. I was happily married, living the sort of big-city life that I had always considered essential for my personal well-being. I was a member of London's "Top Twelve," as we were then called, by virtue of my designing for one of London's leading creative fashion houses. I was happy in my work, pursuing my chosen occupation.

The years can pass very quickly when the world is being good, and London was always good to us. My wife adored London, but spent most of the summer in Germany with her daughter. Perhaps I should say *our* daughter, because I have always regarded her as ours from the day of our marriage. My collection for the autumn and winter was always shown in July, and so I joined them as soon as the press shows were over at the end of that month. Indeed, it was on the morning of such a press show, during one of her visits to Germany, that our son Patrick was born.

We moved into a larger flat, but otherwise life continued much as before. Walburga was now at boarding school near Lake Constance, but came over to join us for Christmas and Easter; Thaddäa and Patrick went to Germany during the summer. One day it dawned on me that Walburga was coming to the end of her school days. If we were ever going to move to Germany, perhaps this should be the time. So far as my work was concerned, I had to be in London during certain critical months, but I could live in Timbuktu during the normal selling season.

One summer evening in 1962 we went for a walk on Primrose Hill. It was dusk by the time we had strolled to the top. Below us the hill sloped away to the London Zoo and to Regent's Park, while the rising, everchanging London skyline formed the glittering backdrop of the horizon on every side.

"I've been thinking," I said, as we looked down on the lamps of the park shedding little pools of light. "Don't you think we should go and live in Westphalia?"

She turned around, taken by surprise. When she smiled, I could sense immediately how happy the suggestion had made her. She looked away for a moment, thinking perhaps of the place that she had always regarded as home since her first marriage.

"Yes, it would be good if it could be done," she said very quietly. "There are many things that we should be looking after, as I know from my visits. Since we have been here in London, *viele kleine sachen* have crept in, that I don't care for. Last time I was there, strangers were wandering on the grounds, in the park, and they were *unhof-*

11

lich when I asked them what they thought they were doing. Yes, it would be a good thing." That settled it. A thousand things had to be done. There were endless discussions, arrangements to be made and decisions to be taken. It is no easy matter to uproot. Thaddäa went ahead of me with the boy, while I stayed back for business reasons which included arranging a new set-up at work. It was as though a dam had opened, and things began to happen fast.

But on the estate in Germany, things were also happening that had no bearing on our personal plans at that moment. Of the two self-contained farms on the estate, the more important is the Home Farm, for not only does the land partly surround the house, but the tenant lives immediately opposite, and has the use of all the outbuildings of the main house. No sooner had we finished moving in than the Home Farm tenant received an interesting offer elsewhere and decided to give up farming. We watched him go with regret; his father had had the tenancy before him, and we had hoped his son would carry on.

The search for a new tenant began at once. Our land agent agreed to help find us the right sort of person, and in due course found us Herr Balz, an admirable, experienced farmer with modern ideas. What was more, he had five children, one of them a boy almost exactly Patrick's age. While all this was going on, we began to look at the property with different eyes. Little by little we saw that there was much to be taken in hand. For example, it was obvious even to a city person like myself that the waterways were suffering from neglect. The big house stands on an island in the center of a roughly circular moat, with about six acres of ponds in addition. But dikes were broken, water levels were low, and every square inch of water was covered by a trefoil water plant that turned the whole liquid area into what looked like a solid mass. Along the banks, water iris and reed flourished like nobody's business; on one stretch of the moat, where an oak bridge had been destroyed after the war, the reeds stretched from one bank to the other.

In an effort to get some idea of the original plans, I poked around in the archives and unearthed old maps, and anything else that would give me the information that I wanted. Never one for half measures, I kept harping about the mess, since the problem was now uppermost in my mind.

"We've simply got to clean up the moat. But how?"

"I have no idea," Thaddäa replied with her usual calm. "I suppose that we could spray the green stuff with something. But if you are referring to the banks and to the bridge, we would have to get a contractor, which would cost a lot of money."

The new tenant was requesting all sorts of improvements, and there was simply no money available for luxuries. When I went out once more to study the jungle, it suddenly struck me that there was virtually no wild life about the place. When I had come from London to spend the summers with Thaddäa and the children, I had loved watching the ducks that the previous tenant had kept. He must have had at least fifty farm ducks of one sort and another. But now the water was depopulated, except for the little waterhens and some visiting flights of mallard. It must have been the ducks who had kept the waters clear of weeds. I dashed back into the house, bursting with pride at my momentous discovery.

"Duck, ducks, ducks and more ducks!" I shouted into the empty vastness of the hall. Thaddäa peered down from the top of the oval oak staircase. "What are you so excited about now?"

"Ducks," I shouted up the stairs. "Waterfowl to eat the ponds clean. And if they don't, we'll eat them!"

"Well, we could always give it a try," she replied, descending the staircase slowly. "We would have nothing to lose, as you say. I was thinking how nice it would be to have a pair of swans. There have always been swans here, and they look so lovely on the water. So you have your ducks and I'll have my swans, and we'll both be happy."

"Oh, yes, swans, by all means, you have swans."

I confess that my bubbling enthusiasm was ebbing fast, as the picture flashed into my mind of my rowing days at University College, Dublin, when we rowed in eights and fours on the river Liffey, and kept an anxious eye on the monster cob and his pen who nested on the bank near the weir, a little downstream from the Trinity College Boat Club. The cob used to wait for the boats to turn above the weir, a slow process with much "Touch her, stroke two" and similar instructions from the cox. As soon as the boat was in position, its bow heading upstream toward our home slip, the cob would emerge grandly from the bank. The moment the cox called "Backstops, ar-r-re you ready, paddle," the cob would begin to surge after the slim shaft of the boat. As soon as it was under way, he would launch himself into the air, heading straight for the cox's back.

I rowed at "stroke," three feet at most from the cox's back. From this position, let me assure you, a swan with obviously evil intent is an awesome sight, especially when flying straight at you at eye level. I derived no comfort from having a titch of a cox as my shield. The cob never hit the cox, but always swerved in the nick of time, turning away with a malicious glitter in his eye. I was so scared of that bird that I was heartily relieved when the Captain of the Boat Club put me in a four, rowing at "two" position;

this meant that I had a cox and two stalwarts between me and the swan.

"But where would we get swans?" I asked innocently, thinking of those evil, malicious eyes on the Liffey.

"I don't know. From England perhaps?"

I began to warm to the idea. It would be amusing to have English swans swimming about Westphalian waters. "Yes, I dare say I could buy a pair easily enough."

"Well, why don't you try next time you are in England," she suggested, and there we let the matter rest.

I kept putting off the business of the swans. I wanted to get a group of ducks going first, and I felt that the large birds could come later. The whole place was a frog's paradise at the time. I had never seen or heard so many frogs before: there were literally thousands, and anyone wishing to study the life cycle of the frog would have found a rich and rewarding field at his disposal. There was no escaping them, on the paths, among the reeds, on the courtyards in front of the house, even in the woods of the park. It was a favorite spot of the local people to idle away a Sunday afternoon, watching the frogs disport themselves. When the mating season was at its height, and during the long hot days of summer, the whole place croaked. Some had the strangest voices, full and wholly primitive. Others had a long rolling rattle. The majority just croaked, and even the surly pike, who occasionally surfaced to attack, could do little to reduce the staggering frog population. Little did they know that their days were numbered.

At the earliest opportunity I went in search of the right book.

Experience had taught me that there is always a "right" book for every subject: *How to Catch Trout, How to Rear Poultry, How to Stand on Your Head, How to Do It Your-*

self, and so on. As soon as I arrived in London, I headed for H. M. Stationery Office, then in Oxford Street, handed over my six shillings, and came away with *Ducks and Geese.*[1] I was wholly fascinated, because it offered pretty well everything I needed to know. It opened up untold vistas, suggesting limitless possibilities. The copy is now dog-eared and dirty; I still consult it frequently.

Immersed in *Ducks and Geese,* I began to make plans for the stocking of the waters. As I lay in bed in my hotel, I rolled the names around on my tongue: cayugas, pintails, kahki, campbells, Indian runners and the Lord knows what else, from shovellers to any other breed that you care to name. I studied the lot, before deciding that we might as well keep some ornamental waterfowl, as well as the more utilitarian species.

Bursting with this newly acquired knowledge, and full of my usual enthusiasm, I announced major plans the moment I returned to Germany. Only then did we discover that neither of us had the first idea how we should set about getting such stock there. England was the only place for me: so I wrote immediately to a well-known breeder in Suffolk, who kindly consented to let us have fertile eggs; it was kind of him, since he normally only sells adult birds. But alas! We fell foul of import regulations, and the permit to import the eggs was refused.

Time was slipping away, and nothing was getting done. But one day my wife and I were driving home from a horse show when I saw some splendidly fat white ducks in a field. I stopped the car, and we marched over to the farm house. The fact that they were Pekin ducks impressed me deeply because I thought them to be slightly exotic, they having come originally from China. Half an hour later I came back to the car, clutching a carton of thirty-five carefully wrapped duck eggs. "Well, darling," Thaddäa said as I started the engine, "all you have to do now is to get them hatched out." I could swear that I detected a note of quiet malice in her voice.

"Oh, nothing to it," I replied cheerfully.

My luck held. One of our tenants had a broody turkey, which she agreed to lend me so that I might start the great experiment. I confess that this was my first experience of a sitting turkey. In the past, my only relationship with the species had been at Christmas—I with knife in hand, the turkey very dead. It did not take me long to realize that without doubt this turkey was the most pernicious and stupid fowl that it had ever been my misfortune to encounter. She had vicious habits: hacking at my hands, walking into her food, spilling it all over the run that I had prepared and sometimes refusing to eat at all. But, to give her credit, she did her job efficiently, and soon we had twenty-seven plump and beautiful ducklings; hungry ducklings, hungry, I hoped, for weeds. I looked on those ducklings with a pride and a joy that I have never since felt. They opened the door to a whole new world.

Those birds must have been among the most carefully tended creatures in the whole world as they waddled around in their pen. Meantime, their "mother" was up to all sorts of tricks. She liked to get out of the pen, but could never get back in because she was too stupid to reverse the hop and the skip that got her out. She would vanish into the park, and come back at the oddest times. But she was first rate at keeping the brood warm at night, or dry when it rained, or safe when danger approached, assuming that she had not gone absent without leave. Eventually, her antics became so annoying, her wanton hackings so vicious, that we packed her off back to her owner as soon as the ducklings showed signs of changing from downy yellow to virgin white.

At first we fed them starter feed, the kind that one gives to chickens. Increasingly, however, we took an old piece of board and scraped up the trefoil water plant from the nearest pond. We filled bucket after bucket with this weed, and emptied it into the ducks' hipbath. This was an old-fashioned zinc affair, about six inches deep and three feet in diameter, which we had originally given them as their first swimming pool. They gobbled up all of the green stuff and literally asked for more.

When we let them out on the ponds, I knew that I had been right. I remember one particularly hot summer's day, when we were sitting out in front of the house, drinking our coffee after lunch. The ducks were on the moat, fifteen yards away beyond the rose bed. When I began to hold forth in my usual way, I noticed Walburga stretching her long legs and tossing her blonde hair. She gave her mother a sideways look that meant only one thing: he's off again.

"They are definitely making an impression on the weeds. We really must get some more next year."

No comment.

"The only trouble is that they look so farmyardy. We really must try to get some more decorative birds. Ones that *look* pretty."

"Oh yes, I agree," Thaddäa said. "Maybe now is the time to get the swans."

"Don't go near the swans!"

Y ES," I SAID, NOT FEELING TERRIBLY COMFORTABLE about the whole idea. Common fairness, however, demanded that if she wanted to have swans, she should have them. As though to underline this, to make me feel even less comfortable about the prospect of swans, my Pekin ducks came up onto the grass and marched through the rose beds onto the forecourt.

There is no equivalent in the English language that properly describes the German *Hof,* or *Hoof,* as one of my more eccentric Irish friends always insists on calling it. These large unpaved areas in front of castles, manor houses and farm houses alike, are most frequently surrounded by buildings on three sides. Ours is divided in two by a long curving lattice fence fronted by rhododendron and lilac, but this leaves an open view to the south where water and trees, chapel and open spaces delight the eye.

I still had a sense of wonderment at being here. A fleeting jay speeding with its dipping flight to the protection of the huge trees was just as noticeable to me as the fat waddling ducks in the foreground. The jay was on its way to join the community life in and around the trees where countless birds reside: rabbits, the occasional hare and pheasants live and feed under the canopy of sheltering branches.

"I know that the swans your grandmother used to keep came from Hagenbeck's Zoo in Hamburg. They were pretty big ones," Thaddäa was saying to Walburga. "The male was called Hans, and he had a wife whose name I don't remember. It was rather sad really. The wife was trampled to death by the cows on the back meadow and the child was starved to death by the father. They were stabled for the winter and he wouldn't let the unfortunate child eat. It was only discovered when it was too late."

I looked at my family with pleasure and pride and thought what a curious family it is. A family of two nationalities, wife and daughter German, father and son Irish. We speak English or German as the mood seizes us and sometimes mix the two. Not that my son and I are very pure Irish. We can claim German, French, Polish, English and Spanish-Brazilian as well as our native Irish, making it exceedingly difficult for us to be anti any particular race.

I looked around the island and tried to picture a swan gliding past on the moat, remote and silent, like swans that I had seen elsewhere. It was not very difficult to picture. Why, I reasoned, should my wife not have her swans just because I was afraid of them?

I had been scared ever since my early childhood. "Don't go near the swans, dear," my nurse Salmon used to say each time we went to feed the ducks on the pond in St. Stephen's Green in Dublin. "Don't go near the swans, dear, they bite!" An anxious hand would grab at mine. She never let me go near any animal, even Sam, my father's gundog, who was as gentle as a lamb. Salmon was afraid of everything that did not have a human shape. Because of this she taught me fear, and her daily education was to spoil much in my later life and to rob me of great enjoyments.

The Ireland of my extreme youth was the Ireland of "the troubles," as the constant Irish fight for independence was then known. My father was much involved, and had been interned in Ireland. His pro-Irish activities made him naturally suspect, and potentially dangerous to the British, so that when he got to Europe in 1919 and began making anti-British propaganda, his antagonists of that time had every reason not to like him. He was on his way back to Ireland when my mother received a tip-off that he would be arrested as soon as he reached England, which he had to pass through on his way home. It was even said that he would be shot. My mother sent him a telegram, telling him that the whole family was coming to join him "because of his mother's serious illness," so he remained on the continent and waited for us in Rome.

I was four years of age when this happened. Eager to keep the two oldest members of the household staff, my mother gave notice to nurse Salmon, and our cook, Ellen, was put in charge of me, while our house parlor maid, Elizabeth, took charge of my two sisters. With our gentle mother supervising this little flock, we moved to Italy. We ended up in the village of Olevano Romano, some forty kilometers outside Rome, which was built on a cliff high up in the mountains. In fact the whole village seemed to hang there in the heat, ready to slide down to the flat plain waiting below. My mother left us here and went to join our father in Rome. If he had to live abroad for a while,

Rome was the logical place. He had already spent sixteen years of his life at the Vatican, serving under three Popes, and had been created a hereditary Marquis by one of them, Pope Leo XIII. My father was a gay and remarkable man, a scholar and a historian who spoke ten languages fluently. When he came with my mother to visit us on weekends, I used to find him a little awe-inspiring. Apart from having to mind our manners and behavior, there was so much to be learned from him. Everything that he did, he did a little bit better than everyone else.

On the whole, however, it was an idyllic existence for children. We lived in a kind of heaven of olive groves, vineyards and as much liberty as was allowed to children of my generation. But if I was living in the sun and had got rid of the fearful Salmon, I had still not got rid of an attitude that came close to hers. Mules were now the objects to be warned against. "Don't go near the mules, boy. They kick and they bite!" Ellen would say. Mules and women were the main forms of transport; the mules carried the great panniers of grapes or olives or wood, while the women carried the huge pitchers of water taken from the village well. A heave, a swing, a little help from a neighbor, and the big copper vessels were up on the head. They were carried with amazing balance while the bearer walked nonchalantly along, knitting and gossiping, as though she were wearing no more than a light hat. The mules looked gentle enough as they stood parked in the sun and tied to the long wall of the nearby mill where the olive oil was made. They looked so sad and huge and innocent. But they certainly bit and they certainly kicked—with a well-aimed ferocity that I have seldom seen before or since.

I learned precious little about animals in Italy, except about lizards. They fascinated me. They would bask in the sun and sweep off at speed when I approached, or chase vertically up a wall where they would pause, gaze at me with unwinking eyes and palpitating sides, and then dash on about their business.

We were often warned about snakes. We saw them frequently either dead or alive, but usually dead. I remember those sad little cairns of stones beside the road, which covered the battered head; the long slender body would trail away from under them while the trickle of blood, already blackening in the hot white dust, attracted scores of flies.

Our one serious encounter with a live snake took place in a cool little valley where we used to go to gather wild cyclamens. Ellen stood on a stick and the stick came to life. So did Ellen! Suddenly she was airborne, and while she was still up on high, the snake made off as fast as it could. To this day I'm not sure if the sleeping snake or Ellen got the greater fright, but the incident made us cautious about where we placed our feet.

After three marvelous years in Italy, and a few months spent in Germany with our cousins, we returned to our house in Dublin. Peace had come to Ireland. The Irish Free State had been founded, the treaties signed and the civil war was over. My father wanted us home. Above all, he wanted me to be educated in Ireland, the country that had claimed him as its own; he had been born in France, educated there and had lived in Europe until he was over forty years of age—but his greatest longing had always been to go to live in the country of our origin.

I was not so happy about this. As a seven-year-old, I found my native heath cold and wet and different, and I longed for the heat and the sunshine of Italy. To add to my troubles, I had to begin my schooling in earnest and that didn't appeal to me in the least. My sisters and I were put

in the charge of an engaging governess who had the difficult task of making me work. Discipline was strict, in the
manner of continental children about fifty years ago, and
we had to endure long and frequently boring walks each
day, for the good of our health. Even these walks were
under the supervision of an adult.

On the other hand, we were fortunate in that we were
much exposed to the adult world. The cream of Irish intel-
lect found its way to my parents' dining table and drawing
rooms, and somebody interesting from home or abroad
would always seem to turn up at the house in Upper Fitz-
william Street. A child was to be seen and not heard. Small
fry were not expected to pipe up and to voice opinions in
the presence of Governor Generals, Foreign Ministers, the
President of the Free State, Professors, Papal Nuncios and
personages of that ilk, but expected to answer and answer
politely and intelligently when addressed. It was surprising
how quickly we learned the rules and how much we
learned by having to keep our mouths shut.

Naturally my sisters and I had our favorites. The gentle
and lovable Dr. Douglas Hyde, Gaelic scholar, founder of
the Gaelic League and later first President of the Irish
Republic, was one. He kept a white cockatoo that I ogled
with interest and kept well away from. He also owned a
splendid Model T Ford, with a gleaming brass radiator;
since my father loathed motor cars, Dr. Hyde often used to
come to collect my mother and take her for a drive. If I
happened to be about I was invited to join them. I was
allowed to drive that car along the road from the Gough
to the Phoenix monument in Dublin's Phoenix Park, and,
oddly enough, nearly ditched the car in front of the Vice-
regal Lodge, now known as *Arus an Ucterain.*

Another one of our more frequent visitors, one who

etched a permanent impression on my mind, was Dr. Oliver St. John Gogarty. A dapper, witty and brilliant man with a love of the classics, he was a surgeon, poet, aviator, horseman, scholar, politician, and also a senator of the Irish Free State. Senators were among those who were listed by the rebels to be shot on sight, and he was kidnaped on January 20, 1923 by those opposed to the Provisional Government. He was taken to a house by the Salmon Weir on the river Liffey, which did not suit the good Doctor at all. He decided to escape, and requested his captors to take him outside to relieve his bowels which, he said, had become loosened with fright. The captors eventually obliged. The moment he slipped outside, he flung his great coat over the heads of those accompanying him and dived into the Liffey. The river was in spate and icy cold; while swimming in the raging waters, he vowed to present a pair of swans to the goddess of the river if he reached the bank.

After a quarter of an hour, he landed safely. He kept his promise. On March 24, 1924, in the presence of his wife, his two sons, his daughter, W. T. Cosgrave, the President of the Irish Free State, W. B. Yeats and Mr. and Mrs. Lennox Robinson, the ceremony was performed.[2] Because of this I always associate swans with Gogarty.

Swans fascinated this gentleman. He and his friend Yeats enjoyed the classic story of Leda and the Swan as a favorite conversational theme. Moreover, Gogarty's first published book of poems was entitled *An Offering of Swans*. The swans he gave to the Liffey were placed on the waters at the weir below the Trinity College Boat Club, so that it is not beyond the realm of possibility that the cob who liked to chase the boats was the original Gogarty cob, since mute swans can attain ages of from forty to fifty years.

There is a tradition in Dublin that there were no swans on this river before that pair was placed on it and that the present-day flocks find their origin from them.

I loved my rowing even if my father did not. He held, not without some justification, that my studies were affected by the hours I spent on the river. In addition to rowing in the "four," I liked to go out alone in a scull and to feel the slim shaft of the boat slipping away under me at the completion of each stroke. Sculling is a bit like riding a bicycle. If the balance is not perfect, if one hand is raised above the other, the result can be an unexpected bath in the river. Apart from the pleasure I derived, I remember that I used to try to stimulate my own courage by going down to where the swan was. Sure enough, he came out and I went in. The rule was that the boat could not be left: one had to sit on the upturned bottom or right it if one was skillful enough. I was happy to sit on the bottom and happier still when I was rescued. The swan did nothing to me, but it kept cruising around with an evil look in its eye until the merciful moment of my delivery.

Fear can be vanquished even if the process is somewhat painful. I shall always remember from my Dublin days my horror whenever I saw a dray horse fall. At that time, horses were as common as lorries today, pulling milk floats, bakers' vans, laundry vans and, of course, coal drays. The coal drays always seemed overloaded, and accidents happened on the cobbled streets. A horse would come down, struggle to rise to its feet and, in the ensuing tangle, the helplessness of the animal was something that I could hardly watch. When I was a bit older, I made the interesting discovery that provided I could take an active part in raising the horse, my cowardice could be controlled.

"Don't go near the swans!"

Perhaps if I had to deal with swans every day, I argued, I would be able to manage. Of one thing I was quite sure: if we had to have swans, they must come from the Thames. It would be fun to look daily upon birds that had sailed with stately grace near Cookham or Windsor or further down near Hampton Court.

When I was in England that July, I drove with some friends to visit their son at Bradfield College. It was a beautiful warm day, humming with bees that were busy at their work, and we went on the river to try out the son's boat. This marvelous vessel had taken him about a year and a half to build and carried us gently on the waters. But what might have been an enjoyable trip was made hideous by the fishermen that lined the banks. Portable radios blared, each set to a different station and competing to drown each other. It was too much. When the boat had been pulled up onto dry land and stowed away, we fled to Pangbourne.

Here there were no disturbing radios and, at a tea-place opposite a lock, we settled down on a terrace to relax by the water's edge. We amused ourselves by feeding crumbs to a greedy fish that should surely have fallen into the creel of one of the musical fishermen upstream. After a while, we were joined by a swan. It came gliding up to us without making a ripple on the water. It sidled up, looking for food. We gave it bits of scone and we watched the lumps making their way down the long throat to the gizzard. It was a very peaceful swan, slim and exceedingly white. It was far enough away so that I could pitch it the pieces of food without letting it approach too near.

"That's the kind of swan I want," I said to myself. "Quiet and unaggressive. Just the sort of bird for me." Then it dawned on me that I was in exactly the right place to find out about buying a pair. The local riverside people, on the very banks of the Thames, would know all about buying and selling swans.

The proprietor of the place was taking his ease, enjoying a pipe as he sat with his back to the wall of the cafe. He looked far from busy so I approached him without any qualms about disturbing him.

"Good afternoon," I greeted him, standing so that I did not prevent the sun from getting at him. "I'm looking for a pair of swans and was wondering if you could help me."

He removed the pipe from his mouth and studied me for a moment. I believe that he was not quite sure if I was being serious. At any rate, he gave the matter lengthy thought.

"If I were going to buy a pair of Thames swans," he told me at last, "d'you know what I'd do?"

"No. What would you do?"

"I think I'd go to the Thames Conservancy Board. They're the people who have everything to do with the river." He scratched his chin with the hand that was holding his pipe, gazing without too much enthusiasm at a big boat full of trippers that was about to enter a lock. "Yes, I imagine that you'd be able to get your swans from the Board."

I thanked him politely. But as I drove back to London, a doubt began roaming around at the back of my mind. Did not all the swans on the Thames belong to H. M. the Queen? But what nonsense. My informant lived with the Thames lapping his doorstep, and must surely know. Or maybe the Thames Conservancy Board administered the swans for the Queen? What if the Thames Conservancy Board either did not want to sell me birds, or had no power to do so? I would just have to look for a breeder.

I telephoned the Board next day. To my relief the receptionist didn't think me a lunatic and the official she put me through to seemed to treat my inquiry as quite normal.

"I am sorry. If you wanted to know something about moorings, or locks, or permits to fish, or even floating corpses for that matter, it would be different. But the swans on the Thames belong either to Her Majesty the Queen or to one of the two City Livery companies that have a license to keep them on the river. I would suggest you get in touch with the Lord Chamberlain's office. But don't worry—you'll get your swans. God knows there are enough of them. Between ourselves, I should imagine that they'll be only too glad to get rid of them!"

Feeling like a runner near to the tape, I thanked him and hung up. Get rid of them indeed. Swans-a-plenty, it seemed, and to be given away, just to get rid of them! I had already had visions of writing out checks for respectable sums, and, indeed, was willing to do so. Now it seemed as if the swans were more or less flying into the bag.

Fingers trembling with excitement at the prospect of having to hunt no further, I dialed the office of the Lord Chancellor of England, only to be told that the principal law officer of the state did not deal with swans. Maybe I was looking for the Lord Chamberlain's office? That cut me down to size. I was somewhat abashed; as a former practicing barrister at the Dublin Bar, I ought to have known.

I tried the Lord Chamberlain's office. To whom did I wish to speak?

"I have no idea," I said, "but it's about swans."

"Will you hold the line a moment, please."

The pleasant voice that followed appeared to belong to

somebody who knew about swans, and I launched once more into the whole rigmarole of how I wanted a pair, about the Thames Conservancy Board and how I would be only too happy, of course, to come along with my checkbook.

"Well to begin with," the voice told me, "there would be no question of your having to buy the birds. All you have to do is write down the details that you have just given me and send them to us. Oh, by the way, how much water did you say you have?"

"A large pond, moats and a fishpond. I suppose about five or six acres of water in all."

There was what is often described as a pregnant pause.

"Well, that ought to do. Could you give an assurance that the swans would be happy?"

It was my turn to pause. "I can't say. I don't really know what makes a swan happy. For that matter, I don't know what a happy swan looks like, do you?"

"Can't say that I do," the voice replied with a chuckle. "Where are the swans to go to?"

"Westphalia."

"Oh!" During the lengthy pause that followed, my correspondent was obviously engaged in some rapid rethinking. "D'you mean to tell me that there are no swans there?"

"Yes, there are, but I want English swans." I was riding high, already visualizing the rapt expression of delight on my wife's face when I came home with a pair of Thames swans for our beloved moats and ponds.

"But why do you want English swans?"

A reasonable question, but a difficult one to answer. It is one of the curses of the telephone that it denies one the subtleties of facial expression.

"Well, I want to make a present of them."

"Don't go near the swans!"

There was a frozen, almost a pained silence at the other end of the line. When the voice returned, it was with a chiding note as it passed sentence. "I say, my dear sir, isn't it a bit much to ask Her Majesty to give you a pair of her swans so that you can give them as a present to somebody else?"

I humbly admitted that this seemed reasonable. The swans were receding rapidly into the land of dreams. His argument and point of view were valid. It would have been bad taste on my part to point out that I had come not to request largesse, but with the bona fide intention of purchasing, and secondly that the recipient was to be my wife. It seemed too late to say that.

"Oh, well," I sighed, "I don't suppose that you know where I could come by a pair of swans."

The voice became warm, even gay again. The reproof had been given and accepted. Honor had been upheld, the world was good once more.

"Why don't you go down to the Norfolk Broads. There are hundreds there which don't belong to anybody. All you have to do is to catch them."

"But do I sound like somebody who could catch a pair of swans?" A terrible vision passed through my mind of myself clutching the leg of a flailing swan, the two of us floundering about among the reeds and shallows of the Broads.

"Quite frankly you don't, but if you have no stomach for that sort of thing, you might get in touch with one of the City Livery companies, the Vintners or the Dyers, and get a pair from them. Good luck anyway. I hope that you get them."

So that was that. While I was disappointed that I had not got my swans, I was honestly pleased that the Queen's property had been so prettily and so honorably protected. Anyway, there were still the two Worshipful companies to turn to. And turn to one of them I did, as soon as I had replaced the telephone on its hook.

"It's about swans," I said, and was immediately put through to the secretary of the company. The charming gentleman listened patiently to my story, before he spoke. "Look, it really isn't that I want to be difficult or unfriendly, but I've got a meeting this afternoon and I'm in the middle of getting it ready. I'm so hard pressed just now that I'm starting to go round in circles. Would you please not fail to phone me tomorrow when we would have a few minutes to discuss this fully?"

I am ashamed to say that I never did telephone again. My London days were drawing to a close and I ran out of time. I returned to Westphalia without any swans in my baggage, just a little crestfallen. Next time I was in England I would try again.

I told my wife. I told her the whole story from beginning to end, feeling that I had failed her. She just laughed.

"Never mind," she said. "It's a pity about your English swans. But did you ever stop to think that you might have had just as much trouble importing them as you had with the duck eggs?"

"No, it never occurred to me. You may be right."

"Suppose that you *had* got the swans, suppose that they *arrived* at Düsseldorf Airport, and were then *turned back,* what would you have done?"

"Probably crept up the wall, but backward!"

⤶ *Six Came Flying*

A S A CHILD I ALWAYS WANTED TO SHARE THINGS: THE dreadful marshmallows that I could buy at six for a penny, or the bag of toffee or anything else. As time passed I wanted to share with others the joy I had experienced in a place. When I had to go to Paris in September 1963, I tried to induce my wife to come with me. I hoped that while I was choosing materials for the new spring–summer dress collection, she would enjoy the shops and life of the city.

I have no idea why, but one always expects Paris to be warm and gentle and friendly. During that autumn it was anything but warm and gentle. A cutting wind swept the streets from Faubourg to Faubourg; a slate-gray Seine drew its color from a leaden sky and fallen leaves swirled and eddied in the gardens of the Tuileries. Window shopping was strictly for the Spartans. Neither of us was sorry to leave Paris; neither of us had ever felt so cold in our lives. When we changed trains at Dortmund we discovered that although it was several degrees warmer in Germany, it was still remarkably cold.

Fortunately we had arranged to have "Jonathan," my wife's car, left at our local railway station. At about one o'clock in the morning, my wife swung the car off the road onto our entrance causeway at home—and we both gasped in wonder. In the long cold beams of the headlights, as they swept across the chapel pond, we caught a fleeting glimpse of floating, unfamiliar forms.

"I don't believe it," said my wife, "but I could have sworn that I saw swans."

"I thought so too. But we'll probably find that the ducks refused to go into their stable this evening and decided to spend the night on the water."

"You may be right but I don't think so. Let's have another look." She put the car into reverse, backing carefully so as to take the same angle across the water. Sure enough, gliding slowly toward us like a flotilla of ghostly boats came a group of swans. They came hesitantly but with supreme elegance, their heads moving up and down as they swam over to inspect us.

"Six," she said, "can you believe it? Not two, but six!" There was a fairy tale quality about the whole thing. If at that moment they had vanished before our eyes as suddenly as they had materialized, spirited away by the wave of a wand, we would have accepted it. The warmth of the centrally heated house, to which we had been looking forward for so long, was forgotten. We must have sat there for five minutes or more, wholly enchanted, staring at the swans, before Thaddäa started the engine again. Although we wanted to stay on, we were afraid that we might disturb them.

After all the talk, all the inquiries, the telephone calls

and the rest of it, six had come suddenly of their own accord, as though they were aware of the welcome that would await them. "It's really too good to be true," I said, pouring a liberal amount of whisky into two large glasses. We were so excited that we felt like dancing around the big dining room like a couple of schoolchildren, and might have done so if others hadn't been asleep in the house.

"But where do they come from?" Thaddäa kept asking. "They must belong to somebody. Did you see how they came to greet us? Maybe they are used to people!" Her eyes were literally shining with joy.

"I wonder how long they've been here. I wonder when they arrived."

"*Gott weiss.* We'll have to ask Patrick in the morning. Maybe he saw them come. But the important thing is that they should *stay!*"

"I'm sure that they will," I muttered, far from convinced myself.

Later, as I pulled the bedclothes over me, I still had a clear picture of those ethereal shapes, gliding silently toward us without disturbing the still water. But how, in the name of heavens, was I going to induce them to stay? At that moment I wanted nothing more in the world. I racked my brain but could not think of a single constructive idea.

"I'm sure that they'll stay," I announced once again in a loud voice that was without real conviction but full of hope. Whereupon my wife, ever the reasoning and practical member of the family with a tinge of the skeptic, pointed out that if they could come they could also go. It would be more probable that come the dawn, not a tail would be in sight.

I slept uneasily that night and had bad dreams of empty waters and of being attacked by dark green swans. I got up

35

earlier than usual, washed and dressed hastily, and dashed downstairs to find out the worst. I looked out of one of the windows in the hall and saw a fairyland of white grass and filigree trees covered in hoar frost. The forecourts looked cold and the ice covering the puddles glinted steel gray in the weak sun. A thin wisp of smoke rose upward from the chimney of the tenant's house, making the scene look colder and more wintry. The tenant himself was carrying a bucket, walking smartly from the direction of the cow-byre, from which I could hear the lowing of cattle. Over the trees of the grounds, wood pigeons were stirring, coming up above the tree tops and dropping back into them again. Not for the first time, I thought it was like a Breughel painting.

I looked at the moat in front of the house as I put on my coat. There wasn't a swan in sight. I felt a moment of something akin to panic. What if they were gone? I went out of doors and made for the chapel pond, where we had seen the birds in the headlights of the Volkswagen. Not a swan to be seen. I crossed the causeway to the public road, and went to the spot where we had first seen them. Unbelievable relief. All six were there; I ran back to the house. "The swans are still here," I shouted triumphantly as I rushed into the breakfast nook in the dining room, without bothering to take off my hat and coat. "Give me a slice of bread."

"Well, that's wonderful," she said, pouring me a cup of coffee. "Now you can sit down and have your breakfast. If they're there now, they'll still be there after breakfast."

For all her seeming calm, I do believe that my wife hurried with her breakfast. I gobbled mine, in my anxiety to get back to the pond. I cut a few thick slices of bread as she put on her rubber boots and her coat, then dressed as warmly as I could. When we got as far as the front steps, we saw that the swans had moved from the chapel pond to the moat. They must have followed me, swimming under the bridge near the chapel. We crossed the grass to the side of the moat and began to throw bits of bread to them.

My wife, in rapture, was smiling with pleasure as the beautiful creatures came closer and closer to where we stood. My feelings were mixed. They might be the most marvelous beings on earth, but they were still swans and, as such, to be regarded with great respect. I didn't like it at all when the big cob came up out of the water onto the grass; I put as much distance between us as I decently could without looking too much of a coward. Apart from my nurse's warning, I had read somewhere that swans are especially dangerous when they have young, and this was obviously a family. Nonetheless, I was determined to make the swans stay with us, although at that moment I hadn't the faintest glimmer of an idea as to how that could be achieved.

We soon ran out of bread. "What you'll have to do," Thaddäa said after we had stood looking at the swans for a long time, "is to go off and buy some maize. I remember that we used to feed the old swans maize."

Delighted to have the chance of doing something useful, I got into my car and drove off to the farmer's cooperative. I handed over 4 DM and emerged with ten pounds of yellow maize. I also managed to cadge some stale bread from a bakery.

"Feed them," I told myself as I sped back in triumph toward the house, "that's the way we'll keep them. Feed them until they burst. They'll stay because there's so much to eat!"

When I arrived laden with the goodies, she grabbed

them from me and began to feed them again, while I stood back at a respectable distance.

I knew that the father was called a cob, the mother a pen and that the young were cygnets, but beyond that I knew precisely nothing about swans. Three of the youngsters, I noticed, were of mixed gray and white plumage and the fourth, which always seemed to hang a little behind, was pure white except for a little gray on the top of the head. I also noticed that they approached us in a certain order: the cob, the pen, the three dark immatures, then a little gap, and finally the white youngster who was always a little more nervous than the others.

"Swan talk" now became the dominant topic of conversation. Over lunch, my wife kept urging me to do something positive about keeping the birds. It was all very well our standing there feeding them to excess, she argued. It might be a pleasant way to pass the time; it might even hold them for a while. But in the end they would be bound to fly away and we would have seen them go forever. After all I was a *man* and should be able to *do* something. I agreed that I was a man, but didn't really see what that had to do with it. What did *they* care about my being a man?

Afterward, we would find frequent excuses to go out of doors in order to find out if the swans were still there. Sometimes we would meet, quite by accident, bound on the same mission, each pretending to be busy with another errand. No one was fooled, and the swans feasted day after day.

The swans were now getting to know us. We had only to raise our voices a little and say, "Come, come," and there they were, eager and willing. They readily ate whatever we gave them in the way of bread and corn. But despite these regular handouts, they continued to regard me with about the same amount of mistrust as I regarded them. If I went too near, they would allow themselves a long reptilian hiss that seemed to have a note of warning in it. I would hastily retreat a yard or so and fling a handful of corn as a peace offering.

As the days passed, the swans stayed put, to our delight and pleasure. But we were making none of the progress that my wife hoped for. My great plans to secure them were as far away a week later as they had been the day after they had arrived. I could think of no way of getting them that would not endanger life and limb: *my* life and *my* limbs. Short of hurling myself into the water and grabbing each individual, I could see no prospect of making them captive, and this I was not prepared to do. The Papa swan was a strapping fellow. Come to that, I could see little difference between him and his brood.

This situation might have continued indefinitely if the ice had not begun to form. The ice begins as a skim on the water surface, a sudden steely calm that produces a gray glint in the late sun. It is easy enough to break this first ice with a long wooden pole, and the waterfowl will congregate around the ensuing hole and keep it open. But breaking a hole becomes less and less amusing every day. As the weather gets colder, the hole becomes smaller, although the ducks will have worked on it and widened it quite considerably by late afternoon. If it freezes hard for a few days running, then the breaking of the ice becomes little short of a Herculean task.

I viewed the ice that winter with mixed feelings. On the one hand it helped us to build a bridge across the moat to the meadows that we had been planning to build all summer. This was to replace the old bridge that had been deliberately destroyed after the war, when there was danger of looting from the Russian and Polish workers who had been coerced into working in Germany.

Herr Balz and I had made all sorts of plans; to drive the piles, which we had felled, into the bed of the moat—which is twenty-two meters across at that point—we had thought of building pontoons to serve as platforms from which to carry out the work. Which was fine except that we had never got around to building them. But as soon as the ice was thick and strong enough to bear considerable weight, Herr Balz and Herr Schütte, another tenant farmer, set to work aided by some casual farm workers. The whole plan of the bridge was drawn on the ice with the edge of an axe. When holes had been cut into the ice, the oak piles, about twelve feet long and over a foot in diameter, were lowered through the holes and literally screwed into the bed of the moat with rope and chain, while somebody hit the top of the pile with a sledgehammer. The pile was left with supports until the next day, by which time the ice had closed in to hold it upright in a vice-like grip. The job took a week but when it was finished we had the satisfaction of knowing that in the future the cattle could be moved quickly from byre to meadow without having to be driven through the main entrance gate and onto the public road.

But if the ice was a boon when it came to bridge building, it became little short of a curse as far as the swans were concerned, and we viewed our chances of holding them with some apprehension. We offered them water in Patrick's plastic baby bath, but they disdained this, preferring to wander off to the stream. It was true that they were coming readily for food but we were beginning to feel the strain of our constant searches for them. It was obvious that we were in for an exceptionally hard winter, and that the birds would not be able to get at any natural source of food. Our only remedy, we reasoned, was to intensify the feeding and to feed often during the day. But we knew that the birds might take off any day and that would be the last we would see of them.

At this point my wife took matters into her own hands. She reached for the telephone and made an appointment with Dr. Helmut Reichling, the director of the Münster Zoo. We drove to see him one Wednesday at his office; while we were eager to hear what he had to suggest, I have to admit that I was quietly hoping that I would not have to become involved too closely with the swans.

The first thing the director wanted to know was what sort they were. "Well, just white swans," I said stupidly. "Ah, but there is more than one kind of white swan," he explained. He questioned us more closely, but we were unable to answer, and so he went to his bookshelf and took down a large volume by Jean Delacour, of whom I had never heard, and asked us to identify the swans from Peter Scott's illustrations.

We felt rather ashamed of our complete lack of knowledge. When we pointed to the illustration of a mute swan, I think that he was disappointed. Dr. Reichling told us that the mute swan is quite a common kind of bird: did we really want to keep them? Oh yes, we wanted to keep them very much, we said, and once more felt a little bit ashamed at wanting to keep anything so ordinary. The kindly director went on to explain that in that case the whole thing was extremely easy. First, we would have to construct some sort of enclosure and drive the swans into it; there would be nothing to that. My heart began to sink. "It's all very well for you to say that," I thought to myself, "you know how to do that sort of thing!" He told us that once the swans were in the enclosure, he would send the zoo's expert to pinion them. As I had already revealed the almost bottomless depths of my ignorance, I decided that to show a little more wouldn't really matter. I asked him what pinioning meant. He explained that there are three ways of preventing a bird flying. One either cuts the flight feathers, which means that the bird cannot fly until it grows new ones, whereupon the whole thing has to be done again, or one cuts the extensor muscle, which is not always successful, or one cuts off the end joints, furthest from the body, of one wing. The last two operations render the bird permanently incapable of flight and are called "pinioning." The last method would be used on our swans.

We arranged that the expert should come on the following Monday, which gave me four days to get things ready for him. Apart from the question of keeping the swans for another four days under the prevailing weather conditions, there was the small matter of building the enclosure and getting them into it. As I drove home, I had visions of building the pen and the swans taking off the moment we tried to get them into it. I had other visions of the expert arriving and finding nothing to pinion.

Life on a farm tends to slow down during the winter months. The fields are still under their mantle of snow; all the animals are snugly indoors, the cows lying or standing on a deep litter of warm straw. The people who are working the farm are busy with indoor tasks, repairing and maintaining equipment, or doing odd jobs in between feeding the animals and themselves. I had little difficulty in organizing the building of a swan pen. Beloved old Stephen, the old chap who does the feeding, became my right-hand man.

We took five fencing posts from the pile that is always

kept handy and hacked out five holes in the deep frozen
rock-hard ground, behind the old *Brauhaus*.³ We placed
four of these about six feet apart, to form a measured
square. The fifth post was placed in the middle of the side
nearest the moat, which was about six yards from the bank.
When the earth had been packed down, I reckoned that
the enclosure would be strong enough to hold a herd of
cattle. We wired heavy gauge wire netting from post to
post, leaving a three-foot opening through which we could
drive the swans, and sufficient wire netting to close the gap
as soon as the swans were in. We then packed straw bales
all around the enclosure to a height of three feet, thus
making a windproof wall. As a final refinement, we drove
four bigheaded round wire nails into the fifth post so that
we could hook the wire netting on to it as soon as the swans
were in, thus making a kind of flexible gate. There was
no need for netting on top because the birds couldn't fly
away; they're a bit like a jumbo jet—they need a good long
run before they can become airborne.

The birds had learned, by this time, to come when
called, or when they heard the rattle of maize in the aluminum saucepan that I used for feeding them. I had also
discovered that they would readily come to a wild whooping call, which was useful when they were out of sight. So
I wasn't very worried about getting them to come. What I
was worried about was how to deal with them when they
arrived. It's one thing to lay down food and retreat, and
quite another to take the initiative and drive the big
birds. Who said that they wouldn't turn about and go into
the attack?

The Sunday afternoon was fine and clear. I stood beside
my pen and began to call. I called and I called and I called.
Not a swan in sight, anywhere. Not a long neck, not a

pointed tail. I began to whoop and I might as well have been baying at the moon. It was hopeless. I knew then that my worst fears had been realized, that the swans had gone. The expert would come the next day and there would be nothing for him to do. I stamped my feet in cold and frustration, and went on calling.

A stream cuts through our land, one of those nasty streams that are empty one moment and raging the next if it happens to rain heavily. It also serves as the demarcation line between the Home Farm and that of another tenant, Herr Wallmeyer, who rents quite a substantial part of our land. Herr Wallmeyer happened to be walking his bounds along the stream as I stood there calling my head off.

"Are you calling your swans?"

"I certainly am. Are they there by any chance?"

"All six are down on the stream. Wait a moment and I'll drive them over to you." Thaddäa had come to join me and we watched him get through the barbed wire cattle fence and slither down the bank to the stream. A minute passed, but nothing seemed to be happening. "He'll frighten them away," I groaned. "He'll frighten them off instead of driving them over here. How on earth is he going to get them and himself across the stream?"

For some reason it never occurred to me that the stream might also be frozen over, but a few minutes later a swan's head and long neck materialized over the near bank. This was quickly followed by another and then another until we could see all six, with Herr Wallmeyer bringing up the rear.

The drive was agonizingly slow. It is one of the signs of the townsman, like myself, that he is always in a hurry—everything has to be done at speed. The countryman is different—everything has to be done in its own time. The townsman is inclined to look down his nose on the low countryman; the countryman to regard the city fellow with a certain twinkle of genuine amusement. But the countryman moves slowly because he knows his business; when dealing with animals, he knows that it is wiser to move slowly and never to look directly at them. Animals, as a rule, move slowly unless there is danger. Attacking creatures move fast, into the kill.

While I danced with impatience, our neighbor worked the birds ahead of him, hissing through his teeth. Sometimes he talked to them gently. When they broke out to left or right he let them go, then gathered them in again always with the same rhythm. When they moved faster, he moved faster, but he never put obvious pressure on them. They marched in their habitual order, over the rough grass, over a portion of the frozen fishpond, over the dike and finally onto the moat. As soon as they heard me rattling the maize they began to hurry. I moved backward slowly, getting nearer to the enclosure with each cautious step. They climbed the bank and a minute later were making for the opening in the wall of straw. As soon as I saw that, I began to strew grain right in the opening.

"This is going to be a piece of cake," I told Thaddäa cockily. Immediately a mild panic seized the swans, and they began to break formation and to head in every direction.

"Close in on them. Close in on them slowly," shouted our neighbor.

We did as we were told. The birds began to mill about as we moved in. A swan that feels itself threatened can turn very quickly on dry land. It pivots on a foot, and raising its wings as it hisses, holds its head high, its tail sweeping the ground. One of the young ones did just that,

45

and headed straight for me. I felt a surge of excitement, a sudden desire to move out of its way, when a voice said, "Raise your arms and make for it." I obeyed automatically. To my astonishment it worked like a dream. When the bird turned and went back to the others, I felt as though I had won a great victory.

We were doing all right. The six swans were bunching together and we drove them very slowly through the opening. As soon as they were in we whipped the length of wire net across the entrance, hooked it onto the nails and the swans were ours. I looked at Thaddäa triumphantly. We had our swans and if all went well the following day, we would have them for as long as they lived. Secure in this thought, we piled the last straw bales against the opening and settled down to feeding and admiring our capture. We looked at them then as if we had never seen them before.

We spent the remainder of the day coming and going to the swan pen. The birds greeted us with little whickering sounds and didn't seem to be in the least bit aggressive or put out by the morning's excitement. They ate whatever we gave them, flopped down on the straw and seemed to be quite content. As we went to bed that night, we heard the wind howling as it scythed across the flat Westphalian plain. We thought of our six swans safe behind their wall of straw. Yet for all the joy and satisfaction at having captured them, I began to wonder if we were doing the right thing.

The day of the operation dawned cold and clear. The wind had dropped and every expelled breath of air turned into a jet of vapor. When I went to look at the captives, they greeted me with their little whicker and lifted their heads. They seemed to have spent a reasonable night because none of them looked as if it were suffering, or half dead, or anything drastic like that. They readily accepted the food that I had brought. I was beginning to grow quite fond of them in the pen. I stayed much longer than I should have done, which meant that I arrived at breakfast about half an hour late.

As I watched my wife drive off to collect the expert from Münster, I wondered how I was going to feel when the whole thing was over. The problem was no longer one of how to keep the swans with us, but of how to deal with them. I collected some more bread and wandered over to the enclosure. Resting my elbows on the top of one of the straw bales, I contemplated our captives once more, as I flung little bits of bread to them.

Thaddäa returned at about eleven o'clock with the expert, Herr Emmerich. "Do you know, I've never been here before," he said gravely as we shook hands. "If you don't mind I'd like to have a look around before I get to work. The job doesn't take very long, you know."

There was something very reassuring about his approach. As we wandered around together, he looked at the stretches of water, or what would normally be water, on which the swans would live. We had the distinct impression that he was summing up the situation, and ourselves along with it. "Plenty of water, grass, water plants. In fact I wish I could take some of that green stuff home to the zoo for the waterfowl there." He commented with enthusiasm on the great weeping willow trees whose foliage literally drips into the water. As we turned away from the last pond, he looked at me and said slowly and precisely, "Yes, I think that swans would be happy here." I smiled, thinking of Her Britannic Majesty's loyal subject who had first made me think about the happiness of swans.

It remains a matter of pride to this day that Herr Emmerich was so complimentary about the enclosure that old Stephen and I had built. He leaned on the topmost bale and looked down at the swans over the wall of straw. Six glittering pairs of eyes looked back at him. They studied him with their heads cocked on one side, in the charming way that swans have when they are looking at something above them.

"I'll need some place indoors to work. And some sort of table. Is that possible?"

Fortunately we had built the enclosure just outside the old *Brauhaus,* where there was an unused stable. It took only a few minutes for Herr Balz and me to rig up a temporary table just inside the door, using four bales of straw for the base and an old door for the top.

"A good place to keep the swans," Herr Emmerich commented. "It's very important to keep them indoors, so that the intense cold does not get at the wounds." I watched him as he unpacked his surgical instruments, which consisted of a wooden mallet, two irons of an ordinary wood plane, a huge folding knife (to call it a penknife would be to insult it), a bottle of some disinfectant and a hank of fine pure linen thread.

"Would you like to help by holding the swans during the operation?" That threw me. I had no intention of putting a hand on the swans. Had I not learned at a very early stage in my life that a swan can break a man's leg with a blow of its wing? If anybody was going to end up with a broken leg, I wasn't going to be the one.

"Maybe Herr Balz would be best at catching and holding them . . ." I suggested. "Perhaps I could open and close the pen for him?"

If my wife thought the less of me for my cowardice, she never told me. She very probably made allowance for my

city-bred fears which were as foreign to her as her under-
standing of animals was to me. We watched Herr Balz
catch up and carry in the first cygnet, and I did my little
trick with the opening and closing of the gate. When he
came back within a surprisingly short time, I followed him
as he carried in the second cygnet, because he told me that
it was interesting to see how Herr Emmerich prepared it.

Herr Emmerich was standing beside his makeshift table
on which all the tools of the trade were laid out. As the

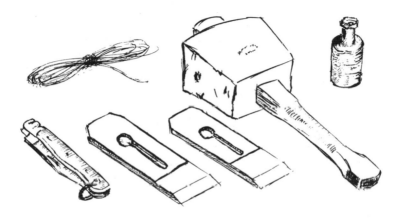

young swan was brought to him, he gently pulled the left
wing into a stretched position and bound the linen thread
around and around the portion above that which was to
be dealt with. He made a kind of binding band about half
an inch deep. When he had done this, he reached for the
mallet and one of the irons . . . as I beat a hasty retreat for
the outside world. I couldn't bear the idea of seeing the job
done. I had watched the behavior of the cygnet; the poor
thing had been so quiet and helpless that I came away with
a feeling of shame.

As I stood by my splendid pen, I began to wrestle anew

with the problem that had been worrying me since the previous evening. Were we doing right in robbing these creatures of their ability to fly? Had we the right, just because we wanted to have swans, to treat them in such a way that they would *never again* be able to take to the air? Standing next to my wife in the biting cold, I looked down on the parent birds; he so proud and powerful and she so elegant. I thought of how they had led their young of the previous year into a situation from which there was no longer any escape. They had come to us seeking open water and safety, flying before the menace of the winter, and they had flown into a life-long trap. I felt an acute sense of betrayal on our part. If we operated on the proud cob and his pen, *never again* would they be able to wing their way across the heavens. They would be earthbound like their children, until the day that they died. Worse still, they would *never again* be perfect and whole and completely beautiful as they were that moment in the pen. I thought about this as the third and fourth cygnets were successively carried in to have the operation performed on them, and I hated every moment of it.

You may consider me a sentimental fool and a romantic, and you may think the less of me for it, but the combination of the words *never* and *again* produced in me an inward shudder. I looked at my wife and it seemed to me from the expression on her face that her thoughts must be running along the same lines.

"Darling," I said rather shamefacedly, "I don't think that the parents should be pinioned. If we leave them alone, they'll surely stay with the children. If they fly away, we'd still have the children. Four swans ought to be enough."

"I think that you're right," she said reflectively.

"Of course it's up to you. In a manner of speaking, they're your swans."

She hesitated a second, looking at me with her level brown eyes, a little frown on her forehead. "Let's leave the parents. We'll take the chance."

I went in to tell Herr Emmerich of our decision. "I think that you are right," he told us. "Why don't we cut the flight feathers of the old ones so that they remain here until the next moult. Then if you decide to let them fly when the new feathers grow, they'll be as free as a breeze. If you come with me," he added, "I'll show you how it's done."

This time I had no qualms about looking on, and so I followed him inside while Herr Balz fetched the cob. He spread the wing and reached for the knife. "Look. Here are the big feathers at the end of the wing, the flight feathers. The knife has to be razor sharp so as not to drag and maybe hurt the bird. If I cut these feathers on one wing only, the bird will become unbalanced, because this wing will no longer exert the same lift as the unaffected wing, so the bird won't be able to fly. Now watch!" With one deft and practiced movement that seemed very easy, he cut through the quills of the last six feathers at the tip of the wing; a speedy and completely painless operation. The same was done to the pen, and a few moments later the work was finished.

I had learned two things that morning. I had learned that the swans were not as fearsome as they seemed, and I had learned from Herr Emmerich and Herr Balz's whole approach how easy it seemed to be to handle the creatures, provided one was both gentle and thoughtful of *their* comfort; two lessons that I knew that I must take to heart if ever I was to deal with them myself. Meanwhile, inside the *Brauhaus*, warm and on straw, away from the wind, parents and children settled down quietly to await events, well looked after and probably indoors for the first time in their lives.

I no longer felt guilty about the swans.

The Swan Man

WE CHERISHED THOSE SWANS. WE WERE A LITTLE BIT mad about them. We spent a great deal of time with them not only because we were anxious about how they were doing after the operation, but also because we wanted to enjoy them. I liked to go into the stable and look at the birds. They were extraordinary to me, much more than six swans. Like children in a fairy story, we had wished for swans and the wish had been granted. All the old Celtic blood boiled to the surface, and if the birds had turned into swan-maidens, I guess I would have more or less taken it in my stride.

They didn't do anything remarkable. They remained six swans, and six swans that were doing rather well at that. As far as we could see without picking them up and looking at them—and my enthusiasm didn't go that far—the wounds of the cygnets were healing nicely. Certainly no blood was to be seen on the flanks of the pinioned sides. All of the birds were alert and glad to see whoever came to them.

53

They had a pretty regular stream of visitors bearing gifts of food. The Balz children would visit them, as did old Stephen, to whom all animals are infinitely preferable than human beings. Even Herr Balz would drop in to have a word with them. Like everyone else, he would say that he had just stopped by to see if the swans were all right. This steady stream of visitors, coming at irregular times of the day, made the birds accept humans. As all of these humans, whether young or old, brought food or came to talk, the swans became increasingly trustful with the passage of time. They would come up to the wooden side of the old stable, uttering little snorts and lifting their heads as soon as anyone entered the passage to look over the low wall of the loose box.

Outside, the temperature had risen sharply during the two weeks that we had kept the birds inside and the ice had melted away. We had been told that it would take a fortnight for the wounds to heal fully, after which, if it became warm enough outside, we could release the birds onto the moat. One sunny morning we decided the moment had come, and we opened all doors with a flourish. It took the swans a little while to realize what was going on, but when they did, they came out fast. They marched out in line and passed the spot where we had built the capturing enclosure, which old Stephen had since demolished, and made speedily for the water.

"They *are* beautiful," I murmured admiringly as they passed us without so much as a glance in our direction.

The very first thing that they did was to wash themselves thoroughly. When they had done that to their satisfaction, they made off under the new oak bridge in the general direction of the chapel pond, with the cob swimming proudly in the lead. We dashed to the other side of the island and watched the procession as it rounded the bend. We were full of a sense of proud proprietorship and we stood there like idiots, bread in hand, waiting for the swans to come up to the bank on which we stood.

They swam rather grandly up to us as though they were conferring an enormous favor, and accepted our offerings. They snapped up the particles of bread, backed away, hissed, came forward again, circled each other and watched expectantly, waiting to see where the next bit of bread would land and who of them would get it.

"Come Hans," said my wife to the cob, "come Hans."

"Hans?" I said. "And where did you get that from?"

"The old swan used to be called Hans, and this one is going to be called the same," she announced casually. "And the wife is going to be called Leda."

"But Leda was a woman, not a swan," I objected. "It was Zeus who took the form of the swan."

"I know that much too, but she's going to be called Leda just the same. Anyway, you can't deny that she's female, can you?"

The oracle had spoken, and as far as I was concerned it sounded all right. It made quite a rhythmic combination. "Now, what about the others?" I asked, only to be told that that would be considered later. But somehow or other, we never did get around to naming the children.

It soon got about that the swans were out on the water. Strangers and neighbors began to come along with stale bread. This was also to the advantage of the Pekin ducks, still active, but somewhat overshadowed by the glamorous swans, for they too got their share of the handouts from the townspeople. Feeding the swans on the dike leading to our entrance gate became a local vogue; the swans were on a good wicket. Because they were now getting their food both naturally and in handouts, we fell into the habit of feeding them with maize at regular times of the day. I instituted the morning feed after our breakfast, the after-lunch-coffee-time feed and a final feed at about five o'clock in the afternoon, at about the time that the domestic ducks presented themselves on the forecourt of the "back house," the annex built onto the north gable of the manor house. I called them if they were in sight, or whooped if they were nowhere to be seen. Then I put the food on the grass and retreated to watch them from a safe distance. I still wasn't keen on getting too near to them.

They learned to answer these calls very quickly, until in time it was only necessary to call from the front doorstep for all six to come along. Swans have remarkable hearing and even more remarkable eyesight. What was highly satisfying was the fact that if we called from the house the birds would leave their admirers by the entrance gate.

One blustery day when the west wind was playing with the fallen leaves, whirling them in little eddies over the grass, I was rather later than usual with the after-lunch feed. As I opened the hall door, I took an instinctive step backward. Standing patiently at the base of the four steps leading up to the house was the whole company of swans. As I made my appearance, they greeted me with little whickerings and lifted chins.[4] I threw them their maize and rushed to call my wife, so that she could join me in watching them from my study window.

Coming to the house became a habit. Regular, plentiful feeding and nonaggression on the part of any human being made them trustful. They had not only accepted the situation in which they found themselves but were creating new routines of their own. This was just as well, because the number of the fairweather friends who came to feed them on the dike began to dwindle as the days became colder.

Toward the end of December the bitter wind began to whistle across Europe from the east again. The temperature dropped sharply and the ice, at first no more than a thin crust everywhere, began to thicken quickly, until it was impossible to hold it open for the waterfowl. The swans became a problem. It was a problem that had to be solved quickly and food alone could not dispose of it.

"You'll have to get them indoors," my wife urged me. "It's just no good having them outside. The swans were always brought indoors here when we had them years ago."

I heartily agreed. But there was nowhere to put them. Workmen had begun to tear down the brick partitions inside the *Brauhaus* and so their stable had gone. "We can't very well keep them with the cattle, and the horse stable is full of animals, so where do we put the wretched things?" There seemed to be no way out of our difficulties.

"Let's talk to Herr Balz."

"Let's do that."

Very considerable changes were being made within the old *Brauhaus,* a fine Dutch-style building. Now that the brick partitions had gone, the ground floor was as it had been built about seven hundred years before. Modern pig sties planned for the ground floor were to be built in such a way as not to damage the fabric of the ancient interior.

Above the ground floor, the structure dates from the seventeenth century. The plan was to install a grain-drying unit in the area immediately under the vast roof, with grain storage on the second floor, and milling and mixing rooms on the first floor. But here the planners ran into snags. Great oak beams support the floors of the second and top stories; three hundred years of bearing loads had made them sag seriously. The surveyors shook their heads, produced their slide rules and calculated that the loading planned for these beams, when a harvest was in, would bring the whole building down. The experts agreed that there was no solution and that the plans for the upper floors would have to be abandoned in toto.

A born nosy poke, I had studied the building, because old buildings interest me and because, as a designer, I have long had a particular way of approaching problems. "Impossible" happens to be one of the words that tend to irritate me. Also, we wanted to use that building very much. Twenty thousand two hundred and fifty square feet of floor space was more than we could afford to lose despite the opinion of any expert. I examined the building with a fresh eye. We had seven pillars down the center of the ground floor, which were the center supports for the vaulting. Made of brick, they supported a first floor of brick that was as solid and massive as any wall. Looking at the sagging beams that formed the basis of the second floor, a thought struck me. If the sag could be jacked up and wooden pillars placed vertically underneath, directly over the dead center of the massive brick pillars on the ground floor, the weight on each individual cross beam could be halved.

We called in Herr Schröder, the local carpenter, an expert in half-timbered buildings. He took one look at the huge sagging cross beams, and shook his head when I suggested the use of jacks. A few days later he arrived with his men. They cut their timber to exact measurements and levered the new wooden pillars into position. It took them two days. The massive oaken beams, tough and elastic, were literally straightened out and new floors laid on them. Everything worked out as he hoped that it would, and today each floor is in full use. Not an inch of space is wasted, be it under the roof where the grain-drying units are, on the second floor where the grain is stored, or on the first floor where a modern electric mill supplies flour to a mixer, where the animal feed is balanced before being blown to storage hoppers in the pig sties and cow byre.

Herr Balz came over after dinner for a council of war in the study. When he had settled his short strong figure into an armchair, we got to work on the problem of where to put the swans for the winter. There was no room anywhere, he told us glumly. Since the building work inside the *Brauhaus* had started, he was at a loss as to where to put some of his own animals. Then it suddenly occurred to him—the old pig sties, between the *Brauhaus* and the cow byre. The building had long fallen into disrepair; the cost of putting it in order was too high, and it was scheduled to come down.

"Those sties are not going to be used for anything. All you need for the swans is a shelter. The sties could be made comfortable with straw and that should provide enough warmth, and they are big enough to let the animals move about freely. Also, there is plenty of light and no danger of them becoming stable-blind."

What he said made sense, forcing us to bow to his wisdom. It was the first time that I had ever heard of "stable-blindness" and I asked him if animals really did get blind if the stable was too dark. He told me that it could happen, although it didn't necessarily mean that animals contracting it would become permanently blind.

Next morning I went out and had a look at the old pig sties. The roof leaked in more than one place and several panes of glass were missing, but the half-timbered walls seemed to be sound enough. To add to the attraction, there were brick floors and a row of fine stone feeding troughs that ran the length of the division of each separate sty.

59

There was also a piped supply of water in one corner. Old Stephen got to work and by early afternoon the largest of the pig sties was ready for immediate occupation. Although we had no intention of using it just then, we wanted to feel it was ready as soon as the need should arise.

With the ponds and the moat frozen over, the family of swans had removed itself to the stream and mill pond. There is always plenty of natural food to be found there and it is a favorite place of visiting wild ducks. The pond is partly silted up and there is much foodstuff to be had in the ooze and reeds. Because both stream and pond are lower than any of the other water areas, and also sheltered by high banks and the trees of the grounds, it requires a very great drop in temperature before the water freezes. Secure in the knowledge that they could not fly away, I was all for leaving the swans there as long as it was practicable. It made for less trouble than keeping them stabled. Moreover, they appeared at their new place by the house doorstep at each regular feeding time, treking across grass or ice to be on time.

But one wickedly cold Saturday night, the eve of the second Sunday in Advent, the thermometer dropped to 1 degree below zero. Even the stream froze. Driving back from church at about eleven o'clock on the Sunday morning, we saw the swans on the mill pond. We stopped the car and got out to have a look: they were ominously still, never once changing their position as we looked down on them.

"I don't like it. They seem to be frozen in," Thaddäa said anxiously.

I didn't like the look of them either. They were sitting together in a strange little group. We called to them and they turned their heads to look at us, but didn't make any other attempt to move. With my usual sense of the dramatic, I had immediate visions of their legs being frozen into the ice and my having to free them. I wasn't in the least bit keen to be put to the test.

We drove home quickly. As soon as I got out of the car, I went into the house, changed completely and put on my rubber boots. My wife took a look at me as I came down, and I could see from the expression on her face exactly what she was going to say. Breakfast first.

"No, I must find out if they're really frozen in."

I walked past the chapel pond toward the mill pond, swinging the bag of maize that I had filled hastily before setting out. I kept telling myself that this idea of their being frozen into the ice was probably a stupid one. But if it wasn't, and if I had to rescue them, I was distinctly dubious about my ability to do that. I was afraid, but oddly enough, not for my person. It occurred to me that since I lacked experience, I might injure them through sheer clumsiness and lack of knowledge.

When I arrived on the scene, the swans were still in the same position. They seemed glad to see me, greeting me with much chin-lifting, but they did not attempt to get to their feet. When I went near to them there was a good deal of hissing. I decided to try a ruse, and threw some maize on the ice, just out of reach of their long necks. I tried to coax them by talking to them. But they didn't move an inch, and I began to feel quite desperate. I threw a little more maize in front of the cob. Success. After a struggle he got to his feet with a tiny tearing sound. After that each member of the family followed suit, each leaving behind it an oval of soft breast feathers that had held it to the ice.

They could no longer be left at liberty unless we wanted to risk the same sort of thing happening. I decided that I had no alternative but to bring them onto the main fore-court as quickly as possible and get them into the sty that was ready and waiting to receive them.

Eventually I managed to coax them up onto the dike. But it was a painfully slow process. It was cold enough to freeze running water, an east wind was blowing and I was hungry. I thought of my family having breakfast in the warmth of the house and began to smell coffee. Although considering myself a fool for not having taken my wife's advice, I obstinately stuck to the job. At least the swans were moving in the right direction, even though they seemed to be very tired. They were following the cob who came after me as I walked backward, dropping a grain of maize at a time. If I left them they would certainly go back to the mill pond and I would have to start all over again. No breakfast was worth that.

"Come on good swans, stupid swans, idiot swans." When politeness failed to stir them, I began to call them some fancy names that are unprintable. At least my language helped to keep me warm, even if it produced no great re-sults. It certainly didn't offend the birds in the least. Al-though we were moving along the path that skirts the chapel pond, the progress was still erratic in the extreme. Every now and again one of the birds would take it into its head that the solution to all of its problems lay on the chapel pond. The others would start to follow suit, or try to turn back along the route that we had just covered so laboriously. When we eventually came level with the chapel and had only a comparatively short distance left to go, Hans walked onto the grass by the big lone pine that stands there and flopped down in tired and final protest. This was the signal for a general demoralization. Swans began to move off in every direction to flop down too.

Swearing like a trooper, I rounded them up into a group again; but Hans had had enough. He slipped past me and headed back to the stream. I had no option but to let him go. Better to get five birds into the sty, than go chasing the cob all over the landscape and lose the lot.

By this time I was not only cold and hungry, but a bit bad-tempered in the bargain. My patience was wearing thin. I decided to drive from behind instead of to coax. I drove them relentlessly. They were pretty close to exhaustion and flopped down for frequent rests. Brutally, I made them move on, suspecting that the more exhausted they were the better I would be able to control them and get them into the sty. Luckily this proved to be right; in no time at all they were sinking down gratefully on the thick bed of straw, while I threw food into one stone trough and poured water into another. Hans could wait. If he didn't know what was good for him then he could do without it a little longer.

When I went in for my breakfast, my wife and son were deeply impressed by my performance and looked after me as if I were one of our precious swans. Warmed by the coffee and the central heating and a decent breakfast, I went out in search of Hans once more. I was better humored this time, and felt quite the hero.

When the stream froze, it had been running strongly. The ripples of movement had been arrested and the ice was a different color—a kind of bottle-green. I arrived to find Hans trying to drink this. So convinced was he that if he tried long enough he could get something to drink that every time I got him up onto the dike beside me, he would rush off and make a fresh attempt. It was rather pathetic, but in the end I got so fed up that I drove him in front of me as relentlessly as I had driven his wife and children.

The poor old fellow was dead beat by the time I got him into the sty. But after helping himself to a long drink of water, he settled down with his family.

During that first winter we came to know the swans well. We tended them ourselves. We carried food and water, visited them in between mealtimes and talked to them, inventing anything that would make us use our voices. This was quite deliberate, because animals feel secure if one speaks to them. An animal's enemies are silent and stalking when on the hunt. A gentle voice, the clatter of a bucket, even a pitchfork, has a pleasant ring if it becomes part of the routine.

Although they seemed happy enough, they were always making efforts to get out into the open. There was a little door, about two feet square, in the wall, which led out into what had once been a run for piglets, long since dismantled. We had hidden this door behind a straw bale, but they got wise to this. One day they managed to open it while I was actually looking at them. I was so surprised that I rushed into the sty, closed the door and packed a straw bale in front of it. When I got out of that sty again, unscathed, it suddenly dawned on me what had happened. During the prompt action, I had pushed a couple of the swans to one side without batting an eyelid. They had done *nothing* to me except to get out of my way fast. It was the turning point. I knew then that my whole relationship with the swans had changed. My fears were groundless.

The swans made many attempts to get out through that door and frequently succeeded. Once they knew where it was, they actually pushed the straw bales out of the way in order to get at it. They liked to hightail it for the chapel pond as soon as they got out, but their tracks in the snow soon gave the game away. I would round them up and drive them home. The return to the sty invariably ended up with little whimpering protests that stopped as soon as I produced some food.

Now that the barrier of fear had been broken, my curiosity began to assert itself and I started to study the birds seriously. I believe that the quick darting movement of Hans' snake-like neck started me off. As I made to throw him a bit of bread, he would suddenly shoot his neck in my direction, aiming for my hand in a most disconcerting way. This is a movement that everybody knows; in common with many people, I had regarded it as a form of attack. Now I wondered. I risked holding the piece of bread and let him take it from my hand. It didn't always work. Sometimes he missed the bread and grabbed the hand. I quickly learned to my cost that the upper part of the beak is rough, like a rasp, so I took to wearing a glove. It was a tough, horsehide glove, but it soon roughened about the thumb by Hans' grasping beak.

It is well to sound a warning here, without further ado. According to Jean Delacour, "Very *tame* male swans attack animals and people readily, striking heavy blows with their powerful wings; they can be dangerous to *children*." [5] The italics are mine. It is advice that should not be ignored by people more confident of themselves than I was.

I went to England at the end of December and stayed there for a month. Thaddäa had to tend the swans on her own, with old Stephen cleaning out the sty as usual. She had a time of it. The cold intensified and the waterpipe in the stable froze, so that every drop of water had to be lugged across from the house. Soon the water in the stone drinking trough froze into a solid block of rather dirty ice.

The block became larger each day, as a fresh supply of water was added at each feeding time, and froze before the birds had finished drinking it.

When the ice reached the top of the trough, she had to pour scalding water around its edges to free it, before Stephen could remove it with a crowbar. The hot water gave her an idea: when a new ice block began to form, she brought hot water for the swans to drink. Poured on top of the ice, it cooled quickly and they were quite happy to drink the tepid stuff. My own feelings were mixed on reading those letters; I was sorry not to be there to help, yet glad to be away from the cold.

Thaddäa had her hands full. She was running not only her household but the swans' household as well. We fed them over two hundredweight of maize alone before that winter was over, as well as a mixture of wheat, oats, barley and rye. We gave them whatever green vegetables we could lay hands on, chopped fine and mixed with grated raw turnips and carrots. We were also always on the scrounge for spoiled and waste bread.

Fortunately the swans were still something of a sensation, even if the visitors could no longer feed them by the entrance gate. My wife organized all of the local shopkeepers and everyone pitched in to collect. By the time that she had finished with everyone, if either of us went into one or other of the two nearby towns, bakers or grocers or café proprietors would reach under the counter and produce an offering. One café that serves light meals at lunchtime went so far as to collect the leftovers from their customers' plates. Soon the birds were eating cake, buttered bread and chicken vol-au-vent with equal impartiality and all mixed up together. They seemed to thrive on it so we fed them this curious mixture without a qualm.[6]

I collected a new name in the process. When I went into the café to have a cup of morning coffee one day, I heard the young assistant yell to the proprietress, "Frau Eschaus, the swan man is here. Is there anything for him?"

Another of our contributors was Frau Müller, the tenant of the local railway station's café. She had a soft spot in her heart for the swans; whenever I called in for a packet of cigarettes, she would ask me how the swans were faring. There were always railway workers, or farmhands, or people from the town drinking their Isenbeck beer or *Schnapps,* or even "father and son," which is a small glass of strong juniper berry gin chased down by a small glass of beer, asking all sorts of questions about the birds' size and weight and whether swans are as vicious as they seem to be.

The enthusiasm that people in general had for the swans never ceased to astonish me. We loved the thoughtfulness of all of those shopkeepers. The only disadvantage of this admirable system was that the shopkeepers would become quite annoyed if we didn't happen to come in regularly. We both learned to put on what we fondly believed to be penitent faces when we were reproached.

One day I was going into the station café to buy my Lucky Strikes when a window was flung open. "Are you the swan man?" a gruff female voice demanded.

"Well, yes I am," I replied uncertainly, for some reason or other expecting vulgar abuse.

"Then wait!" the voice commanded.

I stood in the cold, wondering what it was all about and at the same time slightly amused. The window panes were of frosted glass and the window opened in such a way that I could see nothing. After a while an arm, which I could only see up to its elbow, shot out of the window, dangling a bag full of stale bread. I reached out to take the bread, but the moment I started to thank the owner of the arm, the window was slammed shut in my face.

As I drove home, my imagination began to work overtime. I knew that the arm belonged to an old woman, so I had to dismiss regretfully the thought that it might belong to a glamorous swan-maiden caring for her sisters. I am sure that I was unfair, but a picture began to form in my mind of an embittered old dame, a loathing benefactor of the feathered world, with a face like a turnip. Every time I went for my cigarettes the owner of the arm repeated the trick as soon as I approached the station building. The window would open and the arm would shoot out, dangling a paper bag full of stale bread. The voice would rap out "For the swans," in a tone that was anything but friendly, and the window would be pulled quickly shut again. The owner of the voice remains an enigma to this day.

During my stay in London I managed to get some reading done in public libraries. If I couldn't get the practice, I could at least learn the theory and acquaint myself with the literature concerning the birds. I learned, for instance, that the mute swan, *Cygnus olor* (Gamelin), is one of the two species that breed in northern and middle Eurasia, the other being the whooper swan, *Cygnus columbianus bewikii* (Yarrell), which breeds only in northern Eurasia. The mute swan is described by Delacour as a "heavy, powerful bird . . . undoubtedly the handsomest of all Swans, as their proportions and posturing are far more harmonious than any other species." [7] The species is widely scattered and most people in Europe know it. It is easily identified because, alone among the pure white swans, it has a prominent knob at the base of the beak, while the others

68

are smooth-billed. The beak itself is a pinkish-orange bordered with black, which also borders the nostrils. As a general rule, the feet are black. The neck is long and tends to be thick. The tail is long and rather pointed. The female or pen tends to be smaller than the male or cob.

I also learned that Hans and Leda's tail-wagging and foot-drying [8] were very characteristic of this species, likewise the arching of the wings when they were swimming. They ruffle their neck feathers when angry or when showing aggression, and also arch their wings. As I had already observed, they tend to swim with one foot only, except when annoyed. They then use both and move over the water with a surging and rather jerky motion, causing a considerable "bow" wave as both feet apply the power. Although sociable and inclined to become tame, they can be exceedingly aggressive, especially during the breeding season or when defending or establishing their territory— a piece of information that I thought might bode no good for the future, no matter how friendly they might seem to be at the present.[9]

As their English name implies, they are quieter and their calls are less loud than those of other species. They snort, utter a sound like "nuck" and also grunt, but they employ shriller notes and a sharp little whickering note of command to the cygnets. The cygnets have little piping voices. However, the most common form of utterance is a sharp hiss.[10]

I returned to Germany feeling terribly knowledgeable and definitely one up on my wife. The birds were still in the sty. Since they hadn't had a bath for weeks, they were no longer pure white but a dirty gray. Notwithstanding, they were in fine condition and had not become any thinner. Constant repetition had made the parents associate themselves with their names. Thaddäa had talked to them a lot in my absence, so that I naturally fell into the practice when I began to relieve her with the work.

I was determined to find out as much as I could about the individual birds while I had the chance of seeing them daily. From my reading in England, I was certain that there would be marked differences in behavior between the cob and the pen. I might be an amateur, but I had a pair of eyes in my head, I told myself. Disappointingly, nothing tremendous was noticeable. The cob was stronger, the obvious boss and the least timid of the birds; the pen was more delicate in build, very much gentler and rather shy. But as far as behavior was concerned, there was little to distinguish between them. So I concentrated on learning all I could about their recognizable physical differences, with the idea in mind that by the time I was done, it would be quite impossible for me to mistake one for the other if I saw either on its own. This learning to distinguish was far more important than it seems when it is baldly stated. I planned to study the birds; I reasoned that instant recognition would greatly facilitate attributing specific behavior to the sex of the bird observed.

I also learned that the swan's sharp and rather formidable hiss is nothing to be afraid of. All six seemed to hiss when they were disturbed, or maybe a bit uncertain or even scared, depending on the situation. When scared, they would stand up rather high on their legs; with the tail sweeping the ground and the wings spread, they would make a sort of ballet dancer's turn while hissing at the same time. They most frequently did this if I came up suddenly behind them. They would swing about to face me, not with the intention of *doing* anything, or even of menacing me, but simply because they didn't like anybody coming up on them from behind. When this sort of thing happened, they might dart the odd quick blow of the beak. Since it was never followed up by any sort of aggression, I concluded that this darting motion of the neck was more of a warning than anything else.

I also watched Thaddäa, who has an extraordinary way with all animals. I have never ceased to be fascinated when I watch her with them, whether it's a cow or a horse or a dog or a swan. I believe that it has something to do with the expressive way that she uses her hands and the quiet deepness of her voice. In those days, I studied her almost as carefully as I studied the swans in the sty, trying to get at her secret.

I have not got this sureness that she has, although I do get on well with elephants. I have always loved elephants, and oddly enough, the big beasts seem to know this. I remember a circus party given by the late Atwater Kent, the radio manufacturer and inventor, at his magnificent residence in the Bel Air estate in Hollywood. The party took place on his terrace; I was standing well to the back, leaning against a stone balustrade, watching Miss Gene Tierney, who was exquisitely dressed in a confection of white *broderie Anglaise,* when suddenly a heavy hand was placed on my shoulder, a hand that made little snuffling sounds. I looked up at the long gray arm, straight into the bloodshot eyes of a cow elephant.

I very much wanted to meet Miss Tierney. Alas, there were others of the same mind; besides which, I had contracted a nasty dose of impetigo on my face, which made me self-conscious. So I contented myself instead with making friends with the cow elephant. Delightful and gentle though she was, I couldn't help feeling she was no real substitute.

Elephants have fascinated me since my early childhood and I always wanted to own one when I grew up. The wish to own an elephant was born the day my youngest cousin, my younger sister and myself, nobly aided by a splendid rocking horse, played circuses over the sleeping head of King Ferdinand of Bulgaria, who happened to be staying at my uncle's place in Hessen at the same time as we were. We had been warned to keep quiet during the royal afternoon nap, and chose a room to play in with the belief that he could not hear us. Through some miscalculation we chose the room directly above his head.

We had to make a public and profound apology, under the vigilant eyes of mothers and uncles and aunts, as well as more sympathetic older sisters and cousins. The King was gracious; when we had done with this painful business, he gathered us around his armchair to tell us about his two elephants. I think that he had been given these animals by the King of Siam, the same King from whom my father had once received an enviable order which entitled him to sixteen wives. Anyway, he told us how fond he was of his elephants, and of how, when he reigned from Sofia, he would steal a few moments to visit them and file their toenails. For some reason this piece of information engraved itself indelibly on my mind.

I never did make the grade of having an elephant as a pet, but I do have a number of elephant friends in various zoos, who touchingly pay me the compliment of recognizing me when I visit them, or at least pretending that they do. But except for the elephants, I never had a way with animals until I got to know the swans. We noticed that the swans' *family* had a distinct superiority order. Hans was the boss and Leda came after him. Lower down in the pecking order, the three gray cygnets pecked each other about equally, but all of them pecked the one Polish cygnet. We had noticed when the swans were at large, before the big freeze, that this one Polish cygnet always kept its distance from the general family group. So strongly was this in evidence that we had decided that this one must be slightly older than the other cygnets, and possibly only a hanger-on who was not related at all. In fact, I now knew that its color was a phase known as "Polish," or, properly called, *C. immutabilis* by Yarrell.[11] Birds of this color are distinguished by fleshy gray feet and are white instead of gray from birth. They remain white as immatures, instead of wearing the mixed gray and white plumage of the normal immature swan.

It seemed as though that winter would never come to an end. But one morning we woke up and heard a long eerie sighing. The great day had come, and the thaw was setting in. Winter was giving way to approaching spring.

After breakfast we went out to feed the swans. On our way, we stood on the new oak bridge and looked down on the ice. Long, creeping splits were clearly to be seen and a thin sheet of water was already beginning to cover the top of the ice cap. It was a beginning, but the ice was up to three feet thick in some places, and we knew that it would be a while yet before we could let the swans out. The birds were well aware of what was going on. They were restless and came eagerly to greet us, as though they wanted to tell us to let them out right away.

At night the sounds of the thaw were different in the still air. As the ice cap died, a thousand little sounds could clearly be heard. There were uncanny little whisperings and whinings, snaps and crackles which punctuated the gradual formation of the great rifts and cracks that announced themselves with a boom or a long thin

"Whe—e e e," like the noise made by a bullet passing overhead.

By day we could see that the ice was going at the edges with myriad little holes in it, for all the world like those chocolate bars that are made up of thousands of little bubbles inside the chocolate coating. The ice was still strong enough to walk on, so long as one chose to ignore the sounds of it settling underfoot.

"Do you think I ought to let the swans out today?" I asked early one morning in March.

"I think it would be a blessed relief. Apart from which I can't see any good reason for keeping them in the sty any longer."

The moment had arrived. "Liberty!" I announced to the swans as I went in to feed them. "As soon as you've eaten this lot, you'll be free. Think of that, free!" It would have been gratifying to know that they understood what I was telling them, but I might as well have been telling them that they all had sheep's heads on top of their long necks. "At least you can clean yourselves up a bit now!" Perhaps this was unfair, but they had had no chance to wash themselves, and their undersides were stained and filthy from the dungy straw.

I always like my little bit of drama. I opened the sty door with a flourish and dashed outside to witness the exit. All the doors were now open; they only had to walk down a little corridor once they had left the sty, and freedom was theirs. Nothing happened. I called them, but still nothing happened. By this time we were all waiting outside, thronged around the door to witness the great event. The swans continued to sit placidly in their sty.

My wife gave me an odd sideways look, fetched a tin of maize and rattled it. The six got to their feet and began to

74

march toward the door. They came slowly, but they came. Thaddäa grinned at me. It was only fair, I thought, that they should come to her, though I must admit that I felt a bit foolish not to have thought of the ruse myself.

They came to the outside door with great dignity, in their usual marching order, father first, then mother, then the three dark cygnets and finally the light-colored bird. They filed out of the door and stopped, standing very still as they tried to adjust their eyes to the light. Their whole posture showed they were nervous as they stood there, their bodies erect and their necks stretched.

It was the cob who made the first move. He called, looked over his shoulder, and marched for the bank of the ring moat. The bank was steep enough at that point; below, the steely ice was covered with about two inches of water. He stood still for a moment on the top of the bank, obviously made up his mind, calling once more, and slithered down to land with a thumping splash on the ice. He looked a little surprised. One by one, the family slithered down to join him. They all took a good drink, got up on their legs and stood about. They had expected to be able to swim away. When they found they could not, they were not very certain of the situation.

"I wonder if we've done the right thing," I murmured.

"Of course we have," my wife said. "As soon as they get used to it, they'll be fine. They've been indoors for over two months, and it'll take them a little time."

One of the cygnets got bored just standing there, and was the first to move off. Then, without warning, all six were galvanized into action. With outstretched necks and flapping wings, feet paddling like mad, they made off across the moat, snorting and calling to each other in delight. As might be expected, the ice played them false. One moment they were running and the next their feet had slipped away under them and they were skidding and sliding frontward, sideways and on their bellies. No sooner did they skid to a stop than they picked themselves up again and continued the game. It really was a game—they were stretching away all the stiffness and the boredom that they had suffered during their imprisonment.

We watched, entranced, as they chased each other in a game of ring-a-ring-o'-roses. It was fun, and we somehow felt ourselves to be part of it. They rushed along at break-neck speed and allowed themselves to skid sideways along the ice, a maneuver that often ended in a long spiraling stop that was executed on the belly. While the fun was at its height, Leda discovered the open stretch of water at the dead arm of the moat. She made a wing-flapping rush across the thirty or forty yards of ice and landed with an almighty splash. It took the family only a second to get the message and they were after her in a rush, necks outstretched in effort, wings and feet pounding.

What followed was a show in itself. No group of children at the seaside could have shown such joy. They actually threw water at each other, slapping it about with their wings. Over and over again they chased each other in circles, dived shallowly and then, wings, outstretched, rolled over on their backs and lay there for a few seconds, their legs and feet sticking up in the air.

After about half an hour their high spirits had been worked off, and they settled down to washing themselves in the normal way. There was a good deal of shallow diving to raise the water over their shoulders onto their backs. They also pulled the water through the feathers with the aid of the beak, washing flanks and breast carefully by shoveling up quantities of water with the beak and applying it against the growth direction of the feathers. Occasionally one or other would raise itself up on feet and tail, flap its wings and "feather shake," as it is called, to clear the feathers of surplus water.

Having washed themselves for about three-quarters of an hour, they slid breast first up on the ice, where they engaged in a long preening session. When they finally returned to land to loaf, they were wonderfully clean again, the three white swans gleaming and the three dark cygnets a mixture of pure white and gray.

It was, perhaps, the last wholly happy moment that the swan family spent together. Dark days were ahead of them all.

The Guardians

I T IS BEAUTIFUL HERE IN SPRING, WHEN THE COLOR BEGINS
to flow slowly back into the landscape. As each day
passes, one can observe a subtle change. The rising sap
drives away the drabness of the winter months, and the
fields no longer look dead and gray as they did during the
sleeping months.

Soon the tight-rolled buds will open on the trees. At first
there will be no more than a brushing of color everywhere,
but then the whole park will assume a hazy veil of delicate
green that begins to intensify and darken as the days pass.
Later, when the sticky buds have been replaced by leaves,
the great, ancient chestnuts will push up their pink and
white candles.

The snowdrops are the first harbingers of this renais-
sance. We find them sheltering by the bole of a huge plane
tree, green and white in the snow, exposed to the sharp
winds. Even before they go into retreat once more, the
daffodils, or easter bells, as the Germans call them, have

78

pushed their first shoots above the earth, whole clumps of them bedded in the grass.

Spring might have come, but it was very early spring and the lingering finger of winter was still about. Indeed, when the thermometer dropped below 32 degrees during the night, we woke up next day to find the edges of the moats coated with an apron of thin ice. The puddles on the fore-courts crackled crisply as we stepped on them.

Ice is a great problem for the waterfowl enthusiast. Here in Westphalia it can be quite lasting and thick. Ice is an enemy to be reckoned with since waterfowl are not good at dealing with it. At best it is a hardship; at worst it can be fatal, especially to a species that migrates to the south during the winter months. We dread the east wind most of all. Its fangs are made of ice. When the temperature drops below the freezing point, "fast ice," as I call it, forms over-night up to a thickness of one and a half inches. If the sub-freezing temperature and the east wind continue, we can have a six-inch ice cap without the slightest trouble.

"I don't remember anything like this in England," I mumbled as I returned to the house for the umpteenth time, hands frozen from cutting waterholes with the big felling ax.

"I've often told you that it's colder here than you'll admit. We have no Gulf Stream to warm things up."

Many a cupful and more of icy cold water found its way into Patrick's or my Wellington boots when we slipped cutting those offshore waterholes with the felling ax. The swans could walk with certainty on the thick ice, even if their feet occasionally slipped away from under them, de-spite their long sharp toenails. Thinner ice (under three-quarters of an inch) broke under their weight, however, and caused them great trouble when they tried to get out.

They sometimes hesitated for some time before venturing out onto it, as though they were asking themselves if the feed was worth all the trouble.

This reluctance to venture out onto thin ice, in spite of their desire and even need for food, soon had my interest aroused. It was quite clear that getting over to me must have cost great effort, otherwise they would not have hesitated. I fell into the rather unfair habit of calling them when they were furthest away from me. I wanted to study their ice-breaking techniques, and I soon learned to become fairly indifferent to my frozen toes and ice cold hands.

The swan's body is ideal for moving over water. Almost one-third of the bird, from breast to back, is immersed in the water; this section is roughly boat-shaped with a proper bow and stern. The bow, rounded but still relatively sharp, cuts the water and spreads it to the sides—much as a boat does—so that when the bird swims under full power with both feet, it makes a considerable wave and leaves a wake. This bodily construction helps the swans in the interesting technique of ice-breaking.

Once the leader had slithered down the bank and made a hole, I noticed that he (or she) began, with great legs pushing under full power, to heave the breast painfully up onto the shelf of ice in front. Having wriggled forward onto it, the bird would bear down on it with its full weight until cracks began to appear in front of it, whereupon the swan would move forward and repeat the process. Foot by foot the leader would break a path in the ice. Oddly enough, we noticed that they never came toward us in a straight line, but preferred to zigzag, probably because of the wriggle which was necessary to help them break the ice.

The pair took turns of ice-breaking duty. It usually began with Leda starting the whole procedure and Hans following, but after some time the male took over for as long as he could. For all his power, Hans appeared to tire more easily during this exhausting business. Even when the flight feathers had grown again, it never seemed to

occur to either bird to take to the air. Instead, with necks outstretched and crooked in effort, they battled their way along, occasionally injuring their legs quite nastily on sharp fragments of ice.

But ice or no ice, they still came up to the front door-step to be fed. When the weather became milder, local people began to appear once more, and it soon became a favorite pastime at weekends to come and feed the ducks and the swans. "Don't they look lovely?" the tots would cry. The entrance dam became a parking lot. After a while people even ventured inside the gates and parked their cars in front of the chapel or on the grass.

We didn't care for this too much, but we had our own security forces. Followed by Leda, Hans would get out of the water and advance on his well-wishers, marching steadily up to them, wings slightly arched and head tucked down. An adult swan cob is a very imposing sight, big webbed feet slapping hard on the ground, as he advances at the rate of fifty paces to the minute when in a hurry. The swans were no longer quite so lovely.

"Help!" the children would scream, fleeing for safety behind the shaking legs of the parents. In fact, most people were scared. One upright citizen even threatened me with dire penalties for keeping a "dangerous" swan, until I pointed out to him that he was trespassing in the first place, and could he give me a good reason why.

The postman comes at half-past-nine. He wears a smart uniform and a bright yellow crash helmet; from his shoulder, slung with careless abandon, he carries the postbag, a tough canvas construction made to withstand the wear and tear expected of it. The postmen who come to us are young men. They straddle their little motorbike with assurance, with a certain importance, so that when one sees them, one can imagine how it would be if they could take the postmen's curved posthorn from the badge on their sleeves and blow it to announce their coming. How charming, how romantic it would be to hear a clear-blown "tra-la-la-la-tra-la-la-la, ta-ta-ta." But we live in a mundane and rather drab world, so that the golden notes of the horn would be out of place. We have to make do with the ordinary honk of the electric horn.

The postman delivers to four different families here. Apart from ourselves and Herr Balz opposite, there is the gardener, who lives in the park, and the family who "does" for us, who live in the so-called back house. The back house should really be called the end house. It is an ugly annex that was built at the end of the last century to accommodate the staff for the main house. One of its front rooms overlooks the back courtyard, facing the *Brauhaus*. This room is now used by us as our foodstore, and here in the back courtyard the waterfowl gather. The swans take up their accustomed place, standing aloof, expectant, near a certain manhole cover, hard by the house, waiting to be fed. Here they station themselves at odd times of the day from early morning to the last evening feed, their beady eyes regarding every passerby with speculative interest.

When the postman comes at 9:30, we hear the sound of his motorbike as he crosses the drawbridge, turns into the tenant's courtyard and rides behind the rhododendron screen toward the back house. He always delivers the mail to the back house first. The swans are there to greet him. They meet him as they meet all people, upright, their elbows slightly raised, their necks stretched out, hissing. Like the policeman, the postman's lot is not always a happy one. He is at the mercy of the elements for, as all of us know, the mail must get through, despite mud and puddle, in shine and storm, past dogs bent upon aggression and even barriers of snow white swans.

This particular postman never quite understood that a large bird, advancing upon him with semi-arched wings and outstretched neck in the most deliberate stride, was really only looking for food. The five other big birds usually stood their ground, no more than a foot or two away from the door at which he had to deliver the mail, and hissed at him like snakes. Occasionally, however, all six would come right up to him as soon as he reached deep into the postbag. Without any further ado, they would begin to peck at the bag and its contents. They lived in hope that a handful of maize must come out of that bag.

This was too unnerving for that postman, who stuck with it for a while, then went back to his post office and asked for a transfer off the beat. Dogs he could cope with, he said, but swans were more than the call of duty, more than his superiors could ask him to take in his stride. He openly admitted that he was terrified of the birds. I am happy to say that the superior at the post office had sympathy with the man and transferred him. When I heard the story later, after he had ceased to deliver our mail, my heart went out to him. I wished him luck. Maybe he found his working happiness in some elysian beat with no more to contend with than the odd vicious dachshund or alsatian shepherd dog, to save him from monotony.

To his credit, let it be said that he was not the only visitor to be intimidated. The most unlikely people were scared. I was talking not so long ago to one of the members of our local poultry breeders association, who asked me if I remembered the time when he had visited us together with other members of the association. "We were sitting under the beech tree. We all got up and you fed the swans when they came along." I assured him that I remembered it clearly. He smiled. "I was scared stiff of those swans, and still am. I wouldn't go near them for all the tea in China." When the swans are there, they are very much in evidence and they march up to anyone who comes to the house. Nor are they afraid of cars, which they accept as part of the order of things. Indeed, if a car comes too near to them they are quite liable to strike at it with a blow from the beak.

As accepted members of the family, they decided from their early days that they would join in things that went on immediately in front of the house. It is surprising how interested they are in everything that goes on: there is a patter of feet and they are there. Ever hopeful of something to eat, they will watch my wife eagerly as she unpacks the morning's shopping. She might, with a bit of luck, have brought some grain or something good for them. Possibly because they have never suffered in human hands, they trust all human beings. People are their friends, so that they find it difficult to understand how anyone can be afraid of them.

Another of Hans' favorite diversions is to help when I am washing the car. Sidling up and clumping himself down nearby, he will watch me as long as I am there. Often he will patter about and generally get under my feet; but neither he nor Leda has ever shown either fear or resentment when I have thrown a bucket of water over them or sprayed them with the hose. This is not just cupboard love; they are both extremely fond of human companionship, and quite content to sit and watch for considerable periods while one of us washes the car, or is gardening, or just sitting in a deck chair enjoying the sun.

Having a swan as a companion is not everybody's idea of bliss. I remember one woman who had come to deliver a bill. Standing near the chapel about fifty yards from the house, she began to yell. She wanted to deliver that bill, but at the same time had no intention of coming within range of the swans, who were totally unaware of her existence except as a noise. Eventually we made out that she wanted an assurance on our part that the swans would not come and get her. We gave her this assurance, but she decided that it was smarter to play safe, and left the bill in a cleft twig near the entrance gate.

I felt really quite sorry for the poor woman, until I opened the bill. It is easy enough, when you are dealing with animals, to forget how nervous and scared a lot of people may be. Looking back on my own childhood, I remember some agonizing moments of fear, especially in relation to dogs. I recall the time when we were visiting a convent in Ireland with our governess, and I left the room for a moment. A large and fearsome-looking bulldog followed me down the passage and sat down outside the door to wait for me. Its intentions were very friendly, but behind that door I remained, rapidly growing more nervous, for half an hour—until a pretty nun was dispatched to discover what had happened to me. (I was even more crestfallen to discover that the best items had already vanished from the tea table by the time I returned.) The pretty nun assured me that the dog was quieter than a lamb, but I remained convinced that some vital portion of my lower limbs had been in imminent danger.

To say "Don't worry: it will do nothing to you," is all very well, but it does take a bit more than that to reassure most people. What person in his right mind wishes to risk leaving a chunk of himself in the mouth of a vicious poodle, or the beak of a dangerous swan. It is not a pleasant idea to think of oneself having to watch the animal enjoy a meal of one's own anatomy. Nor is the idea of a gratuitous bite or well-aimed peck, while being brave, consoling in itself. Better leave the beasts alone. Call for help, and run the risk of being thought a coward.

We have two friends, a married couple, who sometimes come to stay with us. There is nothing exaggerated about their fear of the swans; all the same they are circumspect and will make a wide detour if they happen to see them about. This can lead to some interesting situations when the birds are actually at the foot of the doorstep. "I wonder if you could do something about those swans?" "Don't be afraid," I call back airily. "Just walk straight through them. They won't do anything."

As I get up from my desk to come to their rescue, I sometimes wonder if a good, faithful, maybe just slightly aggressive adult swan cob might not be the answer to anyone wanting an efficient watchdog. All that I do in fact is to stretch out my arms and march with determination in their general direction, as taught originally by Herr Wallmeyer. Admittedly they hiss and look over their shoulders while they make off, but that means nothing at all.

It can be especially difficult in the country, when people drop in unannounced. On one occasion we were out shopping when unexpected visitors descended. They were passing through and thought to pay a little visit about lunch time. This had started out as a "since we're in the neighborhood, we thought we would drop in and find out when it would suit you to have us visit you" kind of visit. Anyway, when we came back from our shopping expedition, we noticed that their car was parked in the courtyard. Beyond it, sitting miserably on the top step with their backs against our hall door, were our two visitors. Below them sat the swan family, content with the world, while Hans patrolled restlessly up and down. They had been there for the best part of half an hour and were afraid to move an inch for fear of being attacked. The poor people were really desperate about the whole thing. We had to spend a great deal of time consoling them. We also had to eat a cold lunch that should have been our evening meal.

With the warmer weather, the swans became active in a new way, feeling the urge of the new season. With a sudden thrashing of his pinions, Hans would take off and fly a foot above the surface of the moat, to land about a hundred yards away. He would do this a dozen or more times a day, as though to show the world that his new flight feathers had grown, and we began to realize that his attitude to the cygnets was hardening. From time to time all hell was let loose; obviously the family could no longer live together as a unit, because its natural instincts would not fit in with our human plans.

Bringing the swans into the sty for the winter had interfered with their natural rhythm of life.[12] What happened during that March was no more than would have normally taken place during the months of October, November, December and possibly the early part of January. We had been living in a fool's paradise, believing that the six swans could live harmoniously together on the water; the parent birds were beginning to drive off last year's young.

"They're so stupid," lamented Thaddäa, "they're just like people. They have everything and yet they can't live together in peace." I agreed with her wholeheartedly; nature makes few compromises and we were faced with its dictates. Hans had apparently decided on his territory. This was bordered by the chapel pond, the ring moat, the fishpond and the courtyard. Dikes were included, and land within about fifty yards of the banks. For the rest he was indifferent, in the sense that he would only follow other birds for a limited distance of about twenty-five yards, after chasing them from his territory, and even if they were on adjoining territory, he would not follow them as hard or as viciously as he did when he was chasing them from the territorial boundaries that he had set.

Having worked out his boundaries, he set about the task of clearing all swans off the chosen waters as soon as they put in an appearance, no matter what the reason for their appearance might be, through a whole campaign of hostile acts which often went so far as the attempted killing of the bewildered cygnets. This created near chaos in our lives, with free-for-all fights either taking place in front of the house on the courtyard (which were easy to break up), or downright attempted murder on the territorial ponds and on the moat. The cygnets did not wish to leave the parents, but both parents were ruthless and showed very clearly that they no longer wished to tolerate the young.

"The thing I can't understand," I remarked to Thaddäa on more than one occasion, "is that Hans isn't consistent. Sometimes all is peaceful and everything seems to be back to normal. A moment later, Hans and Leda are hunting the poor things all over the place."

Sometimes the cygnets would come up to their parents only to be driven off with classic displays of aggression. On other occasions the parents would permit the cygnets to join them during feeding time, and the old order of precedence would be scrupulously observed. Hans and Leda would take up their accustomed positions, with the cygnets a little in the background, quite content to accept any food that came their way. But as soon as the meal was finished the cob might turn on them and they would have to make off at the greatest possible speed; an unpredictable state of affairs.

A mute swan can work up a surprising speed overland, especially if it makes use of its wings to help. The cygnets often made use of their wings and would run along, their feet slapping the ground, while Hans, his neck ruffled menacingly and pulled well back into his arched wings, would make after them at a slower and more dignified pace, but full of anger and threat. During these chases the cygnets would bunch together and let the cob follow them as though they enjoyed it. Only very rarely would they break up and separate; it never seemed to occur to them that there was a distinct advantage to be gained by doing so. Instead, they would rush away in front of him until they had reached what they thought was a safe distance, where they would stand looking stupid and bewildered, waiting for whatever might happen next.

If they did happen to break up, they always went off in two pairs. The cob would chase one pair for a while, with one eye on the other, until he tired of the whole business. Then he would smooth his feathers and look as bewildered as the children were apt to do; or he would about-face and march back to the feeding place, still assuming a threatening posture, striding out with a great purpose to no purpose whatever. However menacing he may look, Hans has never been very dangerous on land, but he could be a different proposition on water. Many a time we've watched him dealing with one of his young, attempting to kill it, or at least to frighten it so badly that it would leave the territory. These attacks on water were so rapid and terrifying and came about so unexpectedly that we were afraid that the cob would really kill one of the cygnets, as a big swan is capable of doing.[13] But it never did get as far as that, nor even as far as a serious injury, and all that happened in the end was that the cob finished the action with a beakful of

back feathers after he had grabbed the unfortunate cygnet
and tried to drown it.

Naturally enough, the cygnets had no idea where they
were supposed to go. Hans' territory was home to them,
and it must have been very confusing to them to suddenly
find themselves anything but welcome on the water and
land that they had come to regard as home. But Hans
solved the problem in his own way by first making them
take refuge on the mill pond, and then by driving them
over the weir. The other side of the weir, down the steep
fall of nine to ten feet to the tailrace below, was no longer
regarded by him as a part of his territory. Here the swan
and the human didn't see eye to eye. He might want the
cygnets down there, but I certainly didn't. As this driving
over the weir became a daily occurrence, we had no option
but to go and fetch the cygnets back. Back meant across a
meadow, over the public road and the causeway at the
entrance gates to the park and onto the ponds again. The
cygnets were heavy by this time and it was quite a business
to heft them over a distance of about half a mile, but I
did so.

At first we had to bring the familiar food bag with us in
order to entice them. The trick was to catch them by the
neck and to straddle their bodies with our legs before they
realized what was going on. Still holding them by the neck,
I or Herr Balz, who often helped in these expeditions,
would put a right arm around the body and pinion the
bird between our own bodies and our arms. Soon the swans
got so used to what we were up to, and to riding the half-
mile home, that they would waddle up to us when we came
into sight, fold their legs under them, and wait for us to
bend down and pick them up. They never struggled when
being carried; they let their heads hang at the end of their

long necks and gave a rather pathetic little whimper, as we trudged wearily across the meadow, the public road, and across to the ponds. Later, I had to go out and fetch them alone, because Herr Balz was engaged on the farm. "You lazy, nasty devils," I told them, "the good days are over, from now on you're going to hoof it yourselves." So I became a swanherd; I took a riding whip and solemnly drove the swans ahead of me.

A great ditch runs around part of the park. It was part of the original defenses and now encloses the more domestic part of the land: the vegetable gardens and gardener's house, the tennis court and the meadow areas. The ditch is wide and deep, and I believe that it was designed as a great fold for cattle should the place have been attacked. It is no longer in use, but after heavy rains it holds considerable quantities of water, and mallard sometimes use it for nesting. Things came to a head when I was going through the park one day, and saw two cygnets in the ditch. I walked some distance further on and saw something white among the trees near the mill pond. There, looking dreadfully out of place and woebegone, were the other two cygnets, without a clue as to what to do. Their hesitation was obvious; Hans was busily patrolling the length of the stream and the mill pond in front of them.

"I wish that you would do something about those young swans. I can foresee dreadful things happening when you are away in London this summer."

"Perhaps we could make a big pen across the moat for them." I had been wrestling with the problem in my mind for some time. "Then we might have a bit of peace until the breeding days are over and we can let them out again."

I chose the site for the pen between the new and the old oak bridges, where the wire could be lowered from the new

bridge and there was enough of the old bridge still standing to help me get the wire across the eighteen yards of
water of the moat. Poultry wire is dreadfully contrary stuff
and without a boat it was a perilous feat to get the heavy
rolls across at the required length. Strange to say, nobody
landed in the water, although I came pretty close to doing
so on a few occasions when we were getting the oak boom
across. The purpose of this boom was to discourage any
attempts to get under the wire fence. It was designed to rise
and fall with the water level which varies according to the
prevailing weather. When we had finished, though, we had
constructed a pen that encompassed 1,500 square yards of
land and water, including a floating island of water iris and
weed. We felt this was a decent-sized pen and that the
cygnets would be happy in it, as well as safe from parental
attack.

Catching the cygnets was no trouble at all, with Hans to
do the driving, and with the practice they had had at being
driven from the meadows. The next time that the cygnets
were chased over the weir we drove them all the way overland to the safety of the pen. I was just about as smug as
any human being could be. "That'll settle their hash," I
said, thinking of the calm and peaceful days ahead.

The cygnets took to the pen well enough. There was
plenty of natural food and water, a loafing site and grass if
they wished to graze. A really desirable residence, one
might say. We visited them regularly, standing on one of
the banks beside the pen, or on the oak bridge, talking to
them and throwing bits of bread onto the water below us.

But most captives develop a wire psychosis. It doesn't
matter how large or how well equipped the pen might be;
sooner or later the inmates try to get out of it. Penned birds
are not contented birds. The fact that the captives had

everything inside that they would have had outside of their enclosure had little to do with their desire to escape. As soon as they had investigated the possibilities of the pen, they began to patrol the wire. Before a couple of weeks had passed, they were attempting to decamp.

Their restlessness was further increased by the cob. He was quite indignant when he discovered where the missing cygnets were to be found. He and Leda began to patrol the watersides of the pen; while the cygnets were trying to get out, the old fellow was trying desperately to get at them, because the breeding pair didn't want other swans, even their own children, anywhere near the place. The cygnets were getting a bit wiser, in that as soon as Papa came to one end of the pen, they would retreat to the middle or to the other end. There they either ignored the parents in a most obvious way, or idled on the water and watched the technique of attack. So did we, if we wanted to be amused for a few moments. The oak bridge provided an ideal grandstand.

The favorite method of attack was for the old birds to patrol along the length of the oak boom first, before turning their backs and swimming away for about ten yards. Then they would turn suddenly, to come surging forward with the aid of both feet, head pulled well back, wings arched. They would spurt to the fence looking threatening and magnificent, but all to no avail. The attempt at attack would invariably end up with the attacker having to pull up sharply or hit the boom full force with its breast. Of course if they had thought like humans, they would have swam back from the yard-high fence, and flown over it, but swans don't intellectualize like humans, if they think at all, which I'm rather inclined to doubt.

94

When the adults hit the fence they looked surprised and a bit offended, but they never hurt themselves; as soon as they had recovered, they tried to act as if nothing had happened. Swans undoubtedly show embarrassment, just like dogs, either by scratching themselves, or by sudden preening or self-caressing.

As the summer progressed, the swans managed to get out of the pen from time to time and there was furious fighting when the old cob caught them on the water. We were puzzled as to how they managed to make these Houdini-like breakouts. "I just can't understand it. The pen looks fine—there are no holes in the wire that I can see," I would say.

"I know how they get out," Patrick announced airily. "I've known it for a long time. So has Joseph. It's quite simple. They get out under the netting."

"And would you mind letting me know why you didn't see fit to tell me?" I said, spluttering.

"Because I thought that you knew."

"Well. You'd better show me the hole. And fast."

"No, my dear Pappy," said my son in a superior manner, "when the water level goes down, the place where the wire is attached near the far bank is no longer covered with water, so that the young swans can wriggle out under the wire." Naturally, when I went to inspect, I was unable to find anything amiss. Until that night.

Anyone who lives in the country will know what I mean when I say that animals wait for the night before they play their scurviest tricks. No self-respecting bull gets out of its pasture during the day. No herd of cows springs over the electric fence and makes off down the public road during the bright hours of daylight, nor does any pig worthy of its

salt manage to wriggle out of the confinement except at
night. The swans were no exception.

I was in the bathroom, naked as God made me, and was
just emerging from the shower when my wife called to me
from next door. "I think that there's something going on
in the swan pen." I listened for a moment. All I could hear
at first was the rain pelting down outside as though somebody was playing a firehose on the roof under full pressure. But above this din I finally made out the furious
thrashing of wings. Not just any wings, but big, solid
wings, swans' wings.

I dried myself as if the house was on fire, and got into
my oldest and shabbiest clothes—and that's saying something. "I'm going out to see what it is," I said in a voice
full of heroic overtones that invited great sympathy.
"Maybe a fox or a dog has got in among the cygnets."

"You do that, but it's raining. Put on an oilskin or something."

"You bet I will," I snarled.

I went out into the pitch black night, armed with a
flashlight, a stick and a lot of bad humor. Why hadn't she
the decency to say, "Poor darling," or something comfort-
ing. My hasty feet splashed water on all sides. I received a
stream of water from a small hole in the gutter straight
down the back of my neck, and was swearing like a Dublin
docker by the time I reached the swan pen. There was no
doubt about it, a battle royal was going on. What's more,
I, poor mutt, was going to have to break it up on my own.

When I opened the gate of the enclosure, the strong
beam from the flashlight picked up the milling figures,
flailing wings, the five outstretched necks as five swans
raced about in a circle in the lashing rain. What to do? I
was on the bank, swearing none too silently, while the

swans were in the middle of the moat. I switched off the light and stood there pondering, while the rain streamed over me.

"If you let me hold the flashlight, you might be able to catch them," a gentle voice said calmly over my shoulder. "Try a swan call instead of using all that bad language that they're not going to listen to anyway." I grinned at my wife gratefully and called the swans. The result was surprising. A wild group of four frightened cygnets literally hurled itself out of the water at us. I'm not quite sure to this day if they overran me, or if I slipped, but I went down in the mud with a wet thud. I got up quickly but carefully, hands black and slimy, furious, because in spite of her efforts to keep a straight face, my wife was laughing.

"Your flaming swans!" I bellowed. "Where in the blazes have they gone to now?"

Thaddäa turned the beam of the torch on the corner of the pen, where the four young swans were busily trying to climb over each other in their frantic efforts to get away from the aggressor, who was idling out on the water.

"I'll put the lot in the old swan sty for the night." I grasped the first swan and pressed it roughly to me. "You keep on talking and keep that light trained on them." I was in no mood to stand for any more nonsense from any swan, cygnet or adult.

Soon enough, the cygnets were snugly stowed away and the enclosure was cleared of everyone except the aggressor. To our surprise, it was Leda who was trying to get out into the open water once again. After all that nonsense, I had no intention of helping her to regain her liberty, and made for home and bed. She could stay there for the night.

Leda was still in the enclosure when we came back in the

morning. She was swimming up and down, desperately trying to get to the cob who, like a reflection in a mirror, matched every movement of hers on the other side of the wire. I went into the foodstore, got some maize which I fed to the cob just outside the opened gate. A moment later Leda joined him and was at liberty once more.

A Hospital
Visit and
a New Family

H ANS CONTINUED TO DISPERSE THE FAMILY, BUT WE NO
longer got excited about the whole business. The
young birds were now far too strong to allow him
to get a fatal hold.

I was working in the study one afternoon when I heard
a great commotion outside. There was much excited shout-
ing from the direction of the bridge. Going over to the
window, I was just in time to see a fleeting figure dash
around the bank of the ring moat inside of the entrance
gate, a place where strangers are decidedly unwelcome. He
had a big stick in his hand and was yelling like a maniac.
One minute he was in full cry, and the next second he was
tangled up in a rhododendron bush.

By the time I arrived, he had completely lost his balance
and was down in the bush with one foot over the bank and
nearly in the water. I stood where I was for a moment and
looked down on him. His white shirt bore distinct traces
of his encounter with the bush; the bottom of one trouser

99

leg was up around his knee, his hands were filthy and his face was red, but the expression on his face was full of bliss. "Can I help you? Maybe you were looking for something?"

"I've saved him," he panted, "I've saved him. I really have."

"Saved who?" I demanded, knowing perfectly well what he was going to say, but wanting to hear him say it.

"I've saved your second swan. The other one was trying to kill it."

He got proudly to his feet and broke off another branch or two from the bush. "I do beg your pardon," he said simply, but whether to me or to the rhododendron bush I am not too certain.

He was so proud of his achievement that I hadn't the heart to tell him that the cob tried to kill a young bird every other day or so and that we no longer cared very much. He would have blanched in horror if he had known that I was much more concerned by the damage that he had done to the bush. We had removed those huge bushes the previous autumn from behind the tennis court, with the aid of a tractor and four men, and had planted them by the bank of the moat. Several large branches were now looking distinctly unhappy.

At about that time, the story of the four original cygnets, pinioned and incapable of flight, began to draw toward an unhappy close. The four cygnets became rare. They would vanish for days or even weeks. But sometimes they came nearer home, living a mile or so below the weir, in pairs or in a group. Their reappearances were seldom dramatic except when they put in an appearance on the ponds or moat. Then Hans would get excited and go into a full attack, driving them back over the weir. Next day they would be gone, exiled by their father, meeting the fate of the flightless, landbound and confined to the stream.

One day, as I went into the courtyard, I saw a swan in front of the stable doors. It was sitting quite still and made no attempt to move as I approached; all that it did was to lift its chin in greeting. Hans and Leda were on the fishpond and I could see them feeding among the reeds, so this had to be one of the cygnets. The other was nowhere in sight. When I spoke to the bird, it answered with a little nasal whimper. I put out a tentative hand and it got to its feet, hobbled a yard or so and plumped down once again, making no attempt to move. The foodstore was nearby, so I put a handful of maize about a yard in front of the bird. It got up, but with obvious difficulty. When it had finished eating, I carried it carefully into the duck's stable, where I laid it on straw. The bird remained perfectly quiet, allowed me to give it more food and drank thirstily when I brought a basin of water.

The vet arrived two hours later to examine the patient, and diagnosed a broken leg. "But I can't do anything until I know where the break is. I must have an X-ray."

I was all in favor of an X-ray until I heard that the nearest animal X-ray point was a good thirty-five kilometers away from us. I feared the swan would suffer badly from such a long car journey. In any case we had no container large enough to hold it; one of us would have to carry it, which might make it struggle and cause itself further injury. The vet suddenly suggested the local hospital, which we knew well, and vice versa. "The chief surgeon is well-known for his love of animals. But don't say I suggested it!"

I believe to this day that nobody except myself thought my request an odd one. It was taken as a matter of course at the hospital that the swan should be X-rayed. They would be very glad to help. No, taking it on a long trip would be quite out of the question. I was to try not to move the leg or allow the patient to struggle. Would I appear, please, at 3 P.M. during normal surgery hours on the following day?

We were in no doubt as to who should hold the swan on the way to the hospital. That meant that my wife would drive, and that I would sit on the back seat with the bird on my lap, because Thaddäa seldom, if ever, drives a car of mine, and in any event, I owned a low slung fastback at that time, totally unsuited to such an operation. So we chose to drive in her VW, that somebody later described as an improbable car in an improbable episode. But believe me when I say that every word of it is true. We thought that we would have a little trouble. After all, the swan had never taken a car ride; apart from struggling, there might be other unpleasant consequences. I decided that the best thing to do would be to slip the bird into a large plastic clothing bag, leaving its head and neck free.

The following day I went into the stables to collect the bird, which greeted me with its chin up. I talked to it for a while. I then began to put it into the plastic bag, tail first. It seemed to know that I was out to help, because it offered no resistance whatsoever and cooperated splendidly. I carried it out of doors and struggled with it into the car. Swans, even year-and-a-half-old swans, tend to be heavy if they are healthy.

I had been afraid that as soon as I was seated with closed doors in a moving car, the swan would have only one thought—*out!* Nothing of the sort. It sat on my lap, a hog dead weight of about eighteen pounds, looking out of the window with the greatest interest, its head moving from side to side. As we drove out of the entrance gate, the swan moved its long neck to get a closer look at what was going on in the water below and then settled down for the ten minute trip.

I never would have thought it possible that a swan, hatched and reared under natural conditions, could enjoy riding in a motorcar. But enjoy the trip it did, observing every passing vehicle with great interest and absolutely no show of fear. In fact, our primitive creature behaved in a highly civilized manner.

Nor did we have any trouble at the hospital, where it allowed itself to be unloaded without fuss. When we marched up to the reception desk and announced ourselves, the receptionist looked at us rather doubtfully. Would we mind taking a seat in the main hall until she had checked our appointment? I imagine that she wanted to avoid our sitting in line with the other out-patients; they might have objected to such a curious fellow patient.

There seemed to be a great deal going on that day, and the doctors were heavily booked. So we sat and smoked and talked to the bird. It became hotter and hotter as we waited. A swan is quite a heavy object if you have it on your lap for any length of time, but I think that of the two of us the bird suffered more. The hall was well heated and the poor thing was still in its plastic cover; yet it remained passive on my lap, long neck drooping and head almost touching the floor.

People came and went, looking at us with expressions of disbelief. We ignored them, unlike the swan who looked back at them with interest. When no traffic was passing the bird let its head and neck fall downward as swans always seem to do when they are being carried. Normally they

103

utter a rather plaintive little cry when being carried, but this one was very quiet and never whimpered once.

Thaddäa was quite worried by this drooping head position and thought that the swan was feeling ill. It probably was, considering the unnatural circumstances, the heat that it was generating within the bag and the fact that it had had no water for almost an hour. She took the bird's head in her cupped hand and held it, gently stroking it; the patient seemed to like this, and made no attempt to raise the head or to free itself.

When our turn came after half an hour, we had to run the gauntlet of the out-patients as we marched down the long corridor, and there were many strained looks as we passed. But when we arrived at the X-ray room, we were met by the Sister radiologist, a sparkling, white-robed nun, who got to work in a most business-like manner. I held the swan on the table while the radiologist's young Swiss assistant put the plates under the leg to be X-rayed. Maybe the table was cold, or maybe it was the sudden change from the warmth of my embrace or the sudden change of position; but for the first time the patient got in a mild fit of panic. With legs suddenly free inside the bag, it began to struggle violently and in no time at all had shredded the plastic with its long sharp toenails. I hastily placed a firm hand on its back, and lightly stroked its long neck with the other hand, while I talked to it gently. Firmly held and reassured by the familiar voice, it gave up all idea of struggling. After that the X-ray went without a hitch. Except for a "visiting card" on the table and another on the floor, the patient behaved better than most humans; everybody was full of praise.

The X-ray showed a clean fracture of the upper legbone

with no sign of complication. We were advised to keep the bird still if at all possible, because the break could not be splinted and there was no other way of mending it.

When we left the X-ray room, more patients had arrived, and were waiting to follow us in. Once again inquisitive and rather fearful glances followed us as we took leave of the Sister, and walked down the long corridor. When we got back to the car my wife asked me if I had noticed how many of the people had drawn up their legs under them or pressed themselves flat against the wall as we passed by. I told her that I had, and fell to wondering about the curious pattern of fear.

In fact it was probably fear rather than brutality that had brought us to the hospital in the first place. Such a nasty break in the upper leg must have been caused by a hefty blow, almost certainly with a heavy stick. What probably happened was that during one of its absences from home the swan had seen somebody at one of the farms downstream, and boldly marched up in the hope of getting something to eat. The person concerned, seeing the determined advance of the swan, probably thought that an attack was in the offing and decided on defensive action which ended with the bone-breaking blow.

I have a certain amount of sympathy for the poor ignoramus responsible. He must have known as little about swans as swans know about people. If he had met the advancing swan, arms outstretched, the bird would have turned and gone away. The poor swan, on the other hand, never dreamed that a human being would be capable of doing it an injury. It associated humans with food or help; it was the most natural thing in the world to advance on a being which, in all its experience, represented those things.

It never had reason to associate human beings with fear. The whole business in my opinion, must have been a tragic case of mutual misunderstanding.

The journey home was uneventful. We put the swan in a stable; properly housed and bedded down on straw, well fed and watered, it remained quiet for the duration of the treatment, seldom moving from the one position. We had, in fact, no need of any special precautions to enforce immobility; the bird looked after itself and stayed happily in the stable.

The whole episode impressed me greatly, principally because the young bird had so obviously come home for help. It must have been a painful effort because by the time that I picked it up, it was no longer able to move more than a couple of yards. The second thing that impressed me was that when we tried to pay for the X-ray, we were met by an emphatic refusal, on the ground that it had provided a welcome break from normal hospital routine.

It was I, not Hans, who partly achieved the old cob's aim: finally to disperse the family. I caught up one pair and gave them to a neighbor who wanted them to grace the moats of his beautiful home. They lived very happily there, well cared for, until pollution of his moats from upstream caused the death of one of the birds. The second pair went wild, working its way downstream from us and appearing on periodic visits for many years. One of this pair was the swan whose leg had been broken; for all I know both may be alive and well to this day.

With the cygnets out of the way, Hans turned his attention to other birds on the place and soon there were new victims of his aggression. Hans and Leda were relatively sociable normally, in that they would tolerate ducks and even feed with them; but now that the breeding season was approaching, Hans became increasingly aggressive.[14] One day I had to come to the rescue of one of our prize saxon ducks, which the cob was systematically trying to kill, having worked himself up into a great rage. He had her by the back and was trying to squash her against the bank of the moat. He let her go when I came along and I scooped her up to put her on the bank beside me. She was so shaken and bewildered that she had no idea of what was happening to her. It seemed that she was incapable of distinguishing between friend and enemy, because the moment I released her, she went straight back into the water toward the cob—who promptly pounced on her once again and attempted to drown her. I rescued the silly idiot for a second time, and delivered the cob a gentle slap on the head for his trouble. Except for a defiant hiss, he made no attempt to attack me but sheered offshore. From his look I gathered that, given the opportunity, he would cheerfully murder that duck if she returned to the water. I gave him no chance. I tucked the duck under my arm and put her away in a stable.

These rages were puzzling, but once they got started, they just petered out by themselves. They either lasted for a day, or were drawn out over a period of days, which was exceedingly trying for all concerned. Hans never attacked or attempted to attack human beings during these periods, although he would assume threatening postures which, if ignored, soon passed.

It was quite obvious that the territory they had chosen was our total available water area except for two ponds and a length of the stream, and woe betide any other swan pair hoping to breed on it, or even to visit it. The territory was theirs in the fullest sense, even if they did not make full use of it. They had found it and claimed it; and there was no mercy for any bird large or small that irritated them or got in their way. Visits by swans are so rare that they become occasions. When we do have strangers come to call, we tend to account for their presence by believing that they were once reared here. This is not as improbable as it sounds, because doubtless many of the downy cygnets hatched after the first year of the parent birds' arrival have already nested and produced their own young. I once watched Hans chase off one of a group of such swans that came onto his territory. I believe that they had only come down to rest for a while when passing by. They landed on the largest of the fishponds, which is also the furthest from the house. However, a member of the group ventured onto the moat; Hans was after it in a flash. He chased it around the moat, the visitor looking anxiously over its shoulder all the time. When it came to the point of no return, it swam in close to the island bank, and took off while Hans was still twenty yards away. It got into the air with a bare fifty-four feet of water in front of it, and managed to become airborne with the greatest of exertion. It then came down on the third fishpond, where the other swans were waiting. Shortly afterward, all the visitors departed, although Hans had made no attempt to follow the single swan, or even to join the group at a leisurely pace. As far as he was concerned, once the swan had taken off, the matter was at an end. It made me wonder, however, whether the birds have some other means of communication which warns an intruder that the territory is reserved.

A few days later I saw Hans go for a yellow duckling, selected in preference to a number of mallard ducklings around it. His attack was fast and sure; with wings flailing and feet pushing, he took off and flew low, straight at the victim, which he killed with a hefty blow of his beak.

Skidding to a stop, he raised himself up on his tail, called, shook his feathers, dropped back onto the water and idled awhile, just as if he were saying to the world in general "I'm the boss here and you'd all better remember it."

Alternatively, he attacked from a swimming position, grabbing the intended victim behind the head with his beak and attempting to drown it. Should he fail in his grip, as fortunately often happened, he would grip the back feathers and shake. As long as the victim kept on the move the chances of survival were good. For some reason the cob never let go to try to better his grip, and the victim, with a little bit of luck, got away with no more than the loss of a beakful of feathers.

We noticed that these attacks usually took place on sunny days and seldom on rainy ones. On a sunny day the air was filled with the sound of beating wings and splashing water. Despite the relative danger, our small ducks loved to play "ducks and drakes" with the powerful swan. Often they seemed to be doing it for the fun of it, and then laughing at him behind his back. A group of anywhere up to thirty mallards, white call ducks and cayugas would engage in this sport. This never ended fatally; fatalities only occurred when he picked on a single duck unexpectedly and concentrated on it.

The game was usually played in front of a fascinated audience of people from the town, who had brought their children to feed the ducks from the entrance causeway. Hans would work himself up into a rage and launch an attack on a group of ducks. Rising just above the water surface, he would appear to be running on it, wings flailing. The group would scatter in all directions, some just swimming away and others taking to the air immediately, landing again seconds later on the grassy banks in front of the cob. The swan would invariably come down on the water, shake himself, turn and cruise back to where the group had reassembled. The whole performance would then be repeated. I have known this to go on from midday until six o'clock in the evening, with short breaks for refreshments.

While the cob was clearing his territory, establishing his sovereignty, his mate was simply putting on weight. Leda retired to the fishpond, but this did not mean that she also retired from our lives. Far from it. That lady knew only too well on which side her bread was buttered, and we had more personal contact with her during this period than at most normal times. Establishing her own routine, she would keep a weather eye open on the house, to make sure that she was on the spot when one of us put in an appearance in the courtyards.

I called her "the ghost." It became almost impossible to dodge her, as she seemed to materialize out of thin air. When either of us left the house, there wouldn't be a swan to be seen; the next moment she would be there, paddling across from behind a bush, or the bole of a tree, or from around some corner of the house . . . all eager, her body slim and erect, long neck held high and straight, the neat little head cocked to one side and the bright eyes fixed on the prospect of food. "Not you again! I fed you only half an hour ago. Do you never have enough?"

Somehow I expected an answer as she ambled along after me as far as the foodstore, standing hopefully in the back courtyard until the food was put down. She would give me a quick hiss before she began to gobble up the food, as if it was the first that she had ever seen, and the last she would ever get.

I took care not to give her too much, because I knew that

she would merely leave it for the ducks already lingering hopefully about. Unlike Hans, she was gentle with them, or as gentle as a swan could ever be. Hans was rough with the little birds, and would grab them by the back and shake them until the feathers flew, but Leda only pecked them off, and gave the warning hiss.

Her constant contact with us during this period enabled her to come to know us as people. We found that she was quite capable of discrimination, which was a marvelous thing. She would never rush up to *anybody* to demand food, but only to us. What is more, like Hans, she was perfectly trustworthy with the children, because however Hans may attack other waterfowl and the dogs, he has never attacked any child or human being, except myself, and that only when he is ill-tempered and I choose to ignore it in order to establish who is the boss about the place. Fortunately for all concerned, the children were circumspect in their behavior. They might talk with the birds when passing, but they would not approach them too closely. As a result, the swans' attitude has always been negative toward the youngsters. Patrick would feed Leda for me when I asked him, but preferred not to do so when Hans was involved.

We discovered that Leda responded readily to the human voice, and, like Hans, to a fair vocabulary of human words. This simply meant that she had come to associate certain sounds or words with certain situations. "Come" is a command which all of the waterfowl about the place learn to understand very quickly, and none learned more quickly than Leda. "Wait" means just that, and so on. There is actually very little that is remarkable about this, as most of the animals learn a vocabulary in a fairly short time, and their learning of it is generally associated with

food. However, I really do not believe that her hunger was
the only reason why Leda haunted me; all too often, having
broached what had been put down for her, she quickly left
it. I think that her curious behavior was simply a mixture
of associating man with food, and her highly developed desire for human company.

She did some pretty odd things from time to time. She
tried to follow me into the pheasant aviary, pushing angrily
against the wire when the attempt was frustrated. She tried
to follow me through the front door and through the back
door leading to the fruitstore. The steps defeated her in
both cases. I doubt if she would have persevered if she had
made it to the top of the steps. Swans don't like to go
through narrow openings, and I doubt if she would have
had the nerve to face the comparative darkness inside the
house. But her best effort was when she tried to get into
the car and onto my lap. In those days, I had a low slung
little Simca with a body by Bertoni, which gave me a great
deal of joy. One day I stopped to talk to Leda, and opened
the door wide. It was probably just because the car was so
low that she came right up to me, put her neck and shoulders inside, and tried to clamber in. I drew the line at this,
and pushed her gently away; she was distinctly annoyed,
because she reared up and hissed at me angrily. However,
even love can have its limits.

One day we noticed that the whole picture had begun to
change. We heard the mighty thrashing of Hans' wings less
frequently, and his whole behavior pattern began to affect
Leda. One April day Leda came up to the house to be fed;
I put down a few handfuls of maize, watched her feed for a
while and decided to go for a walk. I went around the
south end of the house where the little island is, close to
the bank of the big one on which we live, and there I saw

Hans busily building what appeared to be a nest. It could only have been Hans because at that moment Leda was guzzling only twenty yards away around the corner. "That's strange," I said to myself. "I suppose that he's carrying on where Leda left off." But for some reason that I could not explain a doubt was creeping into my mind. I decided to observe.

The site was opposite where the mandarin and wood ducks have their pen. To the human eye it seemed a good nesting place, fulfilling most of the requirements that ensured safety. I watched as he sat down and began to gather material that was within reach of his long neck and shoulders. He picked up the material with his beak and began to tuck it away under him, crouching down and pivoting on his axis. Anything seemed to go: twigs, creepers, dried vegetation, the lot.

When all the material that was in the immediate vicinity had been exhausted, the cob began to gather suitable material from elsewhere, and went several yards to fetch it. There was a large pile of sticks about four yards away, dating from the time the island had been cleared; I saw him pick up and carry sticks of up to two inches in diameter without difficulty.

Soon after that I learned that it was wise to be a little bit careful when approaching the cob. A swan has exceptionally sharp eyesight. Upon seeing me, at best he would stop his work immediately, at worst he would go into an attack. Sometimes, when I decided to be secretive about my position and he caught me at it, he really did go for me. On one occasion he was building a nest on the dam between the chapel and mill ponds. I was crouching beside a low hawthorn bush and he came straight for me. I shifted quickly and hid behind the bole of the big beech tree. He pounded past without seeing me, although I was only a few paces from him. Another time he attacked me near water. I was in the open, crouched on the bank, so I decided to let him come and then sidestep at the last moment. He came all right, full pelt, as though he were about to take off. By the time that he reached me he was about a foot over the level of the water. I sidestepped neatly, as planned, but missed my footing and went into the chapel pond up to my knees, while the swan shot past me to land on the grass beyond. I was swearing roundly as I squelched out of the water, while the cob stood indecisively on the grass behind me. He thought that I was calling to him, so he walked back to where I was and got into the water in front of me. Quite embarrassed and not knowing what to do, he lingered about while I continued to swear at him. I pulled off my boots and emptied out the water, then couldn't get them back on, because rubber boots are almost impossible to get into again once they are wet inside. I stood there in stockinged feet and gave the cob a piece of my mind before making for home. As I squelched along in my sopping socks, wet trousers flapping against my legs with every step, the swan swam along the bank beside me. At the same time, I saw my son coming toward me at a leisurely pace on his bicycle.

"My goodness," he said, using his favorite expression at the time, "what on earth happened? Did you fall in or something?"

"No," I said, snarling. "My feet were hot so I went in the pond to cool them off."

Hans tried very hard to get Leda to nest on the little island, but she would have none of it, and rejected it very snootily indeed. The next attempt he made was to build a nest on a little islet of water iris, a rather precarious af-

The author and his wife with Hans, Leda,
and a cygnet, watched by a friend.

Above The swan family at their accustomed
place near the front doorstep. *Top Right* Five
of the original six. *Bottom Right* They
will come on call.

Opposite Hans ready to defend the nest
(which is not in the picture) . *Above* The
present Leda, feeding with her 1971 brood
on the fishpond.

Opposite The cygnets, with the author, watched by the parent birds. *Above* The cob on the nest, 1970. *Below* Hans, nest-building, 1971.

Opposite The cob scolding and menacing, after having attacked the call duck (in the background). *Above* Hans showing active aggression in front of the house.

Top Left The cob landing: adjusting his wings and using the feet as brakes. *Bottom Left* The swan pair, breast-to-breast after mating. *Above* A triumph-display after an attack on a call duck.

Above A triumph-display on the dike between the ring moat and the fishpond. *Below* Hans marching across the courtyard. *Opposite* After the attack, the cob rises on his tail in the water and utters his "nuck-nuck" cry. This photograph, which, incidentally, required great good fortune to obtain, shows him on the rise before feather-shaking.

Top Left A close-up of two flying trumpeter swans. *Photograph by Winston E. Banko, courtesy of the U.S. Department of the Interior, Bureau of Sport Fisheries and Wildlife. Middle and Bottom Left* Two photographs of the cob taking off. The photograph in the middle of the page shows the beginning stages of flight. Note the wing position and the extended neck. The lower picture shows the swan nearly airborne. Water spouts are raised by striking feet; at this point, the spouts are about four feet apart. Notice, also, the spread of the primary feathers and how the wings, neck, and body are held. *Above* Hans and the author walking to the feeding place on the back courtyard.

Leda leading a mixed brood of cygnets, with
the "Polish" cygnets in the foreground.

fair which floated on the surface just off the shore of the chapel pond and opposite the chapel itself. We knew exactly where this nest was because we had seen both swans working on it.

One day Thaddäa was in her rose garden. As I have said, she loves her roses and insists on tending them herself. Suddenly she noticed the pen on the nest. She saw it stand up. She took special note of this because the bird was uttering little sounds and whimpers. She soon stopped what she was doing. The pen was in the act of laying an egg. This was no easy business. Leda groaned a great deal; it took exactly ten minutes for the egg to issue from her body and fall into the nest. The swan was fully aware that my wife was watching her; she told me afterward that the pen actually looked at her from time to time. Unfortunately that nest was too unstable, and in due course the eggs went through it and ended up in the bottom of the pond. But I have always envied my wife seeing that big egg issuing from the swan's body. Indeed I might have seen it myself, had I not moved off toward the poultry runs a few moments earlier.

We thought the loss of the egg might make the swans give up the whole idea of breeding that season, and our joy was unbounded when we found that they had selected an almost ideal nesting site on top of the dike between the chapel and the mill ponds. It was an excellent site, surrounded by three sides of water, ooze and reeds, while the two main water sides gave easy access to the water itself. The whole topography of the place was such that a very young brood would have ready access to an abundance of food, which literally grew on the doorstep. The site was surrounded by huge trees, which gave some shelter from the heavy rain; hawthorn bushes and low shrubs broke the wind, and yet there was complete vision to all cardinal points of the compass. The only open and easily approachable entrance to this site was from the park, but except for animal intervention there was no danger.

Leda seemed to agree with Hans that this was a good site, and she soon joined him in building the nest on it. She took over in the center when it was partially completed and allowed him to bring material to her. Using the same system as he did, she began to tuck the material in under her and to enlarge the nest itself. As the days passed, I began to watch Leda's movements carefully for any sign of egg-laying. Speculation was rife among the family about when she would begin to lay again and how many eggs she would produce. She was visiting the nest frequently, and remaining within the vicinity for long periods, which I took to be a hopeful sign.

She did in fact get a clutch together but I never saw it, because I was too scared of frightening the swans to go near. The result was that I had no idea of how many eggs the pen had laid and was going to sit on. Not that it mattered really, but it would have satisfied my curiosity. With her clutch laid, she settled down seriously to the business of incubation, displaying the characteristics of a first-class broody hen—a general reluctance to get down from the nest at any time. If the weather was dry, she would put in an appearance at the doorstep at about lunch time, but if the weather was really wet, we might not see her for days on end. It took us some time to realize that she was not leaving the nest at all during these wet days, and when we did so, we began to get anxious about her. Admittedly, I had watched the cob on one or two occasions bring leaves of water iris to the sitting pen and, I thought, feed her, but I

could not be positive about this. He certainly did not bring
the leaves as additional nesting material.[15]

Anxiety on our part eventually led us to risk going up
to the nest and feeding the pen while she was sitting on it.
But we had to be careful that she continued to sit on her
eggs. We had to be careful, too, of Hans; idle and bored,
he had now given himself over to what humans would
regard as "defending his territory," but there was nothing
to defend it from. How easily we got to the nest depended
on Hans' mood of the day. Like most males, he was full of
varied humors; there were days when he would not only
tolerate either of us but positively welcome our visits.
With the rain dripping off my hat, I would creep cautiously along the dike between the chapel and the middle
ponds to the nesting site, announcing my arrival in advance. If Hans was at the nest, the rest was plain sailing.
As soon as he heard a familiar voice, he would turn in my
direction, while I advanced on him "making sounds like
food," rattling the maize container. He would allow me to
go right up to the nest and put down the maize without
molesting me. He didn't even indulge in a threat-display.
"Now my silly ones," I'd say to the pair of them, keeping
a careful eye on Hans all the while, "dinner is now being
served by your room service."

Leda would regard us with placid interest, chin-lifting a
greeting and watching the food bag with a shiny, speculative eye. Either my wife or I could approach the nest to
within a yard and put down the food for her. We always
put it down within neck's length, so she could feed without
getting down from the nest. If Hans happened to be there
and was prepared to leave us in peace, we would feed both
birds; he would gobble up most of the food put down for

him with the greatest of amiability. Neither Thaddäa nor I would linger. I was always careful not to overdo the time spent during such visits, in case I might disturb the incubating bird to any great extent.

But on the days when one had to be careful, and they came often enough, it was possible to test out the cob's humor by going within thirty to thirty-five yards of the nesting site. Sometimes he would come with elbows raised and primaries almost sweeping the ground, his march deliberate and swaying a little from side to side, his neck ruffled and drawn back but with the head on a level with his breast; we knew then that this was the moment to pretend that we were only passing by. We would get back to the house as quickly as we could and call him from there. As soon as he arrived, we would lay down food, get into a car, and drive around the park so that we could beat a hasty path to the sitting pen over the concrete bridge crossing the river. If we set off to visit the pen on foot, it was a different matter—the old boy was not to be fooled. Before anybody could get as far as the big beech tree near the nesting site, he would be winging his way across the water in full-blast threat. But the car fooled him every time, as it seems to fool most wild things, and he never paid the slightest attention to it.

The lawn mower was a different proposition altogether. One day I decided to mow a path, in order to have easier access to the dike and the nest. Both of the swans were well used to my coming over to feed them by this time and they would seldom show any sign of hostility. I was mowing away happily, perhaps fifty yards from the nest, when I heard the familiar sound of wings. A moment later Hans arrived in a great rage and began attacking the roaring mower with savage pecks and blows from his wings. But it was quite evident that he did not associate the machine with me; when I switched it off, he just stamped about a bit, eying it angrily. I calmed him down a bit by talking to him, and decided to stop the mowing, but he remained suspicious. As soon as I decided to pull the machine away, his neck ruffled and he started to take up what Heinroth described as the *Imponiergehabe,* the imposing posture, and to again advance purposefully on the machine. Later that year I taught him to disregard the machine to some extent, but he never really trusted it, and would linger offshore, on the water, keeping the progress of the machine under his vigilant eye.

The wet weather passed, and days of glorious June sunshine followed. After lunch, with the hot sun blazing overhead, I would collect the long cushions from the hall and throw them down on the doorstep outside. We would idle for a while, saying little and enjoying our coffee.

On one very hot day, I took my cup and moved toward the shade of the big copper beech that grows about ten yards from the doorstep. I put my cup down quietly.

"Hey," I called to Thaddäa, trying to sound calm, "they're coming under the bridge. With a whole crowd of little ones!"

"How many?"

Neither of us could be certain of the number, as they were hidden behind Leda's tail. As they came toward us under the bridge the swans looked rather like two battleships with attendant destroyers, except that the formation was wrong. Afraid of stopping their progress, I went back to the doorstep and sat down; the birds were now out from under the bridge, in the middle of the moat. Leda was leading and calling sharply over her shoulder to the six little balls of fluff that were close to her tail, while Hans, a proud father, brought up the rear.

"Let's go down and have a look at them," I suggested, as excited as a schoolboy. Thaddäa was more realistic. "I think we should look at them from here. It might frighten them off if we go too close."

As the swans neared the land, they seemed to vanish below the top of the bank. A pause, and then Leda appeared, still calling sharply over her shoulder, followed by the six little babies and Hans. With mounting excitement we watched the mother lead the family across the grass toward us. They came slowly, and with much maternal encouragement, stopping frequently for a little rest: six little gray or white powder puffs with black shiny eyes, with black or fleshy gray legs that would suddenly fold underneath them, so that their owners collapsed on the grass.

"Do you think Leda will bring them right up to the doorstep?"

"Let's wait and see," replied my ever practical spouse.

"I'll be back in a minute," I told her as I went off to get some maize from the foodstore.

When I got back, the family was still approaching slowly. But when I began to rattle the maize, Leda lost all sense of maternal devotion, and came scampering over the grass, Hans hot on her tail. While the parents rushed to their accustomed place by the doorstep, and were promptly fed, the chicks waddled nearer of their own accord, with occasional stops and flops, until they reached the edge of the grass. There they stopped to look around them. During their slow progress Leda had stopped feeding every now and again to give a sharp, commanding call; now, she called again, until the whole family was united near the doorstep, with the babies sitting in the shade looking slightly bored.

Every available camera was produced to capture the scene of our new family. Over and over again we told our swans how clever they were and how beautiful their family was. It was a great and memorable moment. We now had our swans and our swans trusted us. They had brought their family to us within a week of their hatching—probably within three days. Moreover, they had brought them to a place from which, had we chosen to take advantage of it, the family could not escape. Now all the family had been introduced to us.

Icarus, Romeo and Juliet

W AKE UP, WAKE UP. THE SWANS ARE BACK!"
It was Patrick storming into our bedroom in
the early morning who brought the news this
time. Katja, a heavy weight, landed on my feet, panting
heavily, and I looked at my son out of one eye as he tow-
ered over the bed.

"Are you quite sure?"

"Of course I'm sure," said Patrick with all of the superiority of a twelve-year-old. "They're on the near fishpond."

I felt the same kind of excitement that I had experienced
as a child, when my nurse would wake me up, shaking me
as she said: "Wake up you lazy thing, there's snow on the
ground outside and you're still in bed and asleep."

"Did you see them come in?" He shook his head. He had
got up at some ungodly hour, taken out his bicycle and
gone for a fast run with Katja, whose long pink tongue was
lolling like a delicious and savory piece of ham.

Suddenly the swans had come, as though they had been there all the winter and not away from us for months. I realized with a mild shock that the new year of 1968 was already not so very new at all. Gradually, day by day, the sleeping world would start to wake up. With the sun shining, I would feel good right down to my bones and full of hope. Out in the park the woodpeckers would be getting to work. Little clusters of snowdrops would soon push their way up near the trees and along the big ditch by the wood. The birds would soon begin to think of pairing. Best of all, the swans would start the routine of living, half wild, but always a part of our daily lives and our way of living.

I jumped out of bed, put on a dressing gown and made my way down to the bathroom at the end of the corridor. The swans were there all right, floating gently on the open water, just off the thick ice. When I opened the window and called them, they looked up with quick movements of their heads as they located me, and began to make their way to the courtyard below. By the time that I had finished dressing, they would be there, waiting for their first feed.

Both birds were in fine shape, and had come through the winter well. As usual, I thought that they had both lost a little bit of weight, but I wasn't concerned because I knew that with regular and heavy feeding they would soon make it up. I stayed a long time with them, enjoying myself, watching them feed while I talked to them. When I arrived at the breakfast table, grinning like a Cheshire cat, thoroughly satisfied with myself, the family reaction was predictable. "Tell me about the precious darlings," said my wife. Finishing her tea, she took a cigarette, fitted it into her long cigarette holder, and settled back to listen. "Now I know that I'm home again," said my daughter, after I had finished busily buttering a piece of toast. Fair enough, I thought. After all, it is virtually impossible not to meet some creature as soon as one goes out of the front door.

"Papa and his swans!" said Patrick, shaking his head at his bowl of cornflakes, thereby earning himself a killing look from his mother: a look that I was not supposed to see.

"Well," I reminded him gently, "you were as thrilled as your sister was when you saw Icarus flying yesterday. Incidentally, do you have any idea who the original Icarus was?"

"He melted in the sun, or his wings did."

I was agreeably surprised. I had first been told the story as a child, when I went out in a boat with my father on the bay of Naples. I believed then that Icarus had fallen into the bay, and whenever I think of the story now, I always see the poor fellow nose-diving into those celebrated waters.

"Have you been learning about him in school?"

"No," he mumbled as though it were something to be ashamed of, "I read it somewhere."

The story of our Icarus began three years before, when we had three Chinese geese in our rearing room on the first floor of the *Brauhaus*. The rearing room is equipped to deal with youngsters who have been hatched out in the incubator. We are rather proud of it, with its assortment of lamps and brooders which we built ourselves in our workshop. Alas, two of the goslings died; the survivor, a strong little gander, peeped and peeped all day and began to feed badly. I was hoping that he would last out until a broody hatched out a clutch of goose eggs, but Thaddäa was less optimistic.

"You'll have to do something about that gosling," she

said. "Or he will die on you and you will be furious."

She was quite right. The poor thing was so miserable; common compassion alone demanded action. It so happened that we saw an advertisement in the local paper that week for swan geese and I leaped at the chance of acquiring some. The swan goose, *Anser cygnoides* (L), breeds in southern Siberia, northern Mongolia and central Manchuria from the Tobol and the Ob' Rivers to the Okhota River and the Gulf of Sakhalin and winters in China. Domestic varieties of Chinese geese, or knob geese, such as we keep, are derived from this species; I was therefore very eager to have some of them. But since the gosling price was steep, I ordered only three.

When the expensive goslings arrived, we saw that we had been done in the eye. They looked like very ordinary goslings to us, but since we had bought them with the object of their affording our lonesome gander some company, we decided to make the best of a bad job. We would fatten them all for the pot.

It was a trifle ironical that soon after the arrival of this expensive trio the lone gosling died. Then all three of the new arrivals contracted some sort of disease. Two succumbed, and the third was left seriously ill. This bird was nursed back to health by my wife and turned out to be some sort of unknown hybrid of white goose stock.

By the time that this youngster was healthy enough to be put out of doors on the grass, the broody had hatched out her clutch. When we put the gosling with the pure-bred group, he immediately took command. He proved to be so excellent a leader that we decided to allow him to boss the flock as soon as he was mature. It had been our experience that a really tame bird will help in the conversion of wild or nervous birds and we believed that a year under the leadership of a fearless gander might help the flock to overcome its fear of the swans.

This nameless gander had only one son by a Chinese goose. We didn't want hybrids, so we put the son in a pen by the water to fatten it up for the pot. The father had become so vicious meanwhile that we exchanged him for a Christmas turkey, and that was the end of him. But the hybrid son did exceedingly well on starter food and grass, later on grain, growing rapidly into a very large bird. We put a couple of young saxon ducks into the pen to keep him company, and they got along splendidly together until the ducks were stolen one dark night.

The solitary goose didn't stay alone for long. He was befriended by a pair of white call ducks, which was fascinating. Then one day the gosling got out of the pen. He began to live a wild full life, and grew up into a strange and wonderful mixture of white goose–Chinese goose, with a mixed white and gray feather coat, a yellow beak with a vestige of his Chinese mother's basal knob, and the thickest neck that I have ever seen on any bird.

"You'd better catch that goose," advised my wife, "before somebody else does. I'm depending on having him for lunch one day."

I went up onto the causeway with a kind of landing net that we use for catching up poultry, in the hope of netting him. But I had no luck that day. Or the following day or any other day.

"I simply can't catch him," I said about two weeks later. "I've tried with the catcher and by feeding and with all of the tricks, but he's too clever."

"You wait. Somebody will catch him."

"I don't think so. He's too wary, and wild. Unless somebody shoots him, he'll survive the winter out of doors."

When the first freeze came the goose vanished. I presumed that he (or she) had found its way into somebody's pot and said so when we were sitting to a boiled egg for supper.

"Don't you know where that goose is?" said Patrick, with the air of contempt that is reserved for rather senile parents. "It's on the stream with the little white ducks."

The winter dragged on. One day, after a spell abroad, I was standing in the courtyard when I distinctly heard the honking of a wild goose coming nearer and nearer. Looking up, I suddenly saw our missing goose passing over the roof of the cow shed and promptly named it Icarus. It was a splendid sight to see this large bird, with its big wide wing span, flying fast and high for the chapel pond. He was not alone, but flying with a group, at the very center of a squadron of little call ducks and mallard, looking for all the world like a great bomber accompanied by fighter planes.

In the time that has passed since that winter's day, his flight has become one of the sights that we love to see. Possibly the most interesting thing about Icarus is his firm belief that he is a duck. He has always believed this, having associated exclusively with ducks since the first day that he saw the light. For this reason he will only accept the company of ducks. Oddly enough he prefers to associate with white call ducks although he tolerates all of the mallards and cayugas on the place.

During the breeding season, Icarus made no attempt to link up with any of the geese. Had he associated himself with the idea of being a goose he would have had opportunity to do so. There were two ganderless Canada geese available that would have served as mates; that is presuming the free flock of Chinese geese did not accept him for any reason. Instead of attempting to identify himself with the geese, either Chinese, snow or Canada, he remained part of a ménage-à-trois with a pair of white call ducks and assumed the behavior of a drake during the period that the duck was sitting on the nest. I observed him, on several occasions, attacking the whole flock of Chinese geese when they approached within twenty to twenty-five yards of the nesting place. Incidentally, it caused him no effort to put the flock to flight.

When the brood came out onto the water for the first time, he immediately joined the duck and the drake, his old friends from the days when he was penned, and proceeded to defend the chicks against all comers. This group was subsequently joined by another pair of ducks, mallards as it happens, and a community life was begun. As undisputed guardian of the free-flying ducks, Icarus now seems to content himself with guarding the chicks of others. Indeed he is an excellent father and it is rather charming to see the brood follow him as he swims ahead of the mother and her husband.

Icarus and his ménage-à-trois is interesting because two different species are involved. But the ménage-à-trois is not unknown in the world of swans, and no less than four experts give evidence of it.[16] Divorce is also known, although according to C. D. T. Minton in his recently published study, the mute swan is pretty faithful on the whole; divorce among breeding pairs only amounts to 3 per cent.[17] I mention this because it is generally accepted that swans mate for life; those exemplary birds, Hans and Leda, must have been mated for at least eight years, if not longer.

Oddly enough, although most people are quite willing to accept that certain species of birds, notably swans, will mate for life, and that it is in the natural order of things for them to do so, not everybody is prepared to believe that the birds of the air and water are capable of something approaching what we call romance. I have had evidence of this among the Canada and the snow geese, but of all our birds, the pair that really thrilled us most was a pair of ducks. We called them Romeo and Juliet.

The story began a long time ago, in the days when we were still searching for ducks, at a poultry show that we visited one day. As my wife and I toured the cages of the exhibition, we stopped to stare at the largest ducks that I had ever seen in my life.

"I want to have those," I said immediately.

"I wonder what they are," said my wife slowly and quietly, as she began to study the catalogue in an attempt to identify the bird and its breeder. I knew instinctively by her reaction that she was as keen on having that kind of duck as I was.

They were really very fine birds. They had the coloring of the mallard, but their great heavy bodies were set low on their legs, and they looked square and massive.

"They're called Rouen ducks," she announced at last.

Before too long we were busily rearing eight ducklings. Maybe we failed to feed them properly, or maybe we were sent the wrong birds from the hatchery, but when the youngsters were full grown they were as much Rouen ducks as I am a tiger. A breeder told me that Rouen ducks take a long time to mature, and so we decided to feed them for a year and see what happened. But although they were naturally lazy birds, not prone to go onto the water, they failed to put on weight and achieved no more than a pretty plumpness and the wrong sort of shape. We were disappointed, to say the least.

"You don't seem to have had much luck with your Rouen ducks. They look like ordinary mallard, only a bit bigger."

"I'm going to have the lot slaughtered in a couple of weeks," I said grimly.

Like all other ducks, the Rouen ducks lived in the duck stables that face the back courtyard. In common with all other domestic waterfowl, they were let out in the morning and locked away at night. One day I noticed that a little wild mallard drake had fallen in love with the smallest of the so-called Rouen ducks. Every morning at about six o'clock, the little drake would begin his patrol outside the door behind which his lady love had spent the night. He was a beautiful little chap, cocksure of himself and with a certain swagger. As soon as I appeared at nine o'clock to let the birds out of the stables, he would hurry forward to greet me and wait anxiously a little distance away until all the waterfowl came out into the courtyard.

The Chinese geese would come out first. Heads high and honking loudly, strutting along with an arrogant air, they would march out to a certain point and form a rough circle. In clear, sharp tones that can be heard a mile away, their necks outstretched horizontal to the ground, they would greet each other as though they had only just met for the first time.

The other waterfowl would follow, among them, the Rouen ducks. No sooner did they emerge than the little drake would rush to greet them and to join his love. She would come out to greet him with her head on her shoulders, her beak crooked while she snattered her greeting at him. As soon as they were united, the pair would vanish for the day while the other Rouen ducks stood about the courtyard and behaved in a most unadventurous manner.

Icarus, Romeo and Juliet

Anyone who has regular contact with animals soon learns to distinguish individuals in flocks. I used to wonder about shepherds being able to pick out individual sheep because, to my eye, all sheep look the same. But after a while I could pick out the Rouen duck and the mallard drake from all other ducks about the place. By observing them morning and evening I was able to tell that the mallard Romeo was serious. Not only did he hang about in the morning until his love emerged for the day but, strange to relate, he brought her back to the stable each evening. Once or twice he even went so far as to go inside with Juliet, but the enclosed space was more than the wild one could bear. Although he had come to accept food from me outdoors, he would panic as soon as I entered to feed the milling mob.

My wife was as interested as I was in the romance of the ducks. When I announced that the moment had come to dispose of the Rouen ducks, her reaction was immediate.

"But you can't possibly kill the duck that's in love with the little mallard drake!" She was indignant.

I explained patiently that the reason for my not having had those ducks killed ages ago was that I wanted to make sure that Juliet wouldn't be among them; that I actually wanted to carry out an experiment to find out if she would go away with the little drake once she was alone. My wife was pessimistic. She asked me what I thought they would do if they did not stay together, and what I would then do with the single duck. I had to admit that that was a difficult one, but I wanted to see what would happen in any case, when a domestic duck went to live with a wild one. I wanted to see what sort of duckling they produced—if they would learn to fly or if they would be flightless like their mother. When the Rouen ducks were slaughtered, I spent three weeks turning the surviving duck out of her home, because I knew the little drake would not go to live with her in the *Brauhaus*. She was so domesticated, and so much a creature of habit, that she would put in an appearance every night and try to get into her stable. It is almost as difficult to turn away a duck that has lived in one place since her childhood as it is to train an adult wild duck to accept a stable as its residence.

When we forced her to do so, Juliet joined the wild ones. Her little mallard drake remained faithful and soon the pair of them could be picked out on any of the ponds.

Then, inevitably, Juliet raised a family. Because buildings meant something special to her, she ignored the nettles and the reeds, choosing instead an angle of the house in which to build her nest. All in all, it was a secure site: the top of a concrete cover to a manhole between the back of the garages and the back house. Beanpoles had been stacked here to form a kind of wigwam and she built her nest of down and dried leaves and bits of twig and straw directly in the center of its protection.

I threw her a handful of grain every day as I passed on my way to the pheasant pens. She would blow up her feathers and hiss at me angrily, but it was all an act. Her face saved by her threat-display, she would get off the nest while I was still there, cover the eggs carefully and then proceed to enjoy a hearty meal. "How is Juliet?" became a standard question whenever I met my wife in the hall, like, "Has Patrick come back from school?"

One morning I awoke to hear a great chattering and quacking from under our bedroom window. I got out of bed quickly, in time to see Juliet with eight little ducklings waiting at the swans' feeding place to the left of the front doorstep.

132

She came back later in the morning, and continued to come along every day for many weeks after that. Nor did she fail to visit her old home. I once saw her, with her brood strung out in a line behind her, march proudly out of the *Brauhaus* one morning. In fact for quite a time Juliet and her brood were to be seen almost everywhere with the little husband in attendance.

When the brood was reared, Juliet and her husband would join the evening feeding sessions in the back courtyard, with the swans and geese and other ducks. Then, little by little we saw less and less of the pair. Although she had slimmed down a bit, she was still easily recognizable among the sixty-odd wild or tame ducks that haunted the place, for the good and simple reason that she was larger than any of the others.

About a year after their first brood together, we discovered that Juliet had learned to fly. We knew that it was Juliet, the domestic duck, because although slimmer she was still bigger than the other mallard ladies. She behaved in much the same way as she had done before, and even went so far as to visit the *Brauhaus* and go inside it. It would be fun to say that Romeo had taught her to fly, but what really happened was that she mastered flight because, having "gone wild," she could not live the life of a wild duck without this essential ability; she could neither follow her husband, nor fly with the new group. I thought that this was wonderful and possibly even unique, but to my disappointment I later discovered that this was not the case. Be that as it may, firsthand experience is always more exciting than reading that it can happen, and in any case it was fun.

Both Juliet and Icarus had a great deal in common, although their motives were different. Both birds gave up their relatively secure lives and habits because of outside influence, and joined the wild ones. Both learned to fly, and both, bred of domestic stock, reverted to nature and were able to deal with whatever unaccustomed rigors were imposed on them.

Although Icarus has vanished, I am glad to say that Juliet, now six years of age, is still about. She has lost most of her old habits by now, but she sometimes comes near us, hopefully looking for food, and is seldom disappointed. The spring gives way to summer, at night the voice of the nightingale has given way to that of the owl and by day the cuckoo still calls, illusive and far in the distance and the mew of the buzzard is not heard any more. New broods of ducks are on the moat and on the ponds. New generations are on the move, little skuttling balls of fluff that race across the water in a flurry of sudden sound, leaving wakes behind them like miniature speedboats. We get to know the broods, and count them whenever we can, keeping a tally as nature takes its toll.

The dividing line between tameness and wildness is very thin and not as absolute as one might suppose.

Seeing contented birds loafing near the doorstep, swans in particular, many people have jumped to the conclusion that we must have taken great pains to tame them. This impression is heightened when they see other free-living waterfowl following much the same behavioral patterns on the estate. "It's quite obvious that you must spend *hours* working with your animals in order to get them so tame," they say. "Of course I'd never have the patience." I point out gently that it is not really a question of time. It was the swans, not we, who decided on their loafing site by the front door, and the other activities that they engage in; but we have, of course, encouraged them. Love and interest are the main ingredients in the taming recipe. Time is not of the essence, so much as infinite patience.

Neither my wife nor I spends hours with the animals. We lead busy lives that preclude a great expenditure of time. Neither of us spends more time than a decent gamekeeper would spend with his pheasants when feeding them and certainly less than a gamekeeper would spend with the broods on the rearing field. Three to five minutes daily per species is the average of what we spend. This is quite enough to get the animals as tame as we wish to have them, for it must be remembered that tameness in this context has to do with preventing a pheasant flying up and damaging itself on the overhead wire, or with encouraging a mandarin duck to come along to get its food. We call this the establishment of trust rather than the taming of the animal.

What we are trying to do, and have succeeded in doing, is to get free living creatures to associate with man under certain given conditions and to tolerate him as long as these conditions continue to exist. The object of the exercise is not to rob a creature of its freedom and to make it utterly dependent on the human for *everything*, in other words to domesticate it fully. Yet a wild creature that has entered into such an association with a human being retains all of its character as a wild creature once it is outside the area in which the association takes place. Indeed, if the relationship is not continually fostered and kept alive by the human partner, the animal, however tame it may appear to be, quickly reverts and within a few weeks or months, depending on the individual, becomes totally wild again.

I suppose that everybody who deals with animals has his or her own method. The whole thing is experiment and theory anyway, with the single, but vital common ingredient of patience. If one is not prepared to deal with oneself and to go in for a bit of muscular as well as mental control, then as they would say in my country, "you can throw your old hat at it." Without patience, there is no point in trying to establish a relationship with any essentially wild animal.

Tameness and trust come through the stomach. First feed: then convince, is my method of dealing with all the creatures with whom I wish to establish a firm relationship. When I get down to work with an animal that I want to have tame for any reason, I work first through the stomach, or the gizzard, as the case may be. Initially, for ducks and swans the medium is bread, and for geese and pheasants, simply grain. This of course has nothing to do with normal diets which will subsequently be fed.

I call my way of working the "a little nearer" method, which almost speaks for itself. The animal that is to be subjected to the whole unnatural business is usually confined in a large aviary or a large pen, and has to accept two prerequisites: it must understand that it can get away from me or escape from me, in other words, it must have a circumscribed escape distance; and it must get used to the human presence. From that point on, it must accept the fact of being fed and look forward to the time of feeding.

Ducks and swans are not usually penned at all but are free to swim wherever they are at the time. Also they are normally full-winged. I therefore behave as most people do when they are feeding the ducks in a park. When the fowl have got used to being fed at a particular place, I merely begin to feed them daily a little closer to myself, until at last the subject or subjects come of their own accord.

Penned creatures are treated a little, but not much differently. I enter the pen and walk about in it, never directly looking at the creature and never attempting to go near it. Because I do not fix it with a stare, the animal is, as it were, at liberty to say to itself, "the fellow has nothing to do with me." But the food is laid down, always at a special place and always with the whistle or the call that I have decided upon for that particular bird, so that in time the bird begins to form an association of call–man–food. As soon as the bird begins to show signs of accepting food readily at a distance, a day's feeding is left out, maybe even two days'. There is no cruelty involved here because the pen or enclosure has sufficient natural food and water to nourish the animal all the time if need be. However, when I do come next time, having deliberately avoided the pen in the meantime, the animal is waiting.

At this stage I crouch down and wait, rattle the grain in the container and spill a little on the ground. In the early stages the subject gives me a nervous look and tries to make up its mind to come nearer. It takes some steps forward, retreats, moves forward again and stops, maybe hissing in the case of a Canada or snow goose. I stay for a time, not looking directly at it, then put down the food, before walking away in the opposite direction. The idea beginning to form in its head is that there is no danger; I have talked to it gently, I have given the call or whistle that signifies food, I have even added a word to its vocabulary. As I slowly spill out the grain onto the ground, I always say in a low voice, "Come, come."

In a pen of about a hundred square meters, escape is always possible even if it is pinioned, or the flight feathers cut, but with each session the animal comes visibly nearer. When the day arrives that the bird comes within half a yard, I begin to spill food more slowly out of the container before moving away. The next time I extend the food in my hand, and fling a few corns at the bird who has now gained enough confidence to pick them up. The next feeding time, I flip them a little nearer to my own hand, until finally I more or less surround my hand with grain on the ground. I then wait, still as a frozen statue, until the bird approaches and picks up the food. After that, there's nothing to it. I put my hand on the ground *with* the grain, then the grain *in* my hand, and bingo! the captive is pecking merrily away at the palm of my hand.

One small tip: don't be disappointed if after a peck or two, the bird stops and moves away. After all, the soft feel of the hand and the warmth emanating from it are unaccustomed factors. Put the food down gently and persevere until the bird eventually comes to the hand of its own volition.

The rewards? It's all a point of view. Contact is one. No pheasant is as beautiful as the healthy, shimmering creature that pecks out of one's hand. Victory? Of course, over oneself and one's patience. An achievement anyway, a coming to terms with a lot of things, an ultimate pride in being trusted. Mishandle that trust, frighten the creature just once, and you may have to start the whole business all over again, if not from square one at least from pretty close to it. But the real reward, I believe, is that the animal that you are keeping does not fly up and injure itself when you come near to it: so you can now study it in peace.

Talk plays a great role in dealing with all animals; the softer the tone, the better. Tone is vital. People who have heard me are inclined to laugh because I say "please" and "thank you" to our dogs, but it is actually the *attitude* rather than the words that is important. It costs nothing to be polite and the animal instinctively understands it. I hasten to add, in case anyone is thinking that I am near the lunatic fringe, that the animals do not understand politeness *as such,* but rather the tone that belongs with it. If one pauses to think about it, the more logical it becomes that one should talk to animals. Most large predators, from a lion to a cat, stalk their prey silently and by stealth. So it must be instinctively doubtful that any animal that comes with food, making odd noises into the bargain, is going to attack; even if the animal smells uncomfortably of flesh and wears its eyes to the front of the head as most carnivores do.

We humans can have very odd ideas about animals because we have the capability of distinguishing *intention.* Observers of animals living under wilderness conditions have noticed that lions, for example, live with their prey and that the prey is able to distinguish between a hunting lion and a lion that is just there for no other reason than it lives about the place. The dead-silent attitude of the attacking animal, plus fixation of the victim with the eyes, gives away intention; but the expression of *good* intention cannot be conveyed to an animal unless it is known to one, or to be more exact, unless it knows one. In this connection, many humans believe that all animals can divine good intention, as can be seen in any zoo anywhere and any day.

Speaking of good intentions, I am reminded of one wet and dreary winter's evening as I was walking by Grosvenor Square, when the paper man at the top of South Audley Street gave me a goldfish that he had brought to town for some youngster. The paper man had not forgotten his promise, but the child had forgotten to collect it. I took the fish home to our flat in Regent's Park Road and transferred it tenderly from the jam jar to a Pyrex bowl. Next day being a Saturday, I went down to the pet shop in Camden Town and bought another goldfish, one with long trailing fins, and a tench as well as an aquarium, pebbles, good water plants and other good things of life.

The following day the original goldfish was dead. I now had an aquarium, a goldfish and a tench. On the Monday the second goldfish died. On the Tuesday the tench was still spry and remained so until the following Saturday, when I bought another goldfish and another tench, this one slightly larger. On the Sunday the first tench died. I kept on replenishing the aquarium with fish for about two years, but the story ends with my having a large aquarium and no fish, all because of my good intentions toward one goldfish from Grosvenor Square which came, I believe, from a pond in Hackney Wick or somewhere like that.

I still get all kinds of mad ideas. I once was in a sort of pheasant breeding phase. I bought a cock and two tiny Wyndott hens which were to become broody and to hatch out the pheasant eggs. The miner who sold me the birds also succeeded in selling me a golden pheasant cock and two hens, a vast Australorp cock and his four hens. If he had had his way, he would also have sold me the pens and aviaries, but I managed to get away in time.

The delightful dwarf hens were utterly charming and greatly resembled the fat nannies that one used to see in the environs of the Round Pond in Kensington Palace Gardens or *Peter Pan*. They had a rather comfortable way with them, a sort of patronizing air of benign self-content that was very appealing. They reminded me of certain women that I have known from time to time during the course of my life. I thought that they were great fun; what's more, they were so good at the job of hatching that I decided I must have more of them.

I was a bit green behind the ears in those days so I

searched all over the place for more of the birds. It so
happened that one day, just by chance, I saw a whole group
of these hens in an imposing aviary, in a backyard that was
tucked away among some buildings near the zoo in
Münster. I went to have a look at them. They were very
nice and well kept and each one had a splendid yellow
label of plastic attached to the left wing. I stood there lost
in admiration when a man came along and said, "Can I
help you?" This was obviously his way of saying, "Get out
of here."

"Are you the breeder of those hens?" I asked.

"No," he replied. I could see that I had rattled him.

"Do you know if they're for sale?"

"No."

"If you don't know, do you at least know who owns
them?"

"No," he said and I could see that he didn't like the
turn of the conversation.

"I think," he added, drawing himself up to his full
height, "you'd better come again and see Dr. So-and-so. He
might be able to tell you."

"When will he be at home?" I asked.

"I don't know, but he won't be at home here. This is
the Department of Zoology of the University of Münster.
As far as I know the hens belong to it and Dr. So-and-so
is using them to make experiments regarding their intelligence."

It was in this way that a few days later I was to acquire
the hens that came to be known in our family as "the
University Ladies." Due no doubt to their superior education and the fact that they had been at the University,
they were a cut above all other hens. I can say this in all
truth—never before or since have I met hens of such deli-

cate refinement. Naturally they were so tame that it was almost indecent. They required a great deal of handling in order to ensure their personal happiness; they would actually line up to be fondled at the drop of a hat. In fact, only the Favaroles that I had later, who were beige in color and wore white beards and whiskers that made them look like Father Christmas all year round, approached them in gentility of manner and permanent search for human affection. Although we loved the University Ladies dearly, we found it a little irksome to have to stop and stroke the back of each hen when we let them out in the morning. But we had to do this, otherwise the beasts refused to go out for the day.

They came to us full of some wonderful tricks. They could select a pill box with the grain under it, because it was marked with a plus sign and not a minus; they could ring a bell when they wanted to get through a door, and other marvelous things. Alas, their fine education went to pieces because I was not using them for scientific experiments, so they soon got dreadfully out of practice and forgot all that they had ever learned at the University. I am sure that at first they were very puzzled by the problem of too much free time—they had their fixed working hours before that—and they must have considered their new and natural life little short of barbarous. We just couldn't live up to their high standards, and meeting us must have been a frightful comedown in the world for them. They ended up by dying from some obscure kind of liver complaint, but not before teaching me that humans can teach birds a great deal, if there is a purpose and an interest in doing so.

Even though I did not keep those little hens in practice by making them do what they had been taught, their extraordinary trust taught me how to deal with the birds of the air, and how to behave myself with the animals. They had become so used to human beings during the time that they had been used as the subject of behavioral studies, that they responded to the human presence by presenting themselves and expecting to be handled and talked to. It was they who made me want all birds in my care, especially the swans, to react in the same way.

By the end of June, most of the late broods are on the water in a world that is a riot of color. We watch the ducklings run across the water lily pads, touching the opening yellow flowers as they pass. The big rhododendrons are in bloom, their greens, pinks and whites reflecting in the still water. Closer to the house, Thaddäa's roses are in full bloom.

Unfortunately the ducks love that rose bed too. Ruthlessly, in single file, they march through it into the courtyard swinging from side to side on their busy little legs.

"Oh–O-O-O-O," sighs my wife as a few buds or blooms are sent flying. "It's just no good, no good at all. It's always the same."

It's too bad. In the spring the waterfowl regularly trample a whole bed of expensive daffodils flat into the ground along the bank of the moat, where we had optimistically planted them in the hope of having a host of golden daffodils nodding and dancing against a background of water. A five-pound goose and a twenty-pound swan and a two-pound duck can do marvels of steamrolling if the great feet are placed squarely on the tender shoot of a plant.

But nothing would induce us to give up the birds. They have become a part of our lives, of the very scene, and the work that they have done so efficiently is evidence enough of their value. We would not exchange a whole garden of expensive plants for the thrilling daily sight of the birds on the wing, fleet and free above our heads. At any time of the day, a glance upward may be rewarded by a circling brace of duck as it comes lower and lower to drop down onto one of the ponds.

But this involvement with the waterfowl and other creatures is not sentimental. I will wring a neck without too many qualms, especially if a bird is badly injured and my killing it can put an end to unnecessary suffering. I also go out with a gun quite regularly, much to the horror of people who know my love of animals and my interest in conservation. I'm quite unashamed of my shooting. I shoot mostly for the dogs, not to provide them with food, but because I love a good working gundog.

"Do you mean to say that you shoot?" Hands are raised in horror. But I say that shooting often helps to conserve. We have discovered, for example, that if we keep down the number of rabbits, we also keep them healthy. The survivors don't get myxamatosis, and if I were a rabbit, I'd rather die by a good clean shot, than by that filthy, slow, starvation-killing, man-introduced disease. Anybody who has seen rabbits affected in this way will understand my point of view.

I'll shoot ducks, but only on other people's estates. I never shoot my own birds, because I couldn't bring myself to shoot somebody that I might know. However, I'll work the dog if another gun is shooting the surplus ducks and drakes, paring down the flocks to the ninety or one hundred birds that we keep throughout the winter.

It is quite wrong to think that conservation means the maintenance of large flocks or herds of animals. Conservation really involves the preservation of the habitat. Clean water, the assurance of an ample supply of natural food, mud banks where the birds can find what they require to sustain life, hedges for the shelter and housing of pheasants and other birds in the wild, where economically possible, the retention of wetlands: these are the factors that influence the true conservationist's thinking. Somehow one always carries away the idea that conservation has to do with great big schemes carried out under the auspices of powerful institutions. This is quite false, a city person's idea of the whole business. Really effective conservation should begin with anyone who has more than a pocket handkerchief size piece of land in a suburban back garden.

At the other end of the scale there is a dreadful tendency on the part of man to interfere with nature, to root out a whole species because individual birds of prey, for example, take a few pheasant or partridge chicks. Once destroyed, a species is virtually irreplaceable. It is one of the miracles of nature's balance that these birds multiply or decline according to the availability of their sources of food. I have noticed this particularly in the case of buzzards, of which we have a number.

I am fond of this species as I am fond of all birds of prey, the great controllers of nature. Consequently, I imposed on the tenant of our shoot the condition that our buzzards should not be shot. I love to see these beautiful birds wheel in the sky and to hear their lonely little mewing cry. Although our tenant saw the point, my prohibition of the use of the gun on the buzzards provoked an outcry on the part of many of the people who come to shoot as his guests, on the grounds that a buzzard will occasionally take a pheasant chick. "How many pheasant chicks were lost each year by adverse weather conditions, by pelting rain, and by the attack of other predators?" I asked with a deadpan face and all innocence. Nobody could tell me. I said that if the answer could be given to me, if proof could be laid before me that the amount taken by the buzzards could be compared unfavorably with the amounts lost by other hazards, then the buzzards could be shot. I was not taken up on the offer.

There was an interesting sequel to this. Some years ago we felled a corner of the woods and planted some thousands of poplar trees. The forester subsequently came to me one day with a long face, and told me that as bad luck would have it, the young trees were being attacked by voles.

"See for yourself," he said. "What the little beasts do is cut a ring around the tree just above ground level. If the ring of bark eaten away is complete, the tree will not survive; if only as much as a quarter of an inch remains, then the young tree will pull through."

A couple of days later we had a man on the job painting the trees with a poison. We naturally kept the situation under close scrutiny, and in due course the forester was able to report that we had lost no more than 1 per cent of the saplings, and that those which had been attacked, and painted with the poison, would survive.

The voles, deprived of the succulent bark of the saplings, had turned their attention to other sources of food. There were large enough numbers around to constitute a virtual plague. What we did observe was an increased number of buzzards about the woods. Presumably they must have been attracted by food. They were very active on the estate and in the woods generally for about six weeks, and it was undoubtedly they who ultimately controlled the pestilence of voles. We were struck by the fact that as soon as the infestation was over, the surplus buzzards vanished, and we were left with the normal stock of six pairs that we knew well. Quite apart from the utilitarian aspect of it, it was a good example of nature balancing itself out.

We would have been pretty poorly off if we had shot all

the buzzards just because of a handful of pheasant chicks that might possibly have been taken and that, under normal and natural conditions, mightn't have survived in any event.

Hans and Leda

T HE SWANS ARE BACK! I'VE SEEN THEM ON THE FISH-
pond!"

Or the chapel pond, or the moat, as the case may
be.

Nearly every year, I have been away on business when
the swans have returned, and my wife has had to call me
long-distance to London or Paris. As soon as my darlings,
as she likes to call them, have appeared on the scene to
again take possession for their annual visit, she has called
me to give me the good news. Her voice is excited because
she knows what this means to me. The news fills me with
deep personal joy and a quiet sense of satisfaction. Each
time, my mind goes back to that fateful day when we decided not to pinion the old birds; their return each year
is my justification for that decision.

We stopped cutting the birds' flight feathers after their
second brood. Free to fly once again, they took to leaving us
at the end of August or September, taking their cygnets with

them as they vanished silently and unexpectedly over the horizon. Although we had no evidence of where they went, we presumed from our reading that they left to join a flock. Some youngsters can fly by late September, and it is known that the parent birds sometimes accompany them to the nonbreeding flock which they join. Once there, the swans live in harmony and the parents leave their cygnets behind them when they return to their breeding ground in early spring.

When Hans and Leda returned in late February or early March,[18] they always took a little while to settle in. A lot depended on the weather, but at the minimum it took about a week. After this they separated, as though allowing themselves a short holiday before settling down to the months of hard work ahead. Soon enough the air would be filled with the familiar sound of beating pinions, as Hans set about clearing his territory of all opposition, real or imagined.

Since he loathes and detests the geese that we began to breed successfully some years back, his first bit of business is to make life on the water intolerable for them. This is comparatively easy, at least where the Chinese geese are concerned. The geese are quite timid outside their own circle, so timid, in fact, that if they didn't come in each evening to be housed and fed, they might almost be described as wild. Out of doors their behavior is that of wild geese, and it is virtually impossible to approach them; their wildness extends right down to their sentry duty and their cries and calls to each other.

Although unable to fly—flying has been bred out of the Chinese geese that we keep, and I have never known any that did—the birds move very fast over land or water when they use their wings to help them; on land, against the wind, they take off to a maximum height of about six inches. This speed is fortunate or Hans would undoubtedly get one now and then. One year he did catch an immature bird and the injuries that he inflicted to the neck and head were quite dreadful. The goose survived, thanks to my wife's nursing, and is still one of our best breeders.

But when he caught a mature gander, he fared less well. Sore pressed, the Chinese ganders are respectable fighters in their own right. Their special technique is to push breast-to-breast and to try to lock wings. They then grab the opponent by the elbow joint, getting a firm hold with their beaks, and they saw and worry their antagonist for as long as they can hold on. If the enemy disengages and wants out, the bird with the better hold hangs on for dear life and runs along after him, still gripping the elbow joint. I have often had a gander get hold of my sleeve while I have been preparing the birds for shows and it is quite a business to induce him to let go again. Once they have got a grip, they seem able to hold on almost indefinitely.

The gander that Hans attacked must have paid him back, because he came away from the encounter with a fine loss of his own blood.

The injuries to the swan were typical: the feather coat gone and the skin raw and bleeding. The gander must have also delivered blows with his wing because the swan limped. The gander, like the swan, can deliver a respectable wing blow. I know this from experience—they have bruised my shins on numerous occasions.

Another of Hans' more formidable opponents was a very large and aggressive Australorp duck. These birds, which we keep for exhibition purposes, are utterly fearless as well as being aggressive; if the mood takes them, they will quite happily attack anything that happens to get in their way. We kept a segregated group at the time in the *Brauhaus* where we had trap-nests; they had the run of the courtyards, and, like the swans, enjoyed visiting us during coffee-time after lunch. This group was under the command of a very large cock named Atilla.

Atilla would march up and start to steal maize from Hans, even though he had been given his own handful. Hans would immediately deliver a smashing blow with the beak, then with his wings. But the cock was alert and fast, and Hans invariably missed. Whereupon the great black cock would wade into the swan, get under his wings and attempt to inflict damage by ripping his flank or breast with his huge spurs. A couple of minutes of this was usually enough for poor Hans; although the cock could inflict no wounds through the swan's thick feather coat, Hans would beat a rapid retreat to the water.

In fact, Hans always avoids the west side of the ring moat, where the poultry pens reach down to the water. The cocks are ready and eager to defend their territory, and will launch a vicious attack on any swan that lands on the bank. No swan goes near that section of the moat to this day, and it is now the safe reserve of the Canada goose couple that nest there.

Our collection of waterfowl has increased considerably over the years. Apart from the Chinese geese, we have four Canada geese. Hans is careful of the latter and makes a wide detour of their pen behind the house, which has an enclosed stretch of water. I have seen them assume threat-postures whenever the swan cob or pen passed by. Even when these geese were free, the cob never attempted to attack them, but left them severely alone; likewise the little snow geese. We had to pen both of these species as they became very tame, and because some Canada geese were stolen—an annoying aspect of living too near a town.

With these exceptions, other waterfowl were fair targets for Hans' pre-nesting aggression. One thing that has interested me increasingly over the years is Hans' selection of fowl to be attacked. Even during periods of rage, the full weight of his fury is never directed against everything and anything in sight; he follows an order of attack that seems to be color-linked. For example, after an initial attack on the little white call ducks, he will then turn the full weight of his fury on the household saxon ducks that are light beige in color. I have never seen him attack a saxon drake, probably because of its mixed gray color, although he will chase the whole group from the water, ducks and drakes alike. In general, he will tolerate the mallard and the cayuga unless they happen to be the sole occupants of the water at that time, or mixed with the call ducks.

His method of attack is either to launch the full weight of his body on the victim from the air, delivering the fatal blow behind its head with his powerful beak, or to approach from the surface of the water. He will then grab his victim at the base of its head and attempt to drown it. Should the grip fail, the duck or goose has a fair chance of escaping, because the swan will only grab a beakful of back feathers. For some reason the cob never changes his grip; if the other bird keeps moving, it can usually wriggle away, leaving the aggressor with a beakful of feathers as a souvenir. Then Hans will lose all interest.

The question of establishing, holding and defending territory appears to be fundamental in the life of the swan. The instinct is shared by both cob and pen, but the predominance of interest, I should say, lies with the cob. His whole energy, at least during the incubation period, seems to be devoted to patrolling the territorial waters, and this inevitably leads to attacks on other waterfowl. We love to stand far away and call Hans when he is at his most aggressive so that he feels himself forced to defend his territory against us. He will then take off and come on the wing— a foot or two above the water—always a beautiful spectacle. I incite him to do this because I enjoy watching him come straight at me, and also because I like to watch how he comes to a sudden stop. If I get up quickly from a crouching position and stand my ground, he will put on all his brakes and come to a dramatic stop. Sometimes this throws him completely off balance, so that he almost falls over backward or tilts to one side, feet outstretched and wings cupped as he skids to a halt.[19]

While all this was going on, Leda was usually eating as much as she could get. If there were cygnets of the previous year still on the territory, she would help Hans chase them off; if anything, she was far more aggressive and consistent about this than he was. But as far as other waterfowl were concerned, she showed no interest. If there was ice about when she and Hans arrived, they stayed together until it thawed. What she liked to do then was to retire to the nearest fishpond and to spend most of her day there. As soon as we saw this, we knew that Leda was going her own way and that she was beginning to engage in the intensive feeding activity that signaled the approach of the breeding cycle.

I have always loved the truly feminine. Leda incorporated, in her swan-like way, all the attributes that human women long to find in themselves and go to such pains to achieve. She was endowed with gentleness, grace and elegance; she had the secret of eternal youth. Yet she also had great strength of character, for all her modesty, while being

153

shrewd enough to make her interesting. Lighter and more delicate in build than her husband, she carried her neatly modeled head with assurance, on top of a long and slender neck. Her sleek body was smaller, while her legs and feet were a delicate gray, in contrast to her husband's, whose legs and feet were black.

This ultra-feminine bird was rather a special friend of mine. Although I can summon, control, even direct the handsome cob, Leda came to me in a totally different way and was also handled differently. The pair were as different in character as they were in appearance or physique. Hans, colorful, changeable, tending toward violence; Leda more posed and balanced, indifferent to the flamboyance of her mate. She could play rough with him too if he drove her too far, though that seldom happened.

There was nothing negative about Leda. She knew what she wanted and she got it in her own quiet way, which was one of the things I liked most about her. She obviously based her movements at this time on ours, keeping a weather eye open for us, regulating her time by our known movements outside the house. Swans have a very sophisticated time sense, as well as an exceedingly keen sense of hearing and sharp eyesight. It became almost impossible to dodge her.

In fact it took me a few years to work out what she was really up to. She seemed to be up to nothing at all, except to eat us out of house and home. This led me to formulate the theory that the swan pen builds up fat during this period. In order to prove this theory, the pen would have to be weighed on arrival, weighed again at the point of taking to the nest when, say, about four eggs had been laid, and again after the brood had pipped the eggs and were out on the water. It would have meant confining her in some sort of container, hoisting her with a mechanical hoist up to a second-floor level and subsequently transporting her to the point of release. I have never considered that the results would justify the possible danger of frightening the bird. She might be put off laying or might even move away from the territory. I therefore decided that the result would not be worth the risk involved, especially as the swans had become personal creatures rather than birds to be studied. Consequently, the theory remains unproven, but I am reasonably certain that I am right, and that the pen is building up a store of fat on which to live during the lean days ahead.

Although Leda's big clutches may not have been the direct result of her very intensive feeding—certainly clutches of from seven to ten are high in a swan—nevertheless the rich diet which she obtained from us, in addition to the natural foods which she found for herself, may well have accounted for the high survival of her young who may have inherited relatively high fat reserves in the yolk sac as a result of it.[20]

I had always believed, before Hans and Leda came, that the swan pen selected a site, built her nest, possibly with some assistance from the cob, laid her eggs and settled down to incubate them. Six years of observation have now led me to think otherwise. If the behavior of our pair was typical (and I can see no reason why it should not have been, except for small individual variations), the whole approach to selection and building of the nest is bound up in ritual. This will hardly be surprising to anyone familiar with these birds: swans are given to ritual or if you prefer, to ceremony. No matter what front they may present to the rest of the world, they tend to be courteous and tender between themselves. Indeed, a mated pair is very much a "married couple" when judged from the human standpoint of behavior, always providing, of course, that the judgment is based on a happily married human couple.

The decision as to where the nest should be built is not taken quickly. We have known it to take a couple of weeks and have followed the process carefully. Clearance of the territory and the establishment of sovereignty begins at the end of February and ends during the middle of March. Then, as soon as the cob has selected a nesting site, he squats down and begins to work, gathering all material in reach of his outstretched neck and pulling it under him. The first material is usually fallen leaves from the previous autumn, twigs, creepers, coarse grass, dried bark, nettle stems and small sticks. He works in a circle, taking the material in his beak, and pulling it toward him. When the material in the immediate vicinity has been exhausted, he goes off in search of more and will carry this quite some distance.

During this time, he will spend a great portion of each day preparing nest sites. During the nest-building, the pen will often come and keep him company; in some instances she may help him in gathering the material, even changing places with him in the middle of the nest to accept the material that he brings. But eventually she will leave him and *reject* the nest that he has *offered*.

The consistency with which this has occurred has led me to believe that the cob's intensive nest-building activity has a positive purpose beyond the mere establishment of the final nesting site. It would appear that his building of nests, which are subsequently rejected, is designed to *excite* the pen to nest in the first place. What became clear to me from this study was that the cob initiated the building of the nest and the pen finally approved the ultimate nesting site. Hans would build nests in various places and Leda would reject them, until he selected a nesting site that she liked. Then, and then only, would she join him in finishing the nest into which she would lay her eggs.[21]

There is nothing neat and tidy about a swan's nest. It tends to be a rough affair and the selection of material depends upon the terrain and what it has to offer. The nests of the Abbotsbury swans, in Dorset, England, are poor little affairs compared with those built here by Hans and Leda; [22] but ours in turn are nothing compared with the monumental nest of a swan on the shore of the Lake of Lugano at Bissone. This pen literally queened it from the height of her extraordinary nest, which was some twenty-five to thirty yards from the main road that runs along the shore side of the village.

This Bissone nest must have been some eight feet in diameter at the base and three feet or more in height. It was constructed from a most astonishing variety of materials: all kinds of flotsam chosen impartially from billets of wood to cornflake packets, tins, rags, reeds, twigs and rubbish. The bird was very tame and very, very confident that she would not be molested; the village people liked to feed her and the presence of a human did not disturb her in the least. Her nest was a construction of one nest upon another, the original being repaired for each nesting season. I visited this nesting site in 1970, but both the swan and her nest were gone, and nobody knew anything about her any more.

When a swan pen lays her eggs in the nest, she does not cover them over with a blanket of nesting material. Ducks and geese cover their eggs very carefully, but the swan, probably because of its large size and territorial domination, apparently finds this unnecessary. Sheer size has its advantages. Other waterfowl are not advised to nest close by. We have frequently found the dead bodies of little white call ducks floating pitifully on the water in the vicinity of their own, and the swans', nesting sites. Swans do not always make very amicable neighbors.

As I have already said, Hans' and Leda's final nest was usually built on the big dike between the chapel and the mill ponds, a fair distance from the house. With the only open and easily approachable entrance from the park, except for animal intervention, there is no danger. Any human going to the nest would have got into serious trouble with my wife and myself, or Hans, and everybody knew it.

The first sign of egg-laying occurs when the pen begins to visit the nest with increasing regularity, and both swans stay close to it at odd times during the day. Eggs are laid at intervals of about forty-eight hours; once the clutch has been laid, the pen settles down on the nest. Although we are always tremendously curious to know how many eggs have been laid, we have always avoided going near the nest before the pen sits on it. We have learned to wait and find out how many chicks will see the light of day. Leda has laid as many as ten eggs, but the average clutch size is nearer seven.[23]

As soon as the pen has settled down to begin the period of incubation, she seldom gets off the nest. Although she would probably live quite naturally if we did not do so, we still feel obliged to do something about feeding her. This is not always easy, even though the pen will let us come within a foot or two of the nest. The fly in the ointment, of course, is Hans, who doesn't always agree with our coming too near and, on occasion, will fly into the attack.

During the incubating period he is a very bored bird. I have seen him sit beside the nest for long periods at a time, to keep the pen company, and I have seen him continue to sit beside the nest when she gets off it to feed and preen herself. He will not venture too far from the nest except to come to the house, or to make short sallies and clear his territory of any other birds that come too near his nest. Apart from these short ventures, he spends most of his time hanging about, and feeding and cleaning himself.

The period of incubation lasts about thirty-five days, after which the downy chicks pip the shell which has enclosed them, and emerge ready to face the world. If the weather is appalling, the pen will keep her new brood safely under her, even if it takes a few days. She now starts to build up her own body strength as well as that of the brood. Although we have not carried out any post-nesting weighings, the mother bird is visibly lighter. The neck is thin, and the body seems smaller and sleeker.

On a fine day, Leda would bring her brood to the front door. We liked to enjoy the pleasant fiction that she really wanted to show us her new brood. But in fact she wanted food and knew where to get it. This foray normally took place within two or three days of hatching, weather permitting, or as soon as the babies were "water sure." It is quite a distance from nest to house and it was one of the highlights of the year to watch the new brood crossing the expanse of the chapel pond for the first time, gliding under the bridge and finally landing on the bank some thirty yards from the house.

Coming toward us across the grass, the babies would stop every few yards as they struggled to follow their calling mother. She would wait anxiously until the children got onto their legs again after each rest. When they eventually arrived under the great copper beech near the house, she would leave them. It seemed as though this tree, with its seats and garden table, represented some sort of private safety zone in her mind. At any rate, she seemed unafraid of leaving the little ones alone there, although they were fully five yards or more from the feeding place.

While the parents fed eagerly on maize, dried shrimps, crabs, fish and molluscs, the young family would sit in the sun and do exactly nothing.

Once this first visit had been accomplished, Leda would bring the family along almost daily, just after lunch. The children would be left to rest at the near end of the rose bed while the adult birds came across the seven or so meters of open ground to their familiar feeding place by the doorstep.

As time went on we began to be aware of the curious behavior of the pen during these feeding sessions. After she had fed for a while, she would do something like a nervous little war dance; she would suddenly begin to trample with her feet, lifting each foot in turn about a quarter of an inch above the ground, moving quite fast from foot to foot at about 120 paces to the minute. When this odd behavior was repeated day after day, I asked myself what it could mean. Was this an avid expression of evasion, or uneasiness, or fear? But when she engaged in this curious little dance, the pen continued to feed with smooth feathers and with no signs of alarm, so fear obviously had nothing to do with it. It might, I thought, be a sign of impatience. I finally convinced myself that the proximity of a person to her brood made her nervous, and that although she continued to feed, the trampling had something to do with calling the young close to her.

I was to find out that I was basically wrong. It so happened that one day we decided to feed the swans near the water because we wanted to photograph the parents and the brood, which was exceptionally large that year, on the shallow bottom near the reeds. I took a bag of grain with me and began to feed the adults from it, attempting to get them into some sort of position for the photograph.

There was a little mud flat close to the bank, and I threw some grain on it. The old birds came at once and began to feed, standing in about an inch of water. Soon Leda began her trampling movement, whereupon the small ones became very active indeed, darting in and out and feeding busily near her feet. Obviously the trampling had nothing to do with nervousness and quite a lot to do with the babies. Beyond all manner of doubt, the parent swan was stirring up some sort of nourishment from the mud.

I decided that I was on to something, and that I should observe them feeding when I was not close by. To this end I laid food in shallow parts of the water, while I observed the family through field glasses from my study window. Most of the grain was eaten by the ducks, which was not on the agenda at all, but I was frequently rewarded by the sight of repeated trampling procedures.

After consulting the literature which reports similar behavior in geese and shelducks, I concluded that the trampling was conditioned by an instinctive reflex when the very young are near and when *the mother herself is feeding*. Under these natural conditions, the mother tramples to stir up food from the shallow water bed. The chicks cannot up-end yet. When she does this, the youngsters will begin at once to dart about and to feed at the same time as the mother. The whole action has the automatic result of keeping the family close to the parent birds, safe from predators. By extension, the mother will still trample automatically, even when she cannot stir up any food for the young on dry land, because it appears to be the natural thing for her to do when she is feeding in the presence of her young.

This trampling reaction is, in my opinion, no different from the frequent drinking motion carried out by a swan when being fed on dry land. A swan will go through all of the motions of drinking nonexistent water at the feeding place; if water is then poured into a hollow in the ground, the swan will drink from it. Once I tried presenting one of the swans with a bucket full of water. But a bucket was too much, too incomprehensible for a wild creature, although I succeeded eventually in training the cob to take water from a low cooking pot. The result of this has been that he is now able to consume more food on dry land and will finish up the portion given to him. What is also interesting is that he came to expect his water in the pot and became quite annoyed if it was not there.

When Leda had finished her meal, she would call to her young, no matter how near they might be. On her sharp note of command, the babies would form up behind her pointed tail to begin the march back to the safety of the moat, mother leading the way, and father as the formidable rear guard.

Learning to Fly

WHEN WE HAVE FED THE PARENT BIRDS ALONG THE bank, the babies have often been kept waiting for a long time. Tired and possibly cold from waiting around, they have climbed gratefully onto Leda's back, and the swans have put out to water again.

"Oh look!" we hear somebody cry out, "the little swans are on their mother's back!"

The young family is always a joy to watch. Within a few days of the brood hatching, people start to gather on the causeway to have a look. Leda's children were invariably a mixture of the normal gray cygnets with black legs, or the white color phase, white with gray legs. Cygnets are very solid citizens and unbelievably obedient, never wandering any distance from their parents. The result is a close-knit family unit, exceedingly difficult for all except the boldest predator to attack. Should anyone feel the inclination to stray, the mother's sharp call brings him back to his proper place, and no nonsense about it either.

This parental piggy-backing is a common feature of the three species of swan who breed in temperate climates: the Eurasian mute swans, the Australian black swans, and the South American black-necked swans.[24] In the first two to six weeks of life, the babies climb up on the parents' back when they become tired or cold, whereas if they are near the nest and the pen is sitting on it, they will creep under her.

For some reason, swans seem to suffer from cold feet; frequently the old ones will tuck their feet away comfortably inside their plumage, either on water or on land, to warm them up. I have seen a photograph of a trumpeter swan in flight, in sub-zero temperatures, with its feet tucked away in its plumage, instead of stretched out behind it as is normally the case.[25] It is therefore quite easy to understand that the little cygnets find considerable comfort in the warmth of their parents' plumage. I decided to investigate more closely. Partly because I knew from experience that swans seldom, if ever, do what one hopes they will on cue, and partly because I had found out that the naked eye often misses important detail, I decided to record the whole thing on film.

Everything comes to those who wait. In due course we found the right day and the right moment to take pictures. When I ran the film through at normal speed, the shots presented nothing that I had not seen before. But when I slowed the projector down, as slow as possible without burning it, I discovered things I had never even suspected.

The first thing I discovered was that the cygnets do not always sit, as I had believed, on the middle of the back, but were held under the wings, along the flank and above the leg of the parent bird as well as on the middle of the back. When I ran the film through again, I found something else.

Leda did not invite the chicks aboard; the cygnets invited themselves. They climbed onto the mother's back when she was stationary. Alternately, they followed her, paddling like fury until they caught up with her, and then hauled themselves aboard by climbing on a point between the folded wing and the tail. Taking a firm grip of the body plumage, they pushed themselves up on the leg of the swan and climbed up onto the back, obviously using their beaks and feet to get up there. For a second they half hung before they got up underneath the wing; obviously they had difficulty in putting their feet onto the pen's legs. But their climbing instinct is strong. For example, a small mute swan is restless when sitting on a human lap, and will not settle down until it climbs up onto the shoulder of the person holding it.[26]

Climbing down was a different matter altogether. When the cygnets wanted to get down onto the water, the swan pen lifted up a wing, and to a surprising height at that, and allowed the cygnet to drop off her flank onto the water. But this was rather less surprising; I had previously seen cygnets using Hans as a floating slipway, in order to get down onto the water from a high bank. The swan cob had placed himself parallel to the bank, so that they could drop down, one at a time, from the bank onto his back, then onto the water. Hans waited patiently for them to do so. The same procedure was repeated when the cygnets wished to get back to the nest on the bank above.

When the cygnets are about two weeks old or a little more, they begin to feed with the parents on land or in the shallows. The food from the yolk sac in the body cavity has been used up, and the youngsters have to find their food where they can. The next three months are pretty boring to most people, as the cute little downy chicks grow into

young swans. I have to confess that this period of meta-
morphosis puts me in mind of Hans Christian Andersen's
story of *The Ugly Duckling*. In the early stages of their life
the babies are far from ugly, but during the seven or
eight weeks until the fledgling time they are rather un-
gainly.

As soon as the young birds are fully fledged, they are
ready to make their first experiments of flying. The parents
don't help; this is something that they have to learn for
themselves, and there are a number of problems that have
to be overcome. With perfect tact, the first (and subsequent) families always chose a runway in full view of my
study window, so that I could observe them from my desk
without even having to get up.

Most people believe that swans cannot take off from
land, which is nonsense. Swans can and do take off from
land, given a long run and a clear view. I often watched
Hans and Leda take off, whenever the fancy took them,
from the causeway in front of the house, between the
chapel and the courtyard. The area allowed a run of
about ten yards, and they would launch themselves successfully. The trick here is that there is a saucer-shaped
decline of the land, a banking really, between the place of
take-off and the ring moat; when there is an east wind or
breeze, there must be a considerable up-draft at their point
of departure.

At first, the young birds merely stood around, flapping
their wings. I failed to pay much attention to this at first,
thinking that it might be mere coincidence that the cygnets should be flapping their wings whenever I looked out
of the window. They would stand on what I term the
"preening site" for the greater part of the day, necks and
bodies outstretched, flapping away for all they were worth.

One would start the ball rolling, and the others would soon join in. They would flap for maybe five minutes at a time, before their legs would fold up under them and they would collapse on the grass for a rest.

In my ignorance, I had always assumed that birds could take to the air as soon as they grew their first coat of feathers; it never occurred to me that they might have to learn the business. The idea that they might be flightless at any time never occurred to me either. It seemed inconceivable to me that a bird of the air might suffer the fate, even for a limited time, of being earthbound like most other creatures. But they carried on with this wing flapping in earnest for several weeks. I grew increasingly curious about it all, reasoning that they were probably strengthening their pectoral and dorsal muscles against the day when they would master the air. What really delighted me was that the proud parents stood around and watched the procedure; their interest could hardly have been described as avid, but at least they gave the odd glance in the direction of their busy offspring. When the wing-flapping exercises were at what must have been judged a satisfactory stage, the parents brought the children up from the preening or loafing site to the top of the causeway. As if to say: "Now you get on with it!"

I am sure that getting up into the air from dry land was a mighty serious affair for the cygnets, but it was equally entertaining for the main spectator. With a grandstand view from my study window, I had only to sit there in the warmth in order to enjoy the show to the full. If I wanted to get a little bit closer, I merely had to reach for my field glasses.

Imagine a gray swan, very young, a bird of the year as one says, in the full pride of its first plumage, standing with its brothers and sisters on the top of a bank about seven feet above the water level. Swans when standing about have a certain forlorn look about them. In fact they don't look over-bright; they stand about rather aimlessly, like bored people on a railway platform waiting for the train to come in. Eventually something would happen: a tractor would come along, or a car would edge past them, or a well-intentioned trespasser might appear to give them some food. They would immediately forget the business on hand and wander off. Swans are easily diverted; I have seen, time and time again, how they set out to do one thing and right in the middle of doing it, suddenly break off and start something else.

The diversion over, they would all stand about again, for all the world like swimmers nerving themselves before taking the plunge on a cold winter's day. Suddenly one of the cygnets, braver than the rest, would decide to launch itself into the unknown, making a dummy run with wings flapping and legs going like pistons, right down the bank as far as the water. Splash. It would then turn around, proud as punch, and march up the bank. Such bravery deserved recognition. But neither parents nor other cygnets reacted at all, which must have been disconcerting, and the hopeful aviator would set off again.

There were days when two or three cygnets would get going simultaneously. That was a joy to see. Although they weren't successful in getting into the air, at least they showed great skill in avoiding collisions among themselves or with anything that happened to get in their way, like a floating log or a duck on the water. Their real problem was that they knew how to fly all right, but had no idea of how to make use of the air currents that would keep them up, and almost certainly the development of their muscles had

something to do with their failures as well. They were literally condemned to dummy runs until they learned how to
coordinate the various factors that would put them in the
air and keep them there.

Often, there were crash landings when the intrepid
aviator ditched at the end of the take-off. It was as if they
had suddenly said to themselves, "This is it," and then
promptly forgot some integral part of the business in their
excitement, so that they stalled and plonked into the water
below from a height of about ten feet, causing a mighty
splash. The really inept pupils would dash down the runway at great speed, fail to get anywhere near airborne and
crash into the moat from the sheer momentum they had
worked up. They would rest for a moment on top of the
water, looking as bewildered as puppies, and shake their
pointed tails. As soon as they recovered some of their com-
posure, they would then either begin to feed as if they were
shrugging it all off, or they would get out fast and start all
over again. Then a volunteer would position itself on the
farthest side of the causeway. Cleared for take-off. Neck
outstretched, wings flapping, and feet pumping like an
Olympic long-jumper, it would dash along the runway
until it came to the lip of the bank, hurl itself over, catch
the up-draft, and find itself bewilderingly airborne. Success at last! Often the pilot failed to retract the under-
carriage; the legs and feet would continue to run after the
bird was in the air. But it was flying. These sessions were
a joy to watch. Each bird was known to me and important
to me, too. Up until then they had been creatures of the
earth and water. Now they were trying to find the secret
that would open up a new element for their future lives.
It became a matter of great personal excitement, even
pride, when the babies finally took to the air. Then, like

children with new toys, they would take off at any time of the day and at almost any excuse. A great new sensation was theirs; they were determined to master it.

To watch Hans or Leda take off from exactly the same runway was quite another matter. The fast wing beat, the sureness, the strength of the legs and feet thrusting at the ground to add even more power, were impressive things to see. As polished and accomplished aviators, they made the first efforts of their young somehow charming and even a little pathetic.

To be able to take off like this, to master the air, to have a good view of the earth and of the lesser mortals below, is a thought that has captured the minds of men ever since the legendary Icarus flew too near the sun. What dreams! But the airfoil and the internal combustion engine have now made flight possible. The airplane has come, and has come to stay. We take it for granted today but it lacks romance. The turbo-props and the jets scream and whine with their familiar voices above our heads and we just have to put up with them. If anyone had ever told me when I was young that I would get on with my work as I sat in an airplane, without my nose glued to the window pane, without ever a glance outside, I would have laughed at him.

When I was a boy I was fascinated by the idea of flight. To go up into the air was, I imagined, magnificent adventure. To attain altitude and to view the world beneath, must surpass all other excitements. Fields, rivers, towns, cities, coastlines, mountains, would delight the eye for hours on end. Those were the days when to fly great distances or to fly to great heights, was truly the work of the pioneer. Names rolled around in my head like pebbles in a barrel. Sir Charles Kingsford-Smith, Amy Johnson and Jim Hollison, Amelia Earhart, Getty and Post, and a score of others, captured my imagination and fired it with the thought of new horizons. I wanted to be one of them as burningly as any youngster of today might want to be an astronaut.

I had my private gods as well. I say private because I had had personal contact with them. There was Lady Heath who, when she was standing by the tail of a Tiger Moth at what is now Dublin Airport, told four of us schoolboys how she had once landed on the parapet of a house. There was Sir Osmond Grattan Esmonde, a friend of my father's, who founded or was involved in the foundation of the Irish Air Corps. Indeed, before their take-off from Portmarnock, on their memorable east to west crossing of the Atlantic, Fitzmaurice, Kohl and the Baron von Hünefeld visited my parents one evening. Alas, I was tucked up in bed and not allowed to come down to see them. But even their presence in our house was enough to make them undying heroes in my eyes.

It was all to no avail; I was not to fly. Parents struck! I was forbidden the air. But a part of my mind will remain in the air, in every sense of the word; a self-built wind-tunnel and models of strange experimental design kept me happy. I convinced myself that I would become an aircraft designer. Unhappily, my mathematical ability did not even reach the big toe of my ambition, and no airplane conceived in my mind ever took to the air, except in model form. By the time my feet left the ground, the days of adventure had passed me by. To fly in the great commercial machines of today bores me; I look back with love on the days when the commercial passenger flew in a plane made of canvas and struts with the pilot a hand's breadth away.

I have spent hours looking at birds. The fast flight of the

swift, the glide of the seagull, the wheel of the buzzard, the jerky flight of the jay, the explosive start of the duck and its arrow-sure flight across the sky—all these excite me. But most of all I love the swans; the beautiful creatures that have the mastery of earth, water and sky alike. I somehow identify with them and remember my youthful dreams of flight, so that a part of me flies with them as they stretch across the sky. Maybe my boyhood dream was associated with a secret longing for a freedom that is denied the earthbound, but certainly there is a grandness about them when they are in the air that for me not even the eagle can rival.

I am always lucky as far as swans are concerned. I have seen flying birds in so many places, suddenly and unexpectedly. Once, when driving down one of the streets in Bath, I saw a swan come low above the street to my left, turn and fly down the street that I was traveling. I have watched swans sweeping over Swiss and Austrian lakes and in flight across the Irish and English countryside. More recently, I have been able to look closely at swans landing and taking off. Indeed, if I was prepared to go near to the nest when the pen was sitting, I only had to make enough noise to attract the cob. On seeing me from a distance of a hundred yards or so, Hans would obligingly launch himself into the air in order to attack me.

Swans are very heavy birds and it takes a bit of work on their part before they get themselves into the air. Because of their weight, the wing-loading is heavy and they are not able to launch themselves into the air with the suddenness of a duck. But although I have studied them on many occasions over the years, I have never observed any pre-flight preparation. The swan just flaps his wings and "runs" along the top of the water, using considerable leg thrust against the resistance of the water in order to assist his wing beats. The water fountains he makes show very clearly the force and the distance between the "steps" as the swan progresses, gathering speed to get into the air.

My friend Charles Harvard Gibbs-Smith, who is an authority on the history of aviation and greatly interested in bird flight, has confirmed, during one of our many conversations on the subject, that aerodynamically the wing-loading of the swan is high. This means that the wing area is small in relation to its weight, and the weight of the swan's body, when the swan is flying. It means that the bird must therefore build up a high speed on the water before the airflow around the wings is sufficient to produce enough lift to enable it to fly.

Most of us take birds and their flight pretty much for granted. This is not so surprising when you remember that we have been accustomed to see birds fly as a part of the natural order of things. To explain how birds fly is another matter and not a terribly easy one. Wings are marvelous pieces of equipment because they are capable of several things. They not only keep the bird up in the air, as an airplane's wings keep an aircraft up, but they also act as the motive power, as propellers, as parachutes and as brakes, all rolled into one. What is more, as the countless photographs testify, the wing planes may be changed, thus allowing the swan a great variety of sensitive controls over its flight. The wing is also the swan's arm, in human terms, although it is actually an elongated foreleg. Supposing we make the whole thing easier by drawing a direct parallel, and build up the wing in terms of the human arm.

The swan has a humerus, the bone of the upper arm; a radius and an ulna, the bones of the forearm; a wrist and a three-fingered hand. All of these bones are hollow and

BONES OF THE WING; ARM AND HAND

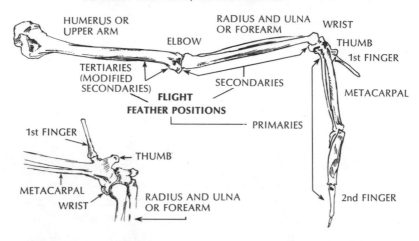

light in their construction, and are covered by a fine sensitive skin, from which all the important feathers grow. There are three groups of feathers, each serving different purposes in flight. The big flight feathers, known as primaries, are attached to the hand or wing tip, and have the job of propelling the bird. The secondaries, which are attached to the forearm, are shorter than the primaries and are the flight feathers of the inner wing, which play a leading part in supporting the bird in flight, and finally there are the tertiaries, which grow from the humerus or upper arm, and are in fact an extension of the secondaries providing a close bearing between the wing and the body, where there would otherwise be a gap.[27]

The feathers themselves are marvelous in construction, and are made of a hollow center shaft, or quill, from which grow a front and a back vane. Each vane is worthwhile examining in itself because the components of these vanes are little branches that grow out diagonally toward the tip of the quill, like the branches from a tree. In turn, each one of these branches supports a further group of branchlets, if you like to call them so, which have tiny hooks on them and which bind the feather parts together in a kind of net. While we are on the subject of feathers, it is amusing to note that somebody once counted the feathers of a Bewick swan, and recorded a total of 25,216, of which 80 per cent were taken from the head and long neck.

What results is a cambered wing, like the wing of an airplane, thick and rounded at the leading edge over a spar of bone, and thin at the trailing edge, the leading edge thickness tapering off toward the tip of the wing. In flying the bird raises and lowers its wings, or flaps them, thus setting a series of actions in motion. Each feather of the wing, the closer it is to the root of the wing, is over-lapped by its neighbor. As soon as the bird engages in a downstroke in flight, the air pressure forces the midwing feathers together to produce an air-tight surface. The inner half of the wing, not having the same distance to travel, appears to stop in flight and to become the supporting plane which keeps the bird in the air, while the outer half drives on downward to finish the stroke. Then, on the up-stroke, it loosens and the feathers open up to let the air slip through and so reduce what would otherwise be a counter pressure on the upper surface of the wing.

The actions described above may clearly be seen in the wonderful photograph of the two cruising trumpeter swans taken by Winston Banko.[28] The swan to the left in the photograph shows the inner half of the wing supporting the bird in air while the closed outer part of the wing com-pletes the downstroke. The swan to the right shows the upstroke of the wing with the primaries opened, letting the air through. A close study of the picture suggests that

175

the right-hand bird is also regulating its course by slipping air through the wing that is to the right of the observer— the bird's left wing—while altering course with its other wing, the primaries of which are closed. Several photographs of the many which were taken of our swans in flight show clearly that directional changes are controlled by movement, or most probably a whole series of movements and adjustments of the plane angles of the outer wing. This would be the same principle as is supplied in the use of the aileron of an aircraft in order to change air flow directions.

Birds do not fly through the air by beating their wings downward and backward as men use their arms when swimming through the water. Forward speed, i.e., propulsion, is produced by the propeller action at the end of the bird's wings; this is of two kinds depending on the kind of bird. First—and this is *not* the swan's technique—we have those large birds like the crane, with huge and rather thin loose wings which, on the downbeat, roll over into a form of a propeller. This is due to the front spar being beaten downward strongly and the floppy trailing edge twisting upward on the downstroke, and downward on the upstroke; this action produces a thrust component which carries the bird forward.

The majority of birds, however, *including the swan,* have comparatively stiff wings. In these birds the forward propulsion (thrust) is produced by two factors: (1) the stretching apart of two, three or four of its outer primary feathers, like opening the fingers of a hand; and (2) the peculiar construction of these outer primaries which are said to be "emarginated," i.e., they have less vane surface on the front of the supporting quill than they have on the rear vane surface. This means that when the feathers are apart like fingers (see the illustration of the trumpeter swans in flight), and being beaten *down,* far more air pressure is exerted on the wide vanes at the rear than on the narrow vanes at the front, with the result that each individual outer primary feather twists into a propeller. And to a lesser degree the same process is at work, in reverse, on the *upbeat* of the wings.

It cannot be over-emphasized that this is the only means by which these birds can move forward through the air, unless of course the bird is gliding downward with rigidly held wings, when thrust is being produced by the force of gravity.

When the swan beats down its wings, these little propellers on the wing tips are extremely powerful and literally propel the bird through the air by their airscrew action. As they beat down, they are seen in high-speed photographs to be not only twisted but bent up at the ends by the force of the downstroke. Again I would refer to the photograph of the trumpeter swans in flight. The left wing of the swan to your right shows very clearly both the bending and the twisting, as well as the spreading of the primary feathers. What is more, by the time the wings reach the bottom of the downstroke, the propeller action—which is entirely confined to the *tips*—has drawn the wings quite far forward as well.[29]

Then comes the ultra-rapid flip upward of the recovery, or upstroke. If the bird is photographed during one of these upstrokes, the outer propelling primaries are often seen as blurred, because this recovery stroke of the wings is so much faster than the downstroke—which takes half again as long. The setting of many cameras does not freeze the movements, as happens in photographs of the much slower downstroke.

When landing, the swan, with its high wing-loading,

must hold its wings rigid at a high angle of incidence in the last stages of its alighting on the water, presenting them to the air almost vertically as a brake or wing-flap. At the same time the outer primaries are stretched wide. Now that the wings are not flapping, these outer fingers provide a number of stabilizing airfoils which will not stall nearly so quickly as the main parts of the wing; hence the latter are allowed to function as long as possible. As the wing tips are a long way away from the root of the wing, they move with great speed, and it is the rapid up and down movement of the outer primaries that produces the whick-whick-whick sound of the bird in flight. Although some think otherwise, this sound is almost certainly made by the wings and not the voice.

In addition to the use of the wing as described above, the landing swan makes use of the feet and the tail as a water brake, with the neck apparently adjusting the final balance. The big feet are spread outward and thrown forward before the moment of impact, and on impact, take on the function of tobogganing to a stop while the head and neck are drawn back as the swan settles.

Ice, as always, presents a problem. One year we had five cygnets. I was feeding the golden pheasants one day when I saw all five take off from the loafing site, one after the other. I had visions of hard landings on the thick ice and warwhooped at the birds, more as an experiment than in the hope that they would obey the call. To my great surprise, one of the group came down near the little island in the moat, behind the aviary. The others flew on. Dropping everything, I dashed like a lunatic around to the back of the house, and arrived in time to see my brave youngsters as they made their landing near the wooden bridge. Cygnets coming down on ice go through the normal landing procedure, feet splayed at the end of outstretched legs, body up and tail well down and spread. Unfortunately, ice is not water, and the resultant three-point landing can be rather funny to watch. Instead of all these brakes being applied and working, the most almighty skids result. All balances are upset, and I have seen a swan literally spiraling along the ice. They can also fall over on their sides and twist away, and they inevitably end up with necks stretched high, looking bewildered.

The four cygnets had landed by the time I had crossed the bridge; three of them were sitting in the curious positions in which they had ended up, but the fourth had not been so fortunate. It was standing exactly in the center of the moat, and as I watched, I saw an ominous pool of blood spreading under it. I had always heard that a bird can bleed very rapidly to death; if ever I saw a bird ready to do so, it was that young swan at that moment. I dashed around to the front of the house again, yelling "Help, help!" over and over.

"What in the name of goodness has happened now?" Thaddäa called out from one of the bedroom windows.

"One of the cygnets is bleeding like a stuck pig. I'm going to try and get it off the ice with food."

My wife is a great one in an emergency. No matter how gory the job, she is up and at it while I am still wondering where to begin.

"I'll be right down."

I grabbed a food bag and ran back to the swans. They were still sitting as I had left them. The dark pool under the injured one was growing larger by the second. The ice was already showing signs of cracking, and I had no great desire to plunge into icy water. So I began to call, using the warwhoop, and to strew the maize about a foot from the bank, hoping that if the uninjured birds came over, their brother would come too. The three did, but the injured one stayed where it was. I was getting desperate, because it appeared to be too shocked to move. But just as I was preparing to give up hope, the fifth cygnet appeared out of the blue.

Attracted by the familiar "whoop-whoop-whoop," it had taken off and come to see what food was on offer. It made a clumsy landing, tipped over on its side and slithered sideways toward the injured bird. Nothing could have been better. All of a sudden, the injured one came to life and began to limp over to us. As soon as he reached us, we caught him and carried him to the big old kitchen of the house.

Like all injured swans of our experience, he was as quiet as a lamb. They seem to know that one is out to help, and never offer any form of resistance. We put him on a table and got to work at once. About a quarter of an inch of flesh had been torn loose at the knee joint, and blood was welling thickly from this wound. Every effort to stem the bleeding was to no avail until we remembered a kind of styptic cotton wool in the first aid kit. That did the trick; we patched him up and put him in a stable and hoped for the best.

He must have injured a wing as well, because when we put him out to join his brothers and sisters a fortnight later, he did not fly away with them and the parent birds. He spent a lonely winter with us, and when the parents returned the following year, made himself scarce, taking to the stream, where he remained for a month or so. He may have recovered his power of flight, because one day he was gone and was never seen again.

Katja Meets the Swans

ONE FINE AFTERNOON IN THE AUTUMN OF 1966, WE drove eagerly to the Düsseldorf airport to meet two arrivals. The first was a close friend whom I hadn't seen for fifteen years, who was due to arrive from New York, and to stay with us for two days. The second was traveling less glamorously by air freight, in a large transport box, and was due to stay for a longer period.

When we arrived at the airport, my wife and I split up. As luck would have it, the two were scheduled to arrive within five minutes of each other at different places; thus it was my wife who first took the small black puppy into her arms and introduced her into our family. It was right that it should be so. There are some people who have a special way, a special magnetic touch with dogs, and my wife is one of them. The pup came to Thaddäa at once; soon the newcomer was frisking happily at the end of her smart new lead as they walked together from the freight depot to meet us at the main building.

It was almost a year since I had decided that we needed a dog. We had geese, ducks and children, but no dog. To me, a big country house without a dog is like a stretch of water without waterfowl or fish, or a forest without deer.

So the decision to buy a dog was relatively easy, the more so because Patrick had become increasingly keen on the idea. But what sort of a dog should we have? That was another matter. We had endless discussions about its size and shape. My wife had always been a terrier person and had always loved sporty little dogs. I, on the other hand, liked big dogs and made no bones about it.

"All right, then, let's compromise. Let's have an airedale, like Hubert has," Thaddäa suggested. But although I knew and liked the two beautiful dogs that my brother-in-law kept, I did not want an airedale, because terriers, even jumbo-size terriers, are not my kind of dog.

"I think that we ought to have a labrador or a boxer," I said quite emphatically.

"I don't want a boxer. They're so ugly and they dribble. They're so ugly that they're almost beautiful, but I don't want to have one."

"Then let's have a labrador," I said, with visions of training it as a gundog and having lots of fun going to shoots. "I'll see about getting one the next time that I'm over in England."

"They're so big and they leave their hair all over the place."

"They're not all that big, and they're very gentle. Just the right kind of dog for the boy."

In spite of our having lived so long in England, my wife had only a vague idea about the size and appearance of a labrador retriever, which for some reason or another, she had managed to confuse with a newfoundland. Whatever

Thaddäa's misgivings may have been, I had my way in the end, and set about the selection of the pup when I next visited England. But if the choice of the breed was finally mine, the decision as to the dog's name was entirely Thaddäa's. She chose the Polish form of Katharine, and the puppy was named Katja.

As usual, I went in search of the right book, and found it at Wesley Richards in Curzon Street, shortly after I had acquired the puppy. *Train Your Own Labrador* by the Baroness Beck soon became my spare time reading, and I found that my own beliefs were so in sympathy with the author's that I determined to use her methods. By this time I had acquired enough practical experience at handling animals to feel competent to train my own dog. I told myself that the same patience and love devoted to the taming of the pheasant, when applied hourly to a constant companion, could produce nothing but good results. The dog would have to learn to be both house dog and gundog; moreover, she would have to learn to fit in with my peculiar way of life.

Katja's future had been mapped out for her long before her arrival. When we began a rigid system of training, she accepted it with good nature and willingness. For general training on the lead, I used what I call the training whip;[30] a long riding whip used by horsemen in dressage. This whip is carried in the same hand as the lead, and is used to caress the dog when it obeys, or, when applied by pressure to either shoulder, to direct it to the right or to the left. Pushed lightly against the animal's chest at the same time as the word of command is given, it will tell the dog not to move forward. Pressure applied to the hindquarters, above the tail, will make the dog sit. This extension of the hand is very useful in training the dog to understand quietly spoken words of command which are given when the pressure is applied. The dog soon becomes so used to the pressure applied by this whip, that it is possible to take it out for a walk with the whip only, without a collar and lead, and to direct it by simple pressures on shoulder, chest or tail without saying a single word.

Just in case dog lovers say, "The fellow uses a whip on his dogs," perhaps I should add that the whip is never used to beat the dog, and that when I take it in my hand, the dog immediately associates it with the joy of an outing. To her the whip does not spell punishment, but a walk, a game, or a bit of fun. For this reason also, if the dog has behaved itself well, it is permitted the privilege of carrying the whip home.

She was never allowed to leave my side, never put out of doors on her own, never left alone. She was taught how to behave in towns, to sit at a pedestrian crossing or alone in shops, not to sit on the furniture and not to destroy the rows of rubber boots in the entrance hall. Baroness Beck was perfectly right about the exceptional intelligence of labradors. With constant repetition and patience, Katja learned all the rudiments in a remarkably short time, about three months. She really learned it so that it stuck, although of course she is still learning and will continue to learn throughout her life.

Fortunately the swans were away when she arrived; it would have greatly complicated things had they been there. When we came to tackle the next stage, I started training her on poultry and with the domestic ducks and the flock of Chinese geese. As everybody knows, young dogs are full of play and curiosity and I worked on the assumption that "misdeeds" were governed by these two factors. She would want to get close to the living thing and find out for herself what made it tick. The goose or whatever would react by getting out of the way as quickly as possible; the dog would follow, to try and catch it, to satisfy its own curiosity. I therefore told myself that curiosity must be satisfied early, and peacefully, without allowing the dog to form bad habits. Because the dog was intended as a family dog and I was frequently absent abroad, it also became necessary to train the *family* to carry on the good work. They all had to be taught how to handle the dog, so that the training would be continuous whenever she was with anybody other than myself.

There were always plenty of tame birds about the place, which we caught and presented to the dog. Holding them in our hands, we allowed the dog to sniff them all over, repeating over and over again "Not for Katja"—a prohibition that she had already learned for behavior in the house. We repeated and repeated this process until she lost interest in any of the types that we wished her to leave alone.

"Sit steady," from our point of view, was the most important command for work on the courtyards. Given this command, she learned to sit as though on a spot of glue until fetched or called with a quiet whistle. Commanded to "Sit steady" every morning within five yards of the stable doors, she soon learned to passively watch the exodus of the birds from the stable without even bothering to stir from her place.

We were delighted with her progress. Our system worked; we began to realize what a jewel had come into our lives. She learned how to flush a pheasant, but not to worry the captive pheasants. She learned not to annoy tame or semi-tame ducks, yet to retrieve birds injured for some reason, or ducks that had actually been shot. She learned not to attack or chase any of the geese. She learned not to attack or chase poultry. All she had to learn now was to live with the swans. But would the swans learn to live with her?

The swans returned secretly, in their usual ghostly way. I was filled with misgiving when I heard that they were there. Supposing the dog went for the swans, the chances were that that would be the last that we should see of them. When the moment of truth arrived, I put off going out with Katja for as long as possible.

The first encounter took place about thirty or forty yards from the nesting place on the dike between the chapel and the mill ponds, at a point where Katja liked to go into the shallows for a swim. Hans was cruising at the far end of the pond. Telling Katja to sit steady about a yard from the water's edge, I deliberately called to the cob. He came at once on the wing, landing neatly and tobogganing to within a couple of yards of the sitting dog, but a few yards to our right. He settled his wings in a very leisurely fashion and began to cruise up and down looking at us speculatively, as though expecting some food.

Paddling gently with one foot, he languidly came level with us. Keeping his distance, he moved slowly, the head cocked a little to one side, mustering us with his glittering eye, possibly a little suspicious of the newcomer. Although I had confidence in the dog, it remained to be seen how the swan would react to the strange presence. "Oi," I called, "and how is my old Hans? Come, Hans, come!"

He put his head over his shoulder and preened his back feathers, a sign of embarrassment and uncertainty.

Katja was interested. Her tail was wagging, but she sat rock steady, waiting for some sort of command. She looked at the drifting swan and then back at me and continued to wag her tail.

186

On the command "Go," followed by "Go steady," the dog walked along the bank beside me, her eyes still fixed on the cob. Neither swan nor dog seemed to have the least desire to make closer contact. Hans contented himself with gliding along on a parallel course, never letting us out of his sight. He did a little half-dive, to wash and to get the water over his back. Then suddenly he reared up on his feet and tail, stretching his whole body and neck. With chin up to the sky, he flapped his wings vigorously, to shake the water out of his feathers. While doing this he gave out an explosive "nuck-nuck-nuck" before falling back into the water.

This performance was designed to show Katja what a big fellow he was, the big boss man of the pond. She was unimpressed, regarding him with polite interest but no more. So we continued on our way, the cob following us along the water edge, always keeping his distance and never letting us out of his sight. As we walked past the entrance gate and into the courtyard I saw him move grandly under the bridge, still peering at us until we were out of sight.

The next encounter was not quite so controlled. It took place at the same spot and Katja had run ahead of me out of the wood in the park. She was hot and thirsty after chasing a rabbit, and went to the shallows to have a drink. When I arrived on the scene she was up to her middle in the water and barking like mad, inviting the cob to play. She had her bottom up and her shoulders down, legs spread and a silly grin on her face.

Hans idled offshore, looking at her with cold contempt, but obviously intrigued at the same time. When I called her off, the swan followed us along the bank as before, always watchful and keeping his distance. Halfway to the chapel there is a large evergreen; beyond this, I noticed

Leda, the gentle swan, advancing in a distinctly unfriendly manner. Her neck was ruffled, her wings were arched and she was surging forward, using both feet, hissing malignantly. She joined forces with Hans and the two of them advanced to the reeds on the edge of the bank.

"Now we're in for it," I thought, as I watched Katja go down to the reeds to meet them. Her tongue was hanging out and her tail was wagging happily.

The swans back-paddled, hissing and not in the least prepared to play. When I called the dog off, the swans advanced again toward us. When Katja moved toward them, I let her do as she wished and the pair backed off. Hopeless. We could have kept that up for hours.

After a while, I noticed that the dog was getting bored by the game. I began to feel more secure. Neither dog nor swan really seemed to want to come to grips. The only trouble that I could foresee might happen when the swans were on land or the dog was in the water. What would happen when the swans came on land?

Swans are creatures of habit. Not even the presence of the dog could put them off coming up to the house in search of food. One day, when they were waiting at their normal feeding place, I deliberately took the dog outside with me. Better, I thought, to have them meet this way under my control than have them meet by chance when I wasn't around.

There was a great deal of hissing and rearing up on the part of the swans which left Katja completely cold. She simply chose to ignore their existence. This was all very well; but what would happen if I wasn't there? I decided that I would have to take a calculated risk. Placing myself between the dog and the swans, I told Katja to sit steady. I then left the three of them while I went to get a bag of maize. When I returned a minute later, the swans were slightly uneasy. Their necks were bloated and their wings slightly arched, as they shifted their feet under them. The dog continued to look at them without very much interest. To my relief, neither the swans nor the dog had attacked the other or given any ground. The risk had been justified, and I set about feeding the birds while Katja looked on with the rather bored expression that labradors can have at times.

Katja and Hans had evidently decided to keep the peace, because I can only recollect one disagreeable incident. The labrador was dozing in the sun on the cobbles in front of the house when Hans, coming up to the house in search of food, took it into his head to go for her. Suddenly launching himself into the attack, he rushed at her with outstretched beak and beating wings. She woke up just in time. On her feet in a flash, she sidestepped and danced away from him, then rushed him in counter-attack, barking angrily. Fortunately I was near at hand. I got between the pair hastily and calmed them down. But for normal purposes it would seem that Hans had decided that Katja harbored no evil intentions toward him. As for Katja, she had obviously decided that Hans was beneath contempt; at most, he was just a large fowl that might have to be retrieved some day.

That year the swans produced their record brood, but for the first time they did not bring the cygnets up to the steps. It was natural enough. Although I know that the dog would not have touched a single cygnet, the swans didn't. Indeed the swans changed their rhythm of life. They abandoned the chapel pond and the ring moat and moved to the fishpond and the stream. It may have had something to do with sources of food that year, but we were certain that it was the dog. Away from our sphere of influence, the swans became shy and wild. But friendship dies hard where a swan is concerned and they would still come to me when I went to visit them, even though the dog was with me, and take any food that I gave them.

One day early in August they vanished. We called in vain. I tramped the banks of the stream, the ponds, the moats and the waterholes, but there was not a swan to be seen. A great emptiness was there.

"I am sure that that is the last we have seen of them," I told my wife disconsolately.

"I think that's a bit premature. We can only tell next year," she replied. But I knew that she was as troubled as I was.

Our misgivings increased when we heard, quite casually, how it came about that the swans had left. A party of us were having drinks after a day's shooting when one of our tenants, the same Herr Wallmeyer who had helped to pen the swans when they first arrived, came and sat beside me.

Westphalian farmers are sometimes very like their Irish counterparts—their approach to the subject can be indirect.

"The swans aren't about any more, are they?"

"No. They left very early this year."

"They had a lot of cygnets this time, I'm told."

"Yes, ten. The biggest number ever. A record, in fact."

"I suppose that it was the fight with the dog that made them leave."

I pricked up my ears. Had Katja got at the swans after all? But I could remember no occasion on which she had been out of my sight. "What fight with what dog?" I asked, guardedly.

"Oh, I thought you would have heard. Seems to have been quite a fight."

"Was it Katja?" I saw all my careful training, the circuitous routes taken to avoid conflict, all the meticulous planning go down the drain.

"No. Bautz, my little dachshund. You know how he is."

I breathed again. Bautz was a little rough-haired dachshund who was well known to all of us. A first-class dog when dealing with foxes, he was also a notable Casanova. He had a special girlfriend at a neighboring farm to whom he was devoted. When the mood took him, he would cross our land on his way to visit her.

On the day of the fight, it seemed that he had crossed the meadows behind the farm house in which he lived, and had passed along the south end of the fishpond, the end nearest the moat, when he spotted the swan family on the second preening site. Being a rather sporty little gentleman, he must have decided to have some fun and chase them off, as he had probably done many times with our flock of geese. Herr Wallmeyer told me that his farmhand had seen the commotion after it had begun and had gone to find out what it was all about.

According to this eyewitness report, the dog was engaged by the cob for over half an hour. If the dog had planned a little bit of easy sport, he had been sorely mistaken. The cob was frightened and angry; the fact that the pen had slipped into the water with the brood had probably escaped his notice as he went for the dog, delivering hammer blows with his beak and slashing blows with his wings.

The courage of the big swan and the little dog was evenly matched. Both were incapable of fear and equally obstinate; but Bautz was the kind of dog that would attack almost anything and keep on worrying it once he had started. Hans, although injured, apparently went on fighting, while the farmhand watched the grim game being played out on the other side of the stream, without even attempting to come nearer and break it up. Eventually the right moment presented itself and the cob slipped into the water.

The fight was over but the damage had been done. "It *would* happen the very year that we acquired our own dog," I commented gloomily to my wife. By the time we reached home I had convinced myself that we had seen the last of the swans. The territory had become unsafe.

Happily I underestimated their toughness as I had underestimated their adherence to habit. They came back the following spring and they behaved as they had always behaved, clearing their territory, feeding, making ready until the moment came for Leda to lay her eggs and to raise her brood of seven chicks. It seemed to me as though the fight with the dog had only been to them an incident, the kind of incident that can happen anywhere in a swan's daily life. For our part we watched them come and we watched them go again, delighted that they were with us, rejoicing that they had come back. Again, they failed that season to bring their chicks to the doorstep, and I had to go to the water's edge whenever I wished to see them. It may not have been quite like old times, but it was close enough to satisfy me, and they would come to me whenever I called them until the day that they left us at the end of August.

If you have enough to do with animals, there is seldom a dull moment. On Sunday, November 24th, 1968, we were concerned with things other than swans. Katja was producing her first litter of pups.

"Is it never going to end?" we asked each other. Over a period of five hours, she kept on giving birth, at first in bewilderment and then with increasing confidence. She had ten pups and made a neat job of it as far as color was concerned. Five were black like herself, and five were pale yellow like their father, my brother-in-law's beautiful yellow labrador dog. The family grew rapidly and we found homes for them easily. By the end of March, only three puppies remained, our own Lica, Nugget, a boy, and a black bitch who, because she was destined for the United States, had to be kept back for various vaccinations.

Young labradors are great fun to have about the place, even if they do tend to be troublesome and to require a good deal of individual attention. As we are quite used to planning our routines around some sort of animal, we soon accepted the responsibilities that they imposed on us. Still, the idea of keeping this group together for another month caused a little concern. It meant teaching them, collectively at least, the rudiments of good behavior on this estate.

But learn they must. Whether they learn with good or bad grace depends upon the individual character of the dog in question. "Good dog, clever dog" are the words of praise if the puppy obeys and remembers; these words become synonymous with having done something well and correctly for the remainder of its life. The same applies to NO. "Did you hear me say NO! ARE YOU DEAF or something?"

Katja, usually a model of behavior, got it into her head to be of no help whatsoever. Forgetting, or wishing to forget, the iron rules of the normal regime, she began to bark at and chase the waterfowl, probably in order to teach the puppies how to hunt. I quickly put a stop to that nonsense by the use of the lead and forcing her to sit steady when the birds were about. She soon got the message.

It has always been my practice to keep Katja as a constant companion, and when I am away, my wife does the

same. Like so many big dogs, labradors are inclined to be
quiet in the house and to lie down and stay in their selected
and favorite places. We found that if the puppies were
properly and frequently exercised, they were equally quiet
when brought indoors, and would sleep peacefully on the
carpet by one's feet. The type of exercise was not always
orthodox, unfortunately.

"I'm afraid poor Max has had it," announced my wife
resignedly one day.

"What do you mean?"

"Look out of the window and see for yourself. The boys
have got him."

Max was one of the little Dutch hens that we kept about
the place for decoration. These handsome little fowl are
black with a shimmer of green on their feather coat, and
they wear what look like wigs or pompoms of white
feathers on their heads, fronted with a butterfly of black
feathers. Because of this, they are inclined to see rather
badly. They mince with a zigzag walk, but they are very
tame, and perch on the wrist like a falcon. The chairman
of our local poultry breeders association had given them
to Patrick; we called them the "put-puts," because of the
way they talked to each other, and of the way that we called
them at feeding time.

I wasted no time in looking out of the window. I was
out of the house door like the proverbial scalded cat, eager
to short-circuit the catastrophe. I paused for a second at
the top of the steps where most of our dramas seem to take
place, and assessed the situation. Not that there was much
assessing to be done.

Below me three happy puppies were busy pulling a
bunch of white and black feathers in three different directions in a sort of grotesque tug-of-war. Head down and

front legs splayed, their mother stood proudly watching her young. Reaching the spot in a bound, I gave a sharp slap to each rounded, happy backside, grabbed each pup by the loose skin at the side of its neck and shook it vigorously, scolding like a berserk magpie until the pups retreated, suitably chastened. Meanwhile, the victim sprawled spread-eagled on the ground. I paid little heed to him until quite unexpectedly he gave a sort of cramped shudder. "Now, on top of it all, I suppose I'll have to wring his neck," I thought unappreciatingly.

We had started with four of these birds, two cocks and two hens, whom we named Honora and Elizabeth after my two sisters, and Max and Hubert after my wife's two brothers. Usually we name favorite cocks and hens after members of the Westphalian aristocracy, our excuse being that our poultry is very well-bred. This reminds me of my delight when I discovered, during the course of a visit to Woburn, that His Grace, the Duke of Bedford had named a row of dog kennels after the houses of some of his competitors in the Stately Home stakes. Had there been no other attraction at Woburn, this discovery alone would have been worth the few shillings spent on the visit.

Alas, the "put-puts" had decreased in numbers. I was responsible for one: I ran over Honora one dark night. Hubert vanished without trace, and poor Elizabeth had already gone the way of poor Max. I was not on the spot at the time, but it appears that one of the puppies arrived at the doorstep rather triumphantly and without shame bearing the relic, and a very bloody and torn relic it was, in her mouth. She met my wife at her sternest, to a thunder of "Pfuis," and "Bad dogs." This may have impressed her at the time, but not sufficiently to be of lasting avail, to judge from my present predicament.

I was just reaching for Max's neck, when, to my astonishment, up hopped the corpse and made off with a most
comical limp. This so delighted the puppies that they decided to go after him again, only to be stopped, scolded and
shaken once more.

Poor Max, now thoroughly terror stricken, mangled and
exhausted, made for the side of the Canada goose enclosure
and collapsed on the grass. I retrieved the widower and inspected him carefully. No feathers were left on the right
wing, except two of the primaries; a great number of feathers were missing from the ruff. There was a bare spot near
the throat. A bush of feathers pulled out of the hood or
head wig. No flesh injuries anywhere. But where to put
him now? Given a chance, he would live.

I came to the conclusion that the safest place would be
the winter residence of the Mandarin and Carolina wood
ducks. There might be the danger of pecking by the snow
and Canada geese who were also there at the time, but it
would be preferable to the attentions of the puppies. In
any case the Canada geese were scheduled to be set out in
their pen that day, so that the time he would have to spend
in their company would be strictly limited.

When I returned some hours later to collect the Canada
geese, Max was sitting on the rim of the swimming pool,
apparently much recovered. But when I tried to catch up
the geese, one of them objected and panicked; whoop,
there was poor Max slowly drowning in the swimming
pool, with a struggling Canada goose on top of him. I
fished him out, put him on top of one of the stall divisions
and turned once more to the geese. When they had all
gone, I dried him off, packed him in straw, and left him
to his fate. Next morning he was still wet so I brought him
into the house, put him in a transport cage and set him

down by a radiator for a few hours. His recovery was complete.

When the swans returned the following February, we were always fearful that the puppies would attack them. But Hans had long before decided that he was master of the water and the island and had made up his mind what sort of stand he would take. He is nobody's fool, a wily and experienced old bird. Only God knows what he has lived through during the decade or so that followed his pipping the egg. I believe that my real affection for Hans finds its source in his deep-rooted courage; it gave me fresh pleasure each time that I saw him stand his ground and menace the dogs when they shaped up to attack him. The dogs knew that he was formidable and respected him for it. They would stand well away from him and bark at him, but had learned to keep their distance.

On one occasion I was all ready to take the "boys" out for their after-lunch walk when I saw the cob appear on the west side of the moat, about forty yards from the front door. As he was obviously going to march straight across the courtyard, I decided to take the dogs through to the back courtyard. There was something about the look of the swan that troubled me; I had a feeling that something silly was about to happen. I shouted to my wife to call the dogs and to get them inside.

"Don't be silly," she called to me from the study window. "Anyway, you'll get the dogs well out of the way before he arrives."

Fearing the worst, I set about the job of trying to get the puppies to follow me but with limited success. They were wayward as they so often were. There was a little bone to be picked up, an interesting pebble to be inspected, a rhododendron leaf to be pulled. They lingered. Not Hans. I looked up as I heard the beat of wings. Hans was pounding along in our direction, neck outstretched in effort, feet and legs pushing away for all they were worth. He was making straight for Katja, with the obvious intention of causing her grievous bodily harm.

Katja, as always, was tremendously fit. A three-foot-high fence means nothing to her; the term "like a coiled spring" fits her well. As soon as she saw the cob coming for her she swung about with incredible speed and faced him.

"Steady," I bellowed while the puppies made off for the safety of the rhododendron bushes. "D'you hear me, steady up. Oh-oh-oh-ho-ho Hans."

Only her immediate reaction to my shouted "Steady" saved the big bird from a frontal attack. Although Katja stood stock still, I knew that she was dying to savage the swan at that moment. Hans, on the other hand, kept on traveling. He had very little option to do anything else. He was so surprised that he literally stamped on the power-brakes. A moment later he came to a violent halt in front of me, his huge pinions spread, neck bent like a shepherd's crook and body so erect that he all but fell over backward. He literally staggered to a halt, then settled down to look about him, his glittering eye assessing the odds. The odds, in the shape of Katja and the puppies, assessed him at the same time.

I regarded the lot with misgiving, and fingered the training whip in my hand. But the whip was unnecessary; Hans obeyed my voice and followed me meekly to his feeding place. He came like a lamb when called; Katja, who had been told to sit steady, never budged an inch.

The amusing sequel to the whole drama took place when the dogs and I returned from our walk. As if to show us what was what, the cob suddenly appeared and marched in front of the house, ignoring the dogs completely, stamping arrogantly in their midst as though they were ghosts.

When everybody was happy again, I went inside and got a slice of bread. I always feed after incidents, giving a lecture with the meal. Incidents are a daily occurrence and are taken as part of the normal flow of living. I believe that the swan or the dog must be made to feel that we are friends again, and food usually calms down ruffled tempers. It is then important to come as close to the animal as one dares, just to show who is master and that the master is not afraid, even if rather wary. When all is said and done, one is demanding unnatural things of the animals concerned and there is seldom any wickedness or vice behind their actions. On the contrary, they are governed by whole sets of natural reflexes. The instinct of self-preservation is exceedingly strong and the meddling human must be the one who gives the assurance of safety.

Trained dogs are very useful. They can rescue injured waterfowl, or waterfowl shot on the neighboring estates. I have used Katja to go in and rescue somebody's exhausted racing pigeon that had come down on the chapel pond. Katja can carry an egg without breaking it; admittedly this is not usually encouraged, since we keep poultry and there are wild duck nests about the place, but it testifies to the gentleness of her mouth.

Although the dog leaves them alone, she has no feelings of friendship for the waterfowl. All of her instincts urge her to chase them, and were it not for her hard training, that is what she would do. She avoids the swans, not just because she has been taught to do so, but because she is afraid of them as well. She will only confront the swan if *he* annoys *her,* or, on the occasions when she has had puppies, when *he* seemed to menace them.

Normally, Hans will not provoke incidents when I am about. In our relationship, he has learned who is the boss, not once but on dozens of varied occasions. He may threaten as much as he likes, beating about with his pinions or jabbing with his beak for all the good it will do him. All that he will get for his trouble is a chasing, a slap or, at mildest, a severe talking-to.

You may smile at the idea of giving a swan a talking-to or at telling it off, but it works. All animals with which one is in daily contact know only too well when one is angry. A swan is no exception. Curiously enough he will try things on with my wife, although he knows that he will get as little change from her as he will from me. She too has used the training whip on him on a number of occasions.

I was working in the study one day when I heard my wife calling to me for help. She had been in the park with the dogs; returning home, they had found the front doorstep blocked by the swan. He was in an aggressive mood and simply went for Katja and her puppies as they came ahead of my wife.

"What's the trouble?" I demanded, mildly irritated at the disturbance. I could see nothing wrong. Two puppies were sitting on the doorstep, Katja was beside my wife and Hans was in the center of them. The swan was beside the doorstep in his normal place.

"But he's driven poor Nugget in among the rhododendrons and won't let him out. He went for him with his wings." When I looked down I saw poor Nugget desperately trying to get up to where I was standing, which was something that he could not accomplish. The house doorstep is flanked on either side by actual slabs of stone, which are too high for a four-month-old puppy to master.

I fetched the training whip from the hall. When I went down the steps to Hans, he tried to peck at me first, then to beat at me with his pinions. I wasn't having any. When I marched straight at him, he promptly decided to play good swan, changed his mind at the last second and went for me again. He got a sharp tap of the whip on the side of his wing. After giving me a good long hiss, he calmed down. Nugget saw his chance and slipped behind me up the steps.

Life Goes On

ON THE 14TH OF JANUARY, 1969, THE TELEPHONE RANG in my London hotel room. It was a long distance call from Germany, and I was frankly worried. Thaddäa seldom rings up unless there is an emergency. But the voice on the other end of the line was normal, even gay.

"I thought that you'd like to know that Hans is back already."

"Already? It's not possible! What about Leda?"

"Well, we have a pen in a stable, which one of the local miners brought around this afternoon. Patrick is sure that it's Leda, but I'm not so certain."

Hans had come in alone and had been seen on the chapel pond, before he presented himself at the doorstep for food. Thaddäa and Patrick had immediately searched the ponds for Leda, without any result. Shortly afterward, the local police rang up. Would she take in a swan that had come down in a miner's garden? The miner had reported the swan injured and unable to take off; not knowing what to do, he had got in touch with the police. My wife readily agreed to help, thinking that it might possibly be the missing Leda. When the miner appeared with the swan in the boot of his car, she had noticed that the bird was seriously injured, with traces of blood around the nostrils and its flanks.

"There are the pips," she said. "So I'd better ring off."

"Oh damn the pips," I said. "Is it Leda?"

"I don't think so," she replied.

Her uncertainty puzzled me, and when she eventually got off the line, I kept on asking myself how she could be so uncertain. I had quite a lot of work to do in London, but as soon as I could, I raced home, arriving three weeks later, after dark, on the 3rd of February.

I was so eager to see the swan that I could hardly wait when I got out of the car to go to the stables. But Thaddäa told me that she had let the swan out a day or two before. She had nursed that swan for almost three weeks, as it lay on straw in the stable. It was quite gentle, like all injured birds, and allowed her to stroke its back; when it could stand and eat with good appetite again, she had set it out on the moat. Hans had greeted it with evident delight and affection. They were obviously happy to be reunited; except for some difficulty in getting in and out of the water, the new pen seemed well and happy.

As luck would have it, I had to leave for Athens two days later, so I had little time to investigate. Early in the morning, Patrick and I went over to the fishpond. I saw what at first sight seemed to be a swan, feeding contentedly. When I looked a second time, the bird was in exactly the same place and position. We went over to take a closer look. She was very dead, the beak and legs already showing signs of bleaching from immersion.

I examined the carcass carefully. She was a Polish swan all right. But the shape of neck, head and especially the knob was different. She was not our beloved Leda, of that I was quite certain, but her presence and Hans' greeting of her could mean only one thing, that the old Leda must be dead and that this swan must be Hans' new bride.

The flight to Athens was a sad one. I had to face the fact that Leda was dead. Anything could have happened while the swans were wintering away from us—a shot, an attack by a dog or an accident. Telegraph or high tension wires might well have accounted for her, overhead wires often cause death among swans, whether young or old ones; for some reason they never seem to learn.[31] Although I have no evidence to substantiate it, I still believe that Leda met her end this way.

Now her successor was dead too. Some consolation was to be found in the thought that birds are creatures of habit. Once a habit is adopted, the bird is consistent in the practice of it. All things being equal, Hans could not have had it much better than with us, and his sure instinct must be saying so right now, I reasoned. He had his own territory to which he could return each breeding season, secure in the knowledge that there would be no opposition about the place. He would find another wife.

I returned from Athens to learn that Hans had disappeared. Days later I was standing by the poultry runs when Katja suddenly uttered the familiar half yelp, half bark, and her tail began to thump the grass. I watched the swans as they passed overhead, deliberate and beautiful, and felt my heart beat a trifle faster once more.

They were flying close to each other, the big cob a little

in advance of his new pen, maybe a hundred feet above us, their necks stretched long in front of their boat-shaped, streamlined bodies.

"Hans has a new wife, a new wife!" I said aloud to Katja, who responded by thumping the grass even harder with her tail. I called to the swans as they circled overhead, using the old warwhoop. The swan hesitated for a fraction of a second and looked down.

They were magnificent as they banked, and I caught my breath as the cob came through a gap in the trees, came low over the road like an airplane making its final approach, and landed on a narrow strip of open water in the ice.

I waited for the pen to fall in, but she missed the gap and sheered off to the north. I watched as she made a right-hand turn, curved far out over the road and the south meadow, before returning again to make her second attempt at a landing. Just as she was coming in, I heard a familiar engine, and saw a wretched Volkswagen careening down the road, straight into her landing path. She shot upward, banking sharply, and I just caught a brief glimpse of her as she disappeared behind the bulk of the house. She reappeared again for a second, framed between the buildings, before vanishing from sight.

I ran to the chapel pond, with Katja at my heels, and found Hans cruising about with total lack of concern. Suspecting that the pen must have come down somewhere near the fishponds to the north, I called to Hans to follow me. He came up on the ice of the ring moat and crossed the grass, marching toward me at an infuriating slow pace, while I danced with impatience. I looked anxiously in the direction of the fishpond, but saw nothing.

I spoke to the cob for a moment or two, then left him

and went for some maize. When he saw me near the steps with the familiar feeding pot in my hand, he came over and accepted the maize. He was very subdued and docile. As soon as he had finished, he moved off again in the direction of the chapel pond, and I made no attempt to stop him.

No sooner had Hans left than I saw the new swan on the furthest of the three fishponds. I could just see her head and part of her neck above the top of the dike. She was standing quite still, probably in the same position that she had landed in, and I wondered uneasily if she might be injured.

One should always follow one's own advice given liberally to others; a pet theme of mine is that one should avoid meddling with nature. But meddle I did on this occasion. I knew that it would be no good calling or rattling a pannikin of food, because she would probably not react to the sound of grain in a tin vessel and a voice would almost certainly frighten her off. But I was determined to have a good look at her. Not next week, or even tomorrow, but right now.

Dashing back to the house, I put Katja in, seized my field glasses from the gun cupboard, shouted to an empty hall not to let the dog out, and raced back to the wooden bridge that spans the north side of the ring moat. I began to stalk the swan. If you can imagine a rather long stick of an elderly gent, dressed in a heavy parka, with leather breeches, rubber boots, and a green shooting hat from Austria, moving across an orchard in a zigzag, with field glasses glued to the eyes, stumbling from time to time and swearing while doing so, you would have a fair picture of my progress. A stranger might have cause to wonder, but our local people were quite used to these antics, and would probably have concluded that Herr Baron or Mar Kiss was not being any more eccentric than usual.

When I dodged behind a big chestnut tree, I almost fell into a full but iced-over ditch, and settled down to observe. The pen on the fishpond was still at a much lower level than I was, and so I saw no more than a head and part of a neck. Nothing remained but to show my hand if I was to see what she looked like. So I stood up boldly, and began to saunter toward the fishpond. As soon as she saw me, the swan vanished behind a heap of earth near the edge of the pond. I sneaked along the ditch until I was in a position to have a good look.

The pen was a strong one. She was also wild, well-built and black-legged like Hans. In fact she was almost as big as Hans, and had a great strong neck. A mature dame, in fact. I studied her carefully for about ten minutes until I felt a familiar wet nose nuzzling my hand. I swore under my breath. Somebody had let Katja out, and she had followed my spoor. It would have been better if I had taken her with me in the first place and placed her at "stay" in a field. But the damage was done. The dog would almost certainly put the pen to flight. I made for home—in a temper.

Later on, when I went in search of the bird with Patrick, the swan was nowhere to be found. We walked all of the ponds and ditches, the stream and the ring moat, but not a trace of her was to be seen. I was not surprised. "It's no use," I said. "She was a wild one. She's probably gone for good."

I was miserable when she disappeared, driven off by my meddling or the sight of the dog. But habits die hard. Shortly afterward, Hans flew away again, only to return the next day with yet another pen. Once again I heard the sound of the pinions, and once again called to the flying

cob, who came in fast, landing near the little island at the
south end of the house.

I stood in the forecourt, with the pen in full sight as she
mounted the dike, and I called the cob. When I went onto
the bridge with the food bag, I was between the two
birds. The new pen, I saw at once, was not afraid of
people. I talked to her and threw her a few grains; although she pecked at the corn, she was not really interested. Her attention was riveted on Hans, who was
following across the wooden bridge behind me. But when
he was precisely halfway, the old boy got into a panic. He
must have felt himself trapped, because he turned around
and marched back the way he had come.

I made myself scarce, and once I was out of the way, he
got down on the bank beside the bridge, and over the
sheet of ice, mounting the dike to where the pen was
standing. But she was not going to know anything about
him until it suited her to do so. No thank you. As soon as
he was up on the dike, she promptly went down on the ice
and marched off. He checked, altered course, lifted his
elbows and ruffled his neck—then set off along the ice in a
very determined way. I watched as the new pen mounted
the other dike at exactly the spot where Hans and Leda
always used to preen. Seconds later, Hans followed her.
Standing about six feet apart from each other, the two
birds began to preen vigorously.

The pen was not the most beautiful swan that I had ever
seen. She looked as if she had managed to scrape through
life and to survive. She also seemed very young, maybe a
three-year-old; her neck was slender to the point of being
thin, and she did not look as if she would pose a weight
problem if one of us picked her up.

"I'll get my hands on you, my beauty!" I said. "We'll see how you fatten up. You just stick around!"

When I went out with the dogs after lunch, she was no-where to be seen. Then after I had completed a round of the park, I spotted the pen on the chapel pond where she was obviously searching for her mate. I took the dogs home by a circuitous route in order to avoid frightening the swan. But nothing ever runs completely smoothly and I had reckoned without the tenant farmer's children.

The two youngest had some friends visiting them that day, who, to make matters worse, had brought a dog with them. On that day of all days, they chose to fool around by the drawbridge. I watched the pen march under it, making for the cob, neck long and alert, watchful of danger. I heard the dog bark, whereupon she began that odd fast flapping run preliminary to take-off. Swearing like a trooper, I dashed into the dining room in time to see the bird flying strongly over the east meadow. She half-circled once and then headed north. When I came out again, into the back courtyard, having downed a very large whisky, Patrick and Herr Balz's son, Joseph, were playing by the corner of the *Brauhaus* that is nearest to the moat and the wooden bridge. They were firing stones from their latest and most secret weapon, a two-man catapult over five feet high. They were obeying instructions and firing the thing where it could do no damage to man or beast, into a poplar tree.

"Hello," said Patrick, full of good humor. "If you're looking for the new Mrs. Swan, she came down on the fish-pond a few moments ago. Hans has gone to meet her there. Have a look at this, though. Isn't it super?" Wham, an-other stone went speeding off to hit the unfortunate tree in the orchard.

Having thanked the boys, I asked them not to shoot me in the back, got a pitying look for my trouble, and headed off across the bridge. Hans reached the dike between the moat and fishpond at about the same time as I did. He was totally unaware of my presence, concentrating on the pen who was standing on the ice about twenty feet from the nearest bank. She saw him and walked unhurriedly in his direction. With wings arched and necks bent so that their chins were resting on their own breasts, they moved step by step. When they met they touched breasts, and simply stood, not quite knowing what to do next.

They stood quite still, until Hans stretched his long neck so that his beak pointed to the sky, and gave the curious "nuck-nuck-nuck" call. The pen came to life at once and did the same. Like dancers in a slow-motion dream, they twined necks. After some mutual caressing, they turned a half-circle on the ice, came apart, and as though nothing had happened between them, began to preen.

Hans had greeted his new bride with love. I turned away as they made off overland to the open stream.

1970 and 1971

W E COULD SMELL THE SNOW LONG BEFORE IT CAME, and as Patrick and I paused in our work, we agreed that it would soon be falling. Before we lifted the fourteen-foot-long pine that was to be our Christmas tree, we looked over in the direction of the moat where Hans and Leda were watching us hopefully. Then we worked the tree cautiously through the open doors of the veranda, and carried the tree to the spot where it was to stand. Later that day, Thaddäa and Walburga would get to work on it. By the next evening, it would have been transformed into a shimmering, magic thing, hung with hundreds of threads of silver foil that would make it look like an icicle-laden tree in a forest. Then would come the silver balls, the silver cross deep among the branches, the creche at the base and the shining silver star at the very pinnacle.

"Well," announced my son when the tree was standing, "I think that it's the most beautiful one that we've ever had."

I nodded in agreement, and thought to myself that each year brings the most beautiful tree that we have ever had. Shaking my head to clear it of the vision that I had of the same tree as it would look next day, I said rather abruptly, "Come on, let's get the feeding over with."

"O.K. let's do that," agreed Patrick, "but let's do it quickly. It's so cold outside."

When we went out, Hans and Leda, as though aware of our plans, were already waiting for us. They were standing at their feeding place, and although they made a move in our direction, they waited patiently until I went over to feed them. They were so quiet and so gentle that they allowed me to stroke their backs when I had put down their maize.

It was amazing that they were still with us. Never before had they remained so long and so consistently about the place. Even their shy cygnet, the only survivor of their 1970 brood of two, still remained offshore on the long strip of water left open at the outlet between the fishpond and the moat, or stood disconsolately on the thick ice with the snow and Canada geese and the hundred or more semi-wild and wild ducks that were wintering with us.

The following day was the eve of Christmas, a great day with us, because we celebrate our Christmas then, German fashion, before we drive to a midnight Mass. It is always a quiet family affair, shared only with any friends who may happen to be staying with us at the time, and we exchange our presents near the tree, which has been transformed into a fairy thing with its five dozen softly burning candles.

It had snowed during the night and, Christmas morning, a soft, thick blanket of pure snow covered the outside world, garnishing each twiglet of every tree branch, and turning the woods into a setting with the same fairy tale quality that my wife and step-daughter had created for the tree that was indoors.

I went out of doors with a bucket of mixed grain in my hand, ready for what I knew was going to happen. Although the snow was new, the ice had covered the water for many days, and as soon as anyone turned the north corner of the *Brauhaus,* the horde of waterfowl at the open waterhole set up an almost deafening cacophony of sound as they greeted any human being. Then, if a bucket was being carried, a great movement would begin, until, within a few seconds, all the birds were making their way in one's direction.

As I went forward, some ducks, emboldened by hunger, took to the air and came up to me, flying six feet over the surface of the ice, to land almost at my feet in little flurries of snow. Ignoring them, I marched out onto the ice, followed by a veritable trail of ducks as the snow and Canada geese came forward to greet me, the latter with upstretched necks and throwing their white-cheeked heads up and down as they sounded their greeting. My mind went out across the ocean as I recalled when my friends David and Betty Marshall had driven me across Oregon to look for trumpeter swans, and we, under the aegis of their friend John Scharff, the Refuge Manager, had watched about four thousand of the honkers come in to spend the night on a lake of the Malheur Refuge.

As on that occasion, I looked hopefully for swans, this time my swans, but except for the lone cygnet, no swan was to be seen. I fed the assortment of birds and called to the cygnet, but it showed no interest, so I put food down in the shallows and went in search of Hans and Leda. Hans and Leda were not to be found.

I didn't think it possible that they had left us. Earlier in the month, before the ice had set in, I had watched Leda and the cygnet take to the air and circle the territory, huge in the lowness of their flight, but they had remained. Now it seemed to me impossible that the parent birds could have flown away, leaving the cygnet alone on the territory. Yet as the day wore on and the next day followed it, I found that this was what had happened. Hans and Leda had gone with the coming of the snow.

"The swans are gone," I announced dramatically during supper at the end of the third day after Christmas.

"Oh, well, I suppose that that was to be expected." A pause, then, "The young one as well?"

"No, that's the curious thing about it. The cygnet is still on the open water near the fishpond. It didn't come when I called it to be fed."

"Didn't it? That's rather odd, isn't it?"

"It's pretty shy," I pronounced airily, "and it hasn't come when called for a long time. I put down some food for it."

I should have put two and two together and suspected that something serious was amiss, but I had a clear picture of the youngster's shyness, and I presumed that it fed when I was out of sight. It was usually floating in the center of the open water, its neck curled over its back, the head buried in the soft warmth of the feathers. Although it showed little or no interest in me when I went over, the fact remained that the food I put down in the water was always gone, so I assumed that it was feeding well.

One of my sisters-in-law was staying with us during Christmas. It was she who really sounded the alarm. An instinct told her that something was wrong with the bird, and this instinct was so sure that she kept on nagging at me to do something about it. As luck would have it, the cygnet moved over onto the ice of the chapel pond. As soon as my sister-in-law saw it there, she hunted for me until she found me, entreating me to catch it up and see what I could do with it.

I was frankly skeptical as I approached the bird, but I soon had to admit that my sister-in-law was right. Although it ran away from me and sought refuge among the dense lower branches of the huge taxus bush at the side of the pond, it only did so because it was terrified. It was not until I sent in Katja and Lica to work it gently out to me that I saw how much the effort had cost it in energy. I was shocked when I caught it gently and took it into my arms. Hundreds of little beads of ice were attached to the plumage, and the cygnet had almost no weight to speak of.

As I had left the Mandarin and wood ducks out of doors for the whole of the winter, their stable with its built-in swimming pool was free, and I had a place to put the poor creature. As soon as it was safely indoors, we went and got some bundles of straw, and soon had it resting on a warm deep litter that smelled sweetly. Because it refused to eat anything, we did not fill the pool but gave it a container full of water, laced with a good dose of mixed vitamins such as we give to the poultry. This treatment seemed to pick it up, and within two days, I had the joy of seeing it eat small feeds of grain.

Things appeared to be going satisfactorily when I left for England at the beginning of January, but when I visited the cygnet just before I left, I detected a nasty bronchial rattle in its breathing. Knowing my wife and her competence, I didn't worry, and I was sure that with care and treatment, the cygnet would get over its troubles. On the evening of January 11th, the telephone rang at my hotel and Thaddäa broke the news; the cygnet had died the day before in spite of her every effort to save it. Outside, the earth was so deep frozen that the body could not be buried, but had to be cremated in the boiler for the central heating.

The death of that cygnet ended our record for successful rearing. For the first time since the swans had come to us, a whole brood, even if it only consisted of two, had been lost while still with us.

Hans and Leda returned a week before I came back at the end of January. None of us had seen them go, and none of us had seen their return. They were suddenly there, waiting at their feeding table, the manhole cover near the door of the annex. Having only been away for four weeks instead of the usual six to seven months, they were still sleek and in good physical shape, behaving as though they had never been away.

Early the previous October, I'd succeeded in an experiment that I had been trying for years: to make the swans feed out of a container full of water into which the grain could be poured. I had only succeeded because I had held the little aluminum saucepan full of grain over the water container until they had pecked at it and so poured the grain into the water themselves. Now, if the container is not there, the swans look for it, and it has become their waiting place.

I had also succeeded in another experiment which involved very close proximity. To achieve this, I would walk along the wall of the house with the swan on the outside, its wings brushing my legs as it followed me from the door to the feeding place, a distance of about six or seven yards. I would then stoop down and pour the grain into the water, and at the same time, stroke the swan's back from the base of the neck, over the wings to the tail.

This kind of tameness began to wear thin by the beginning of March. Hans had been almost sedentary, since he and Leda spent most of their days waiting in the back courtyard. He soon forsook it and began to move around his territory—gently at first but then with increasing activity, until soon the beating of his wings as he took off on flights a foot over the water became, once again, the background music to our lives.

Seldom had the cob been so aggressive in clearing his territory, or so frequent in his attacks. Also, the dead and lamented original Leda was a pacifist saint compared with the new pen of that name. The new pen, careful and even shy during the whole of 1970, has developed into a veritable virago, an aggressive, hissing female who is almost as large as her mate and very nearly as bellicose.

In April, for the first time ever, Hans really attacked me on three separate occasions at feeding times, once getting me between himself and the house wall and striking heavy blows with his beak and pinions. At last I could tell from firsthand experience, what it feels like to be attacked by a swan, and what the results are.

I cannot rightly remember the effect of the blows or pecks with the bill, but he did manage to hit me repeatedly with his wings, on the upper leg, before I could remove myself. His blows inflicted no outward injury and did not even raise a bruise, but the muscle hurt for a couple of days afterward and was rather stiff and painful. If a swan breaks a man's leg with a blow from its wing, it can be due only to a great piece of ill-luck or a very weak leg. Admittedly though, the result of Hans' efforts was painful enough for me not to want him to repeat the performance.

On another occasion he came racing across the back courtyard with neck outstretched and half-way on the wing.

I was in no humor to take that nonsense, which was after the first incident, so I ran straight at him with outstretched arms, flapping up and down. This threw him into a great state of confusion, forcing him to put on the brakes with everything he had in order to avoid breaking his neck in a head-on collision. He nearly went over backward, then stood rather sheepishly, trying to pretend that nothing had happened and scratching himself in embarrassment.

But I am the soul of kindness compared to a Canada gander who is simply named Gander. Gander is a very humorless sort of bird and even more territorially minded than Hans. Even Hans can learn a thing or two from this five-year-old chap, who is gentle enough outside of the breeding season. However, during the breeding season he's as tough as a boot and absolutely fearless, taking on dogs, humans and swans with equal impartiality.

This year, he and his wife set up house behind the tenant's house, just as they did last year. There, Mrs. Gander is sitting on five eggs, in a nest on a ledge near the water. While she gets on with the job of hatching out the precious eggs, all the more precious because they are the eggs of the only breeding pair of Canada geese left to us (the other geese having been so tame that they were stolen), he patrols his territory. This is made up of the poultry runs, the section of the ring moat behind the tenant's house and a fairly large section of meadow.

We also have a widowed goose called Assie who plays a part in this story. Normally this lady lives with the Gander family, but as soon as the breeding season begins, she is dismissed without further ado. As she is no longer acceptable to the pair and to their year-old son who, oddly enough, is not driven off, she is forced to live on Hans' territory. During the early part of this year, she enjoyed herself by leading that gentleman a merry dance all over the place. It seemed to me, at one time, that he spent the day chasing her for want of anyone else to chase, and that she seemed to be getting some fun out of it. Whenever he got too near, or whenever she got bored, she would take to the air and, honking happily, fly away from him, only to come back a little while later to begin the chase afresh. Odd as it may seem, this goose spent a lot of her time in the company of the swans, swimming and feeding with them, and apparently becoming a good friend of theirs.

But one day Hans so far forgot himself as to follow her onto Gander's bit of meadow, crossing the invisible line of demarcation that seems to be known to the waterfowl. Gander was after him like a flash. I saw it all from the window: the swaggering Assie followed by Hans, and then the low-slung crouch of Gander as he swung into the attack, black shiny neck snaking and head weaving from side to side, with beak open and tongue showing, as he uttered his peculiar threatening sound of anger.

Arrogant Hans isn't used to this sort of a reception and, for the second time to my knowledge, made the mistake of trying to assert himself as boss. He made a darting punch with his bill, missed, and resorted to wing blows which also missed the agile gander. Realizing his faux pas, he wheeled to make off, but he was still on Canada goose territory, and before he got the chance to retire gracefully, Gander was on him. I mean literally; on his back, fastened into his feather coat between the wings. Wings spread, Hans wheeled, trying to throw the gander off, which he eventually did, leaving that gentleman with a beakful of white feathers.

Hans beat his retreat, not quite as arrogant as when he had arrived, with the low-crouched gander following him.

But at some invisible point, Gander left his own territory and Hans was back into the attack. As soon as Gander crossed the invisible boundary, Hans stood still and the pair of them faced each other for what must have been half a minute. Then, with an arrogance matching that of Hans, Gander began to crop grass. This was the signal. Hans dropped his elbows, slimmed his neck, turned his back on Gander, and made off to his own territory; but I noticed with interest that he did not allow himself the usual triumph-display that he would have indulged in if the boot had been on the other foot.

Gander is the only creature about the place that enjoys Hans' respect. All the rest, be they the five other ganders, the dogs, the ducks or even some humans, are there to be chased and intimidated. But Hans and Gander have much in common as the guardians of the future of their species.

When the snowdrops retired and the daffodils began to smile their golden smile at the freshening green of the grass, Hans began to offer nests to his Leda. He would spend his days busily building, hopeful of finding the right site, while she would come to me in search of extra food, just as my beloved and gentle old Leda had done before her. He built her four nests this year, one on the old nesting site which the dead Leda loved, one on the little island, one on the shelf of land by the water of the ring moat, just behind the second garage, and finally, one on the dike between the ring moat and the fishpond.

In the meantime, while the green brush of spring spread its tender wash of color on all of the branches of the great trees in the park, and the first shoots of the water iris thrust their sword-like blades above the water of moats and ponds, lining the banks like marching regiments, the swans could be seen from time to time engaging in the graceful ritual of their love.

"Soon they'll be nesting," I told myself with a feeling of joy, and wondering which of the nests they would take. They took the one on the dike, and by Easter, Leda was sitting on at least four eggs. She is sitting very well and I have only seen her come down from the nest a few times. Hans is often by her side, loafing, preening, keeping her company. He is not aggressive now, he is waiting.

I must admit that my wife's idea of having swans was rather different than mine. She had visions of elegant birds, snow white and decorative, drifting languidly on the broad moats and ponds. She ended up with what she calls the "collection of spoiled beasts on the doorstep," whose comings and goings have become so much a part of our daily routine.

Occasionally one says an impatient "Come" to a dog, only to be rewarded by the patter of swan feet. This sort of thing is quite routine and is only remarkable because it is the swans that have instituted the relationship rather than we ourselves. What is amusing is that people who believe that we have spent "hours taming those birds" are quite unaware of this fact, and disbelieving at that.

When all has been said and done, the swans come to us because they want to come. They come of their own accord, while all we do is to encourage them to keep coming. Except for encouraging them, we have nothing to do with it. They are not our swans. We are their people.

The other day, three wild swans passed overhead, strong wings beating. I raised my hat to them as they passed by, straight on their course, thrilling and wholly beautiful. As I watched them for that brief moment, I felt in my heart that surge of excitement, that strange tingle in the veins, that longing to fly with them that always overcomes me when I see swans in the air. I asked myself if I had once known them; if they were not "my" swans, raised and bred here, the children of "my" Hans whose presence gives added joy to my days when I am here, and whose absence can leave so big a gap. I like to think that those wonderful passersby may be "our children"; I like to think that in our small way, we have helped to keep the white wings in the sky.

What I Have Learned: An Appendix

I THINK THAT AS A YOUNG MAN I HAD A PRETTY EVERYDAY opinion of swans. They meant to me what they appear to mean to most people, and that's not much. When I told a friend recently that I intended writing this book about them, his immediate reaction was predictable: "You're not serious," he said. "You couldn't possibly fill a book by writing about swans. They're dull and bad-tempered."

My feeling is that my friend was wrong on two points. In our experience, swans are far from dull and only occasionally bad-tempered. As for filling a book—no problem. The difficulty is to know what to leave out. Something had to be left out of Hans' and Leda's story, and what was left out now follows, for the reader who wants to know a bit more about these fascinating birds; more about how they behave, and what I did to them in order to learn about them and to understand them better. Because I *did* have to understand them, and getting to do that by outward signs was as much fun as living with them is.

To most people, and I say this after quite a bit of research, the main function of the swan is purely ornamental. A stretch of water looks the more romantic for the presence of a swan, but people's enthusiasm often begins to wane when the swans come nearer. The cob looks threatening in his attitude and provokes feelings of fear as he surges forward, a wave at his bow, his great pinions arched, his neck bloated and drawn well back. A further contribution to this air of menace comes from two unwinking, glittering eyes, emphasized by the marking in black that sweeps back from the base of the orange beak to a point made by the eye. For the most part, except when real fear is aroused, the common attitude toward the birds is distaste. People will throw bits of bread to the birds on the lakes of some public park, or along the banks of a river like the Thames or the Alster, watching them quietly out of the corner of one eye, in case they suddenly throw an unreasonable fit and decide to inflict grievous bodily harm on their benefactor.

I know few swans that are congenitally vicious. One of them belongs to my cousin, the Count Schlitz von Görtz, who keeps a fine collection of waterfowl on the ponds of his private park near Schlitz, in Hessen, Germany. He owns a male mute swan of almost unparalleled viciousness that is so ready to attack and injure anybody passing that my cousin has had to enclose the large pond with a low wire fence. This ill-tempered bird will attack both in and out of the breeding season, and will cross its pond in a full surge of fury as soon as a human being comes into sight; but this male is quite unusual in my range of experience. Fortunately, the normal swan doesn't go in for this sort of nonsense. The male will only show aggression if it believes that its territory is being invaded during the breeding season, and even then, it's quite possible to upset his concentration. For an example, I have often found that when Hans is trying to drown one of his sons, a loud shout and a rattle of maize in a tin can is enough to break off the murderous engagement and bring both parties to my side in search of food. All in all, you have to take the rough with the smooth, and you have to know your swan.

The birds are not all that stupid. In our early days with Hans and Leda, we discovered that Leda responded readily to the human voice and, like Hans, to a fair vocabulary of human words. This simply meant that she had come to associate certain sounds or words with certain situations: "Come," "Wait," and so on. There is actually very little that is remarkable about this, as most of the animals learn a vocabulary in a fairly short time, and their learning of it is generally associated with food.

It is a mistake to attribute human sets of behavioral values to animals, or to attribute human concepts of logic and of good and evil to them. This is fatal to the establishment of any relationship with them. Animals are animals, and humans seem to forget this very easily. It is curious how on the one hand people say, "It's only an animal," and on the other make demands of it that bespeak the attribution of human intelligence and thought processes. I can only speak for myself, but I have always found that it pays to attempt to think oneself into an animal's mind and to simplify.

People in zoological gardens fascinate me. I am inclined to spend more time looking at them than at the exhibits. They seem to long for animal friendship, as you soon discover if you stand long enough before a cage. However, the feeling is not always mutual. There is no question but that animals know "their people" and react to them. This is something I have experimented with over and over again. For example, our snow geese come readily to me if I am alone or with Patrick, but they will hesitate if a stranger is standing about. The golden pheasant will feed from my hand, from that of my wife or from Patrick's, but not readily from a stranger's unless it happens to hear my voice.

The combination of familiar voice and approach is therefore linked. I have watched Dr. Kear, of the Wildfowl Trust at Slimbridge, communicate with various ducks, geese and swans she has worked with since they saw the light of day. All these come readily to her hand. When I commented on the way she talked to the birds, her reaction was instantaneous: "But naturally," she answered. The stranger, confronted with a swan surging across the water, has had no such opportunity. Small wonder that he tends to retreat as he looks at the menacing bird, and labels it dull or bad-tempered.

To understand what a swan is really up to requires a little knowledge of its general behavior. We can only understand what it is trying to show by recognizing the physical signs. Situations may provoke anger or pleasure or reactions may come about because of the swan's response to certain conditions prevailing at a particular time. For example, arching the wings, which the swan does by raising its elbows so that the secondary and tertiary feathers form the arch, is usually accompanied by a ruffling of the neck feathers. The whole posture is no doubt intended to create a fearsome illusion of great size and strength, designed to intimidate the subject against whom this display is being mounted. It usually succeeds, judging from the way most spectators back away carefully. When the swan crosses the water under full power, it uses both its powerful legs and feet at the same time, and surges forward with a slightly jerky movement, pushing quite a sizable bow wave in front of it.

Most authorities very rightly associate this display with aggression, but I have observed that there are occasions when the ruffling of the neck and the arching of wings do not seem to be associated with any form of aggression. Very close daily contact with our pair of swans has made me wonder if the ruffling of the neck and the arching of the wing might not have other meanings as well; neck-ruffling without wing-arching, or with only a limited wing-lifting, occurs when I approach with a familiar container associated with food, the yellow plastic bucket filled with maize, or the aluminum saucepan with maize or mixed grain. Both swans come forward in greeting, their necks ruffled to a greater or lesser extent, their chins lifted, snorting a welcome. They know very well what all this means. They will turn as soon as I have walked past them and run along beside or slightly behind me like chickens: the pen first, her neck upstretched and partially ruffled. In her eagerness and excitement, she will attempt the odd peck at the food container. The pen will run along in this way the *whole* of the distance; the cob lags behind and, at some time or another, will drop down from the erect stance, and advance in what is accepted as a threat-display. He looks aggressive but is not.

At the feeding spot, I pour the maize slowly onto the ground, or even put it down by handfuls, about three inches away from the eager and expectant beaks. The birds begin to feed at once, both wholly concentrating on the food, or on the thought of food. The thought of inflicting

damage is as remote as that of refusing the grain. My conclusion: in such a situation the ruffling of the high-held
neck is caused by *excitement* and anticipation.

When the birds are being fed, the neck feathers slim
down, especially the pen's. But then somewhere overhead,
an aircraft may pass the sound barrier; a few second later
there is the ensuing sonic boom. The swans look up suddenly, obviously startled; they ruffle their necks for a moment, then resume feeding. Or I may make too sudden a
movement, fumbling for my packet of cigarettes. The high-
held necks wave back, slightly sideways, like a boxer
dodging a blow. The necks ruffle for an instant. I conclude
that at such moments the ruffling of the neck feathers indicates a momentary state of alarm, whereas if a swan is
really frightened, he indicates it by a *slimming* of the neck
feathers. For example, the swans might be waiting at their
accustomed place near the front doorstep, when I return
from a walk with gun and dog. If there is one thing that
the swans cannot bear, it is the lolloping gait of a dog.
The necks go up. Giving voice, they set off at a pattering
run for the moat, sleek heads on sleek necks looking anxiously over their shoulders. Sometimes the wings are outstretched and flap slightly in order to increase the speed of
departure. This, of course, is the real thing, an exhibition
of fear in a big way, in comparison with the momentary
alarm of the sonic boom, where the neck is quickly ruffled
and just as quickly slimmed again.

The swans may be feeding peacefully, harried by ducks,
who dart in and out busily grabbing whatever they can.
The swans' necks ruffle as they peck at the little birds.
Sometimes they may hiss a warning; mostly they will just
raise their wings. My conclusion: the swan ruffles out of

sheer *annoyance,* half raises the wings out of *anger,* but leaves it at that.

Alternatively, the cob may be feeding when the breeding cock comes along and attempts to steal the food away. The cock is very determined and will not be pecked off—in fact he draws himself up for an attack. The cob ruffles and lowers his neck. The neck seems to be twice its normal thickness. The wings arch as the elbows come up, and the cob jabs at the cock with his beak. In fact, he is doing something positive about this cheeky interloper. The swelling-up of the neck and the arching of the wings are linked to an act or a series of acts which are followed through. My conclusion: this is definite aggression, as much so as when the cob, or the pen, chases off ducks or mounts an attack on one of the cygnets when it is driving them off.

But while these illustrations deal with typical instances of neck ruffling, there are others when the act is less easy to interpret. Surely the ruffling of the neck during the courtship display, by both of the mating pair, has little to do with aggression. And why would a swan, all alone on a stretch of water, ruffle its neck? Why, too, should a swan that is at peace with the world and preening itself ruffle its neck? It would seem preposterous to imagine that on such occasions the bird is aggressive or threatening.

My own belief, for what it is worth, is that apparently unmotivated neck-ruffling is associated with contentment and comfort, as well as with aggression and acts of war. It may have something to do with ventilation of the skin, somewhat like the opening and closing of the louvers of a heating plant. But I believe that first and foremost one has to observe what the swan is doing at the time, before one can conclude that the bird is being threatening.

Our cob is a great wing-archer. To many people, wing-arching is usually associated with aggression, but this is not always the case. If swans were to attack every time that they arched their wings, everybody around would have a pretty exciting time of it. Threat-displays, as they are called, don't necessarily mean that the bird is actually going to attack. It is simply their way of telling everyone about that they had better move off—or else. All of us know the classic appearance of the swan as it surges across the water under full power, with its wings arched and its neck and head pulled well back between them. Here the secondaries and tertiaries are used in the display, the primary feathers being folded away out of sight. If you happen to be in a boat when a swan comes close to you, there is nothing much to be alarmed about. If you turn toward the swan, it will usually shy away and back-paddle uncertainly. If you row away from it, it may follow you for some distance in the full glory of its threat-display, but it won't do *anything*, as it feels that it has chased you off its territory.

Often, when I have called Hans to come with me to be fed, he will march overland beside me, or slightly behind me, the neck pulled rather back and the wings arched. But the arching is not complete; it is more a raising of the elbows and a slight puffing out of the wings. The wings meet over the back, but the display is poor. It seems that good arching of the wings is not consistent with the effort involved in marching; when the swan strides out like an old general of infantry, he is not quite so much at home as he would be on the water. This kind of half-hearted arching is not really a threat-display. I think it has something to do with strenuous effort, because when Hans actually comes up to me, he does not even take a peck in my direction. He will just stand there, perhaps raising himself to full height with feathers shaking a bit, as he waits around for something to happen.

Then there is the threat-display when he is standing on land or walking very slowly with an exaggerated side to side movement, a ponderous roll that involves the whole of the body. Here the arch is very beautiful and complete, and has the additional attraction that the primaries are dropped and held out from the flank sides. The head is held very low on a forward-shooting and crooked neck, and moves slowly from side to side. This, from my experience, is a posture that is better watched, for it can change quickly to an active exhibition of attack with pecking and beating of wings. Of the three, this final display is the most likely to precede an attack, for the good reason that it normally follows the arrival on land after a flight, and the swan can mean business.

The forms of wing-arching that I have described above are quite straightforward, but some are more difficult to understand. Take for instance the case of the swan, all alone, dead center on the water. He is idling along, paddling with one foot and gliding between strokes. The wings are half arched, the neck is sleek. There is nothing in sight, not a duck, not a goose, not a waterhen. The swan pauses and takes something up from out of the water, or may even have a drink. His wings are still arched. My conclusion: this arching is not a sign of aggression, but rather of contentment. In fact, a swan arches his wings frequently and in many different situations other than in threat displays. These are always obvious, because one can see what or whom the swan is threatening and when. It is not unreasonable to assume that wing-arching serves in some way as a means of ventilating the body, in the same manner as neck-ruffling.

My cousin Schlitz von Görtz once told me that if ever I came across a strong stag in the forest which showed signs of attack (and they sometimes do), I should immediately make a quick assessment of the stag's antler span. I should then hunt about for a dried branch larger or wider than the stag's span, and holding the branch to my head, advance briskly upon him. According to my cousin, he will then turn tail, recognizing that I have the larger antler and should not be engaged in combat.

Something similar applies to the swan. If a swan shows signs of really attacking you, it is quite enough to hold out your arms, crooking them slightly, and to advance on him in this way. He will spread his wings defensively. But he will then turn away and make off. With very few exceptions, swans don't go about attacking people; rather the contrary. A swan will only attack if you are in the immediate vicinity of its nest, or try to capture its young, in which case you richly deserve whatever is coming to you. Hans has attacked me a few times, for no real reason but always on land and in the back courtyard. As soon as I heard him coming at me with beating wings, I turned on him and *ran* toward him, which quickly put a stop to such displays of capriciousness. But these attacks were due to familiarity or tameness. If I may quote Jean Delacour again: "Very tame males attack animals and people readily, striking heavy blows with their powerful wings." [32]

I decided at one stage to find out for myself the extent to which very tame males would attack animals and people. The animals about the place were mostly cows at that time, so there was no real danger to them; as far as the people were concerned, I thought that if I were to tame Hans toward the end of his season with us, those in the main line of attack would be myself and my wife. He never bothered much about anybody else and I felt that we could certainly deal with him.

I made the experiment of feeding him directly from my hand for about four weeks, before what I estimated would be his time of departure. I used horsehide gloves when giving him particles of bread; within a week the thumb of the glove had been rasped rough by the inside of his beak, because the greedy chap tried to take my thumb as well as the bread. It would be an exaggeration to say that he became vicious as a result of this experiment, or that he attacked anybody. But he undoubtedly developed the rather demoralizing habit of dashing up to people and going for their hands, because he thought that they might be carrying a goodie for him. Both the baker and the postman (another unfortunate postman) arrived regularly with something in their hands. Since neither found this new habit very amusing, I dropped the experiment after about three weeks.

Yet looking back, I am not sure that "attack" is the right word for what he did when he became over-tame. Although he showed all of the aggressive characteristics, I am inclined to think that there was more eagerness than malice in any of his so-called attacks. There is a double moral here. If you do tame the swan so that he expects to be fed out of your hands, he will naturally try and take food out of your hands even if there isn't any there; perhaps if you are a trifle naive, you may well think that he is attacking you. The second moral is that having made the swan tame, the swan may not be ready to distinguish among people. It will rush up to strangers and "attack" them in the hope of getting the food which he would normally expect to get from the hand. As a result, the bird will suffer: so if you love your swans, don't make them too tame.

People who have seen me with my swans have often asked what damage a swan could inflict. For some reason people always expect animals to bite, and to bite for no reason at all. I have never taken a bite as such into serious consideration, for the good reason that I have known that it is not a swan's method of attack. From observation and from direct experience I can say that a swan delivers a punch with its beak, a peck if you prefer, and that the more serious attack is mounted with the big wings. However, since people are afraid of being bitten, I thought I might find out how hard a swan could bite, and if it can really inflict any injury in this way. I tried, but I failed. In fact I met with no success at all as far as Hans was concerned. The old boy wouldn't oblige, no matter how hard I tried to get him to bite me. The rasping of the horsehide glove proved nothing as far as I was concerned, because the swan had not *bitten* my thumb; he had merely tried to take it as a part of the food that was offered to him.

I might never have found out but for a visit one day to the zoo at Hellbrunn outside Salzburg in Austria. I love that zoo. It has a charm unequaled by any other that I know. Most of the animals are unbelievably tame, so that you soon have the feeling that roles are reversed, in a huge humorous game of make-believe. I went there one day with my wife and Walburga, who came with her usual assortment of cameras. There was one wonderful enclosure which I privately named The Garden of Eden, because of the mixture of animals and birds that roamed about inside it. Standing near the low railing, making a good deal of noise to attract attention, was a bored-looking Bewick swan.

What I Have Learned: An Appendix

I went up to it and held out my hand. It came at once and obligingly took one of my fingers in its beak. It held on for dear life, but as I didn't think much of its grip on my hard forefinger, I pulled my finger out of its beak and offered instead the soft part of my hand between the thumb and first finger. It took a good grip of the flesh and pulled. As I didn't think very much of that either, I repeated the process and offered it the back of my hand, on which it tried its best. In fact the swan bit various parts of my hand and wrist during the fifteen minutes following our first encounter, repeating the performance for another five minutes later on, when Walburga arrived to take some photos.

Being bitten by a swan is no more serious and somewhat less painful than being pinched by a nice girl. The result was a few contusions and bruises that turned red and blue, and lasted for a day or two. When we returned home I tried again with Hans, for the fun of it. Hans was on the water and I was on the bank. I let him grab at my forefinger and then closed my thumb over his upper mandible. We played a game of tug-of-war, which he did not care for too much, though he did not seem to object to it either. He had a fine strong pull, as he back-paddled away from my grip, but was incapable of hurting me. The lesson that I learned is that a swan's bite is nothing to be afraid of. A word of advice to anyone who wants to try: if you have to choose between being bitten by a swan or a gander, choose the swan. A gander can really hurt, using his beak as both an offensive and defensive weapon in conjunction with his wings.

On the other hand, I had heard since my childhood that a swan could break a man's leg with a blow from its wing, so it is just as well to dispose of that fable here. The wing is the offensive and defensive weapon. Wing blows can be unpleasant, but can be dodged by anyone with a little agility. Swans are not in the habit of attacking people for the fun of it, and, consequently, the chances that one may have to contend with a serious attack are slim. But Delacour tells us that very tame male swans can be dangerous to *children,* and I am sure that if a blow from a wing landed squarely, it could break a child's shinbone. When I talked to Mr. Turk, the Queen's Swan Keeper, about swan-raising, I asked him if a swan could break a man's leg with a blow from its wing. He told me that he did not believe that it could. But he did say that he believed that it could break a man's arm; therefore, it is reasonable to assume that it could break the leg of a small child. The real moral to be learned is to feed them if one wills, but to leave them in peace, which is all that they ask for.

In fact, far from being dull and bad-tempered, our swans have proved charming and sociable birds, very ready to seek human society and quite prepared to allow themselves to be gently managed. They have established their own niche in our way of life, knowing when to come and how, in their own way, to communicate their needs to us, responding readily to our talk, and coming along with us to the place where we want them to be. Close living with them has taught us that they are gentle and friendly by nature, and this far outweighs the odd outburst of temper and aggression. If we do not let them become too familiar, it is on account of the possible dangers to themselves, and to other people, who, because they might not understand the big birds' motives, could possibly do them damage in "self-defense." As far as my wife, our children, myself, and the dogs are concerned, mutual respect is the rule that governs our daily life with the swans, and makes it a happy one.

Far from being in a constant state of aggression, a good deal of the swan's life is spent in preening. This must be a very necessary and pleasant occupation, for they will cheerfully spend a whole morning in this way. Fortunately for me, our swans selected at an early stage a bowl-shaped bank near the entrance to the island as a favorite site for this activity, the same site they subsequently used for the flying lessons.

A really good feed seems to excite a desire to preen, maybe because the birds are content and full and have no need to go searching for more. It also suggests sensual satisfaction, and as Johnsgard points out, is associated with precopulatory behavior, when "mutual head-dipping" movements alternate with various comfort movements, such as preening against the back and flank, head-rubbing movements in the same areas and even up-ending.[33]

Preening is carried out very thoroughly and even methodically. Flanks, breast, wings over and under, and even the neck, all come in for their share of attention. Belly, breast and flanks are preened against the growth direction of the feathers, and with the flat under and underside edge of the beak. The movement along the flanks tends to be fast and seems to involve two actions: tail to front and back again. Both of the actions are different, the important one being that from tail to front, and the secondary but distinct movement being only a quick smoothing down of the plumage. The forward movement is undertaken with the underedge of the beak, which is employed in much the same manner as a good barber will use his razor on a client's face. It means that the head and beak are held at a slight angle toward the tail as the head is moved forward.

The edge of the angled beak is swept along the feathers with a sharp, fast motion that makes the soft feathers ripple ahead of it, and at the same time dislodges any loose feathers from the body. Consequently, loafing sites are always littered with the soft breast and flank feathers from the birds.

The back is preened by laying the neck in a loop, usually over the right shoulder. I have not seen the action of the beak itself under these circumstances, but because the general action and speed seems to be the same as in flank and underside preening, I think it fairly reasonable to assume that the underside edge of the beak is employed. Under and over sides of the wings receive attention from this same position of the neck. During most of the preening operations, the wonderful flexibility of the neck can best be seen. The swan can achieve a wide variety of complicated movements. As the neck feathers are often ruffled to some degree, this has led me to believe that neck-ruffling can also be a sign of satisfaction or contentment, and not only of aggression.

After preening comes a loafing period, although this is by no means invariable, and that is usually followed by a spell of feeding. When loafing, the birds stretch themselves luxuriously, or often lie on the side, the uppermost leg and foot tucked comfortably away among the feathers of the flank.[34] They seem to find this position a comfortable one and often adopt it while waiting to be fed outside the front door.

In common with most human beings, we like to feed the swans. Right from the beginning, we discovered that they loved yellow maize, especially if we fed it to them at their beloved feeding place to the left of the front doorstep. It is their favorite extra food, second in popularity only to particles of bread, with the built-in advantage that it can be fed to them dry, on land, and that they can readily pick it up. At an early stage, however, I noticed that if you put a small heap down in front of a waiting bird, it would take one or two grains at a time with enormous eagerness at first, and then with decreasing speed, and that often they would leave some.

Over the years we have tried several experiments with their food, including one of adding dried seafood to the maize. This is what we frequently feed to the poultry, and is composed of dried fish particles, shrimps and crabs and seashells, which, surprisingly enough, appear to be eaten as well. The swans love this so much that we have now included it as a regular item of their diet. But their appetites are not insatiable; in our experience about one and a half slices of bread and about two hundred grams (the equivalent of a teacupful) of the maize and seafood mixture is about as much as they will take on land.

They have the greatest difficulty in picking up any smaller grain, and on the one or two occasions when we have tried to feed them the mixture of wheat, barley and oats that we keep for the ducks and geese, they could only consume what was on the top of the heap. Anything on the level of the ground was left, to the huge delight of the ducks. Of course the swan requires a good deal of water when feeding, to help in the picking up and swallowing of the food. We have often noticed that it will go through the motions of drinking when being fed on land. This water requirement may well be the limiting factor in the amount of food that they can consume in a dry state. The birds are too wild to drink from any container put out in front of them, and their suspicions are aroused at once if you give them a bucket of water since they obviously don't drink from containers when in the wild.

A winter visit to the Wildfowl Trust at Slimbridge in Gloucestershire convinced me that the most satisfactory way of feeding small grain to swans is in the water. What they do at Slimbridge is pour the grain into the shallows by the banks. This method seemed to be so eminently suitable that I decided to introduce it when I returned to Germany that spring. What was good enough for the famous Bewicks of Slimbridge must surely be good enough for my Hans and Leda. However, neither Hans nor Leda was at home and I had to wait until they returned in February. There was still ice about, so I had to take my ax to break the ice over the shallows. But having done this, I fed them in this way twice a day. Since the swans were obligingly tame, I watched them closely; all I had to do was pour the food into the water from a crouching position about six inches in front of them, and let them do the rest.

When the swans are picking up food on land, you can hear the grain being rolled along the inside of the beak before being swallowed, and then watch its progress downward in the form of a lump. But food poured into the water was another matter. As soon as I started pouring, I noticed that the light, surplus grain did not sink and was immediately sucked off the water surface by both birds. It seemed as though they had Hoovers inside their beaks, because the floating grain was not gobbled and eaten, but literally sucked in. Once this surplus floating grain had been dealt with, the birds set to work on the grain below the water surface. Keeping their heads relatively still, they continued to suck the grain into the beak in a stream, the lower mandible opening and closing very rapidly and

very little. While this was going on, the unwanted water and the air was expelled at the sides of the bill and through the nostrils. There was an almost continuous flow of air bubbles while they were sucking the grain, which moved in an almost perfect triangle into the bill. Every now and then, however, the swans stopped sucking to drink and to swallow. As time passed one could see a column of grain along the side of the neck, apparently stored there. Then a good swallow of water would be taken, the neck would be stretched upward and the grain would disappear.

The fact that the swans relied almost exclusively on the grain during ice periods made me wonder if there might not be the danger that the swans would be fed too little during these times. So when the ice had melted, I decided to undertake a series of experiments, in order to discover just how much food a swan could or would consume at any one time. This became a matter of practical interest as much as one of curiosity. My experiment was divided into two parts. First dry feeding on land by the house, followed by wet feeding in the shallow parts of the water. When the swans had been given a dry feed of one teacupful of maize and one slice of bread, I coaxed them to the water, a walk of about sixty yards. When we arrived I drove them into the water where they waited for me. I lined up eight containers of grain, each filled with a pound and a quarter of mixed grain, and put these on the bank of the feeding place, before calling the swans. As soon as they were in position, I started to pour the grain into the water, a pound and a quarter at a time.

The amount that they took was rather disappointing; no more than two and a half pounds between them, one container apiece. They refused to take any more, but I poured another half kilo into the water in front of them. They took a little, but then left off feeding altogether. Of the two, the pen was the more continuous feeder, but this was largely due to the fact that the call ducks, the mallard and the cayugas had got in on the act, and the cob stopped now and then to drive them away.

When they would take no more, the birds drifted away from the shore, with wings not fully arched but puffed out and held away from the flanks, the upper part of their necks ruffled. Each consumed about a quarter of a pound of maize, one slice of bread and one and a quarter pounds of mixed grain altogether; on this they had reached, or so I believed, saturation point. When they reached the center of the moat they slimmed their necks, but still retained their half-arched wing posture and idled on the water. I threw in another handful of maize on top of the mixed grain and the birds came paddling over to me. Still they refused to eat, content to inspect the remaining food. Since neither of the birds seemed to show any inclination to leave the feeding place or the grain that was still there, I picked

up my containers and made for home. It was then 6:30
P.M.

Every time I looked out of the window of our small
dining recess, I noticed that the swans were still lingering
near the feeding place. When I returned at 8:45 P.M., there
was still plenty of grain to be seen, but it had been
broached: trails of grain extended outward from the banks
for a distance of about one foot. The next check at 10:45
P.M. caught the swans moving away to begin their normal
nocturnal cycle; about half of the remaining food had
been consumed by this time. A midnight check revealed
that the swans had returned and were finishing off the
grain. In all, they had eaten about three and three-quarter
pounds of food between them.

What emerged was that the swan (unlike the domestic
duck, which is a seed eater with a relatively large crop)
cannot gobble all that is put in front of it. Being herbivor-
ous, it eats little but often, more or less all the time, and
this partly accounts for their regular appearances in search
of food. If given food on demand, they will happily eat
about a quarter to half of a pound of maize according to
their appetite at the time, as well as any bread that happens
to be on the menu. Moreover, their appearances for this type
of feeding are so regular that one can almost set the clock
by them. We have conducted these experiments at odd
times over a number of years; their value has been to assist
us in realizing how much food we should give to the swans
and how much they would require over stated periods. We
learned that it was not sufficient to feed the swans, say,
once or twice a day and feed them a good hearty meal, but
that constant feeding is quite in order.

Looking back on it, the third winter after the swans'
coming was a strange and lonely one. We had let the flight

feathers grow on the old birds, and they had left with their brood: the first time that we had risked letting them go away from us. We spent much of our time wondering if they would ever come back. But there was plenty to compensate for Hans' and Leda's absence, and it was at this time that my growing interest in all forms of waterfowl was given plenty of rein to develop. I doubt if I should ever have learned about the early morning flights of duck, for example, if it hadn't been for the loading of one particularly vociferous group of pigs.

The pig dealer calls at the ungodly hour of 5:45 A.M. to collect his purchase of pigs. One morning I was awakened by a tremendous commotion of shouts and squeals. I got up and peeped out of the window to see ten vigorous young pigs scattering in every direction. There seemed to be pigs everywhere, all bent on leading Herr Balz and his wife, old Stephen and the dealer, as merry a dance as anyone could dream of. There was a pig in the middle of our courtyard, one down by the edge of the moat, another behind the rhododendrons, and a pair doing their best to desecrate my wife's rose bushes.

When the fun was over, I went to the bathroom for a drink of water. I was very much awake, which isn't normally the case at that time of day, so I opened the window and looked out again to see if everything was really quiet, and at the same time to enjoy the outside world at that early hour of the morning. I was rewarded by the sight of two mallard and a call duck speeding across the sky. These were followed by another group, then another and another. They all circled the ring moat a few times, before settling on the water once again.

This flight pattern seemed to be much more than a coincidence, so I set my alarm clock for 5:30 A.M. on every third day for the next six weeks and took up my position at a suitable window. My wife murmured darkly that she had married a lunatic who always went to extremes; I soon learned to smother the alarm clock before it woke her up. The result of this lunatic behavior was that I satisfied myself that the half tame mallard, cayugas and white call ducks took ritual morning flights for no other apparent purpose than to satisfy an urge to fly. Merely to watch fast-flying ducks has always given me a sense of satisfaction; this compensated me for the early risings. To be quite truthful, I used to go back to bed afterward.

I had daily contact with these free-living birds, which I distinguish from the domestic ducks which are stabled at night, and from the purely ornamental ducks which are penned. Inevitably, I began to learn where they spent the night, liked to loaf through the day, and something about their daily routine. What interested me particularly was that these semi-wild waterfowl discovered the times of feeding for the purely domestic species. This pointed to some sort of built-in clock, because they were usually waiting at the feeding place long before the domesticated species.

Surely the same rules might apply to the swans, I argued. They came at regular and specific times to be fed, or to keep us company. But if their clock was influenced by human intervention, what would happen if the human element was removed, and the swans were left to their own devices? Would they create a daily schedule for themselves, or would they just swim about, moving from place to place in an unplanned manner in search of food? The more I asked myself these questions, and tried to answer them from memory, the greater became my impatience for the return of the swans. I scanned the sky, listening for the familiar sound of the wings, looking across the ponds in search of missing white forms.

When Hans and Leda returned that year at the end of February, they received their usual welcome. If this experiment was to be a serious one, however, personal contact had to be eliminated or, at the very best, greatly reduced. I therefore decided to call them in for food only twice during a day: at 11 o'clock in the morning and after lunch. It was a difficult decision to take, but I wanted to leave the birds to their own devices as much as possible. What actually happened was that the swans soon began to show their own reluctance to turn wild. But because I did not feed them so often and no longer tried to establish regular contact each day, they eventually got the message and became slightly wild. They began to keep away from the house and from me except at the stated feeding times. My conscience weighed heavy; I felt as if I were betraying my friends by not feeding them as they were accustomed to being fed, and that I was guilty of a breach of hospitality. I decided that I would have to make amends as soon as I found out what I wanted to know.

Because I never go to bed early, I made up my mind to begin my observations at midnight, and to check the swans' positions every hour until about 10 o'clock in the morning. This is not quite so ambitious as it sounds, since I could make most of the observations (except the midnight and four A.M. checks), in complete comfort from various windows of the house, with or without the use of binoculars. As I had no intention of sitting up for more than one night, which I did in order to establish a complete pattern of routine, I established a system of random checks at selected hours of the night. By spreading this random sampling over a period of several weeks, I calculated that I would minimize the loss of sleep and any domestic uproar. In fact, my wife knows me only too well. She was inclined to shrug her shoulders when I got out of bed at strange hours, and put it down to eccentricity.

Under normal conditions, I found that the swans started the night on the west end of the chapel pond, but near the south bank. (See map on page x.) Here there is a floating island of reed that is well loved by both swans and ducks, under which the large carp like to lie. The feeding there must be good, because there are always plenty of birds there, espccially the wild mallard that come to visit us. The swans usually reached this spot during the late hours of the evening, and remained in its vicinity until some time after midnight. They then began their nightly move, traveling slowly along the south bank until it curves east to north. They fed along the fringes of reed, moved out to the center of the pond, back to the banks on the north side of the pond, or, by preference, to the southcast banks.

It is never completely dark here during the night. There are nights when it is so overcast that vision is exceedingly restricted, but complete darkness hardly exists with our open stretches of land. This made my observations relatively easy. I also discovered that as a general rule Hans and Leda spent a great part of their time either feeding along the banks or well offshore toward the center of the water area which they were occupying at the time, making it easier for me to spot them. I never saw them take to the land at night.

At two to two-thirty A.M. they were resting and feeding along the shallows near the dike that leads to the drawbridge. This is the dike (see photographs following page 114) from which adults and children from the nearby town come to feed both swans and ducks.

I discovered that if I spoke to the swans from this dike at night, they would come more or less immediately and swim about aimlessly in expectation of food. Otherwise, night conditions did not seem to affect them very much. They came to the familiar whooping call, or if I called them by name, as readily as they came by day. Even when I was thirty or forty yards away from them, they began to move in my direction, but they were normally slightly uncertain until they identified me by my voice. The one thing that upset them was the strong beam from a powerful flashlight. This confused them and they tried to get out of the beam into the darkness beyond.[35] If I held them in the beam and then called them, they would come toward me slowly and uncertainly, their swimming ragged and uneven; if I then switched off the light, they would at once swim normally in the direction of the call. Unlike the resting ducks that become upset and frightened by such a beam, and will even fly as a result of it touching them, the swans were no more upset than one would be oneself if blinded by the headlights of a car. Their eyes, once adjusted to the dim light of the night, may not be very able to readjust quickly to the strong light of a flashlight.

Some time between three and four A.M. the swans moved under the drawbridge into the ring moat proper. Although they were now opposite their normal loafing and preening place, they never came on land. They idled there for an hour or two, moving back and forth between it and the islet which is the turn of the circle into the east side of the ring.

They then began their journey around the ring moat

toward the north.[36] Between the hours of five and seven
A.M. they were busy in the shallows on the east bank,
directly opposite the house. They remained more or less
in the one spot because the feeding is good there, and it is
a favorite place of the geese. Surplus water flows into the
moat from the drainage system of the big meadow at this
point, and a little further along there is a ditch where, in
season, the frogs like to spawn.

The swans only played the game to a certain extent during the day. Although they had become wilder, it was impossible to divorce them completely from their habitual
reactions when they saw me or heard my voice. Consequently, the experiment became something of a farce
during daylight hours. Yet the swans did observe a daytime
routine, with the human element absorbed as part of it.
They waited on the dike until I came along to call them
for their morning feed. If I should chance to miss calling
them, or arrive late for any reason, they would swim across
the intervening water and present themselves at the door
of the back house, and wait there patiently until I came.

When called on the dike, they came with alacrity, the
pen invariably swimming ahead of the cob. This feed was
usually one of the wet feeds, so that they did not come out
of the water for it, but stood in the shallows. Afterward
they normally returned to the loafing place on the dike
for a long and luxurious preening session which lasted
until mid-day, when they vanished from sight, crossing
the second dike that separates the fishpond from the stream.

They then made their way downstream to the mill pond,
in readiness for the after lunch feed. When the weather is
hot, my wife and I like to enjoy our coffee after lunch in
the sun. Quite obviously we do not do this in winter and
spring, but the time for coffee is sacred to the swans and

they come along anyway. Despite their temporary wildness, they stayed around to keep us company, their alert and beady eyes fixed on our every movement.

When we disappeared, the swans either stayed around for a while, or went back to their loafing spot in front of the drawbridge. There they remained within easy call for the rest of the afternoon until ducks and geese came home to go to bed in their stables by the back courtyard. Everyone came along then: swans, geese, semi-wild ducks, domestic ducks, the lot. The swans would wait patiently until all others had been locked up. For them the day of human association had come to a close. Quietly they would make their way to the water once again, and, following the eastward side of the ring moat, swim and idle and feed their way back to the chapel pond, after spending plenty of time by the islet or near the drawbridge. By eight o'clock they were gone. A session on the mill pond, and at midnight we kept our rendezvous once more. The movement cycle was complete.

I ended all experiments as soon as Leda sat on her nest to lay her eggs. I wanted to get things back to normal, so that life with the swans could resume its gentle rhythm. I had satisfied my curiosity up to a point, and had certainly proved two things to my complete satisfaction. The night routine, undoubtedly the most successful part of the experiment, made me positive that the swans planned their cycle of movement by night. They fed and slept and idled all through the night, much as they did during the day, except that they did not come ashore to rest and preen. The second point that I discovered was that in spite of my attempts to reduce feeding, and therefore human interference, the swans were such creatures of habit that they would appear at accustomed places at accustomed times, whether called by name or not. In both instances, either by night or by day, their cycle of movement was both timed and directional. They began their movement around the pond and the moat at the south, worked their way to the north and then during the day worked their way back to the south, with stops, rests, preening periods and feedings at specific places and at specific times. Finally the swans very quickly became fully tame again, once I had decided to re-establish frequent contact. When Leda brought her new brood to the doorstep, I knew that we were back to normal once more.

The thing that made my studies of swans a bit different from most other people's was that I concentrated on an individual pair—something that I have already mentioned. Because of this, I very often asked myself if all swans behaved in the same way. I had little time to seek other swans and to make a comparative study of them, nor did I want to dig too deeply into the literature, because I was making my own observations and wanted to find out later if I had observed correctly, or if I had come to much the same conclusions as other people had done. Stupid or not, I didn't want to lean heavily on knowledge acquired by others.

Still, somewhere at the back of my mind, was this desire to compare at firsthand. I got my chance after the death of Leda the first, the "old" Leda, as I will call her. As soon as Hans returned with new mates, I had, in a sense, the ideal situation. I had a basis for comparison far superior to any that I might have had with any other pair observed on some river or lake. I had *exactly* the same terrain, I could reproduce *exactly* the same set of circumstances at any time that I wanted to do so, and in addition, one of the partners—the dominant one at that—was *exactly* the same as he had always been. So theoretically, the swans' way of life should be *exactly* the same as it had always been; or that is what I thought.

It was probably reasonable enough of me to expect that since all conditions were equal, or could at least be reproduced, Hans would fall into the old routine of life and that the new Leda would follow. But I miscalculated. I did not allow for individuality. I soon learned that the partnership in a swan's union is absolute, by which I mean that the partners seem to be equally responsible for decision-making.

I was to discover that there is a very wide gap between foreseeable and established acts of behavior; that is, between swans preening or engaging in triumph- and threat-displays, and sequences and patterns of behavior such as movement over the terrain or the choice of nesting sites. In fact, the daily way of life. Hans and the new Leda's way of life, and Hans and the old Leda's way of life differed in the most important single factor of a breeding swan's life: the ultimate nest site and therefore the ultimate territorial requirement of the breeding pair.

What I found out was that the size and boundaries of the swan's territory appear to be closely connected with the probable position of the ultimate nest, by which I mean the nest that is finally used. The daily cycle of movement is based on the position of the nest, even, as far as I could see, when the nest is not in use. Consequently, the whole of the study already described, together with the map entitled "A Day in the Life of a Swan," is only applicable to the Hans and old Leda combination.

The present Leda refused all of the nests offered to her, and in her first year here, 1970, decided on a nest on the little island in the middle of the carp pond (see map), situated between the fishpond and the furthest carp-breeding pond, not shown on the map. By this simple fact, she changed the whole of the territory, and the whole sequence of habitual movements of both herself and her mate, prior to, during and after the nesting. Except when called, Hans virtually vanished from the scene to become almost estranged and wild.

Because the swans remained so long with us at the end of 1970, the pen had become accustomed to us and no longer avoided us. The territory changed because, having had a whole new series of nests built for her by the cob, the pen ultimately selected one built on the dike between the fishpond and the ring moat, and was quite undisturbed when humans came near. Once again, the sequence of habitual movements changed, with both the cob and the pen coming readily to the feeding place by the door of the courtyard. In the meanwhile, the pen had learned, obviously from the example set her by Hans, that she had no need to fear either the humans on the place, or the dogs.

I think that the big lesson I learned was that the birds are highly individual and capable of influencing each other. At first, I didn't think this was the case, but now I have had every indication that this is so. The exciting thing was the transformation of Leda's whole character after she had learned from her mate. Certainly both first-hand experience and secondhand knowledge had long ago taught me that it is possible to tame wild creatures by introducing a tame one in their midst—a technique that I have often used with pheasants, and that the Burmese use with elephants. But I did not know that free-ranging creatures can be tamed in the same way.

I have fleetingly mentioned divorce among swans, and even this is not outside of our experience. After the disappearance of the old Leda, Hans came back with a young pen that was obviously capable of pairing, but not of breeding. When she failed to accept any of the nests that he built for her, he decided to get rid of her.[17] That gave me the chance to see an actual divorce in action.

The whole business was distinctly gradual. Hans became very sour at first, then quite ruthless during the later stages of the unhappy relationship. During the month of May 1969, he began to harry her, never leaving her a moment's peace. He would go for her with magnificent threat-displays, as though she were a strange swan invading his territory. Although he never attacked her as he would have attacked a stranger, he would bite her and drive her among the reeds. At last she took refuge behind the projecting branch of a half-sunken tree, near the causeway entrance between ring moat and chapel pond. There she lived off the generosity of the townspeople who came to feed the ducks, but Hans knew this, and he would come and drive her away, obviously attempting to starve her.

We were very sorry for the gentle little pen who was so tame that we often wondered if she was not one of our own swans from a brood of previous years, but we had no way of checking it since we had never ringed any of the birds. I have no doubt that she would still be with us had Hans waited for a year, but alas, she was too meek for her dazzling and aggressive old husband.

Notes and
a Bibliography

Notes

1. Ministry of Agriculture, Fisheries and Food.

2. O'Connor.

3. *Brauhaus:* Roughly translated, a brewhouse. It is believed that in olden days beer was probably brewed here for the estate workers, although there are no physical indications remaining today. The large building was also used as a bakery—the oven still exists and was used until 1959 and could be used tomorrow—as quarters for farm workers and for storage of grain, etc. Today it is mainly a granary with mill- and grain-drying units, with one room on the first floor kept for old Stephen who likes to spend his summers there. Pig sties, duck and geese stables and a slaughter room occupy the whole of the ground floor.

4. Johnsgard, citing Heinroth, describes vocalizations as "simple and fairly weak. They include a loud 'snore' and softer 'chir' . . ." (p. 27). In our experience, chin-lifting, accompanied by this soft "chir" is the highest form of friendly greeting. It is quite frequently used. The swans used to chir at the same time as chin-lift when we went to visit them in the stable, and this greeting as well as the soft hiss is frequently used when the birds are met for the first time during the day. They almost invariably chin-lift and call when they have been called and are swimming over the water toward the caller. There is another movement, a variation of chin-lifting, which is seldom used by them; the head is thrown up and back and shaken from side to side. This is strikingly similar to, but not nearly as abandoned and energetic as, the head-shaking and head-throwing movement used by the Canada geese when they have been called from some distance away and answer in their loud honking voices.

5. Delacour, p. 67.

6. The mute swan enjoys a staple diet of plant food, feeding mainly on water weeds, very occasionally eating some small invertebrates, frogs and fishes (Delacour, p. 66); which confirms H. E. Witherby et al., who mention that mute swans have been noted to eat "small frogs and toads, tadpoles, worms, freshwater Mollusca, occasionally small fish (*Alburnus*) and insects with their larvae" (p. 177). Both Hans and Leda were observed eating portions of quite large fish, of estimated weights from one quarter to one pound: carp, pike and perch—which had been entombed in the thick ice and had come up to the surface with the thaw. The bleached and already decaying carcasses were only partially eaten by the birds, who, by gripping a portion with the beak, shook their heads to and fro, until the small portion tore away from the carcass and was then consumed. It is impossible to estimate how much meat of this kind was eaten by the swans, or how many carcases were broached because of the number that were floating about. A few hundred fish had been suffocated in the ice that year. The swans have also eaten the long leaves of the water iris which they break off near the tuber—and eat as well. Leaves are often stripped from the willow trees that overhang the water, while grass near the preening sites, and in front of the house, is frequently taken. Supplementary food given to the swans has been described in the text.

7. Delacour, p. 65.

8. Foot-drying, a characteristic that it shares with the black swan, seems to be necessary to the mute swan. The birds may be seen swimming with one leg and foot drawn up out of the water, the foot spread out near the tail in order to dry the web. In order to dry the foot while swimming, the bird keels over quite substantially on to the opposite flank, to the foot that has to be dried, submerging it and a part of the folded wing. This can give the illusion that the drying leg and foot are resting on the back, though in fact the leg is extended backward and sideways on the flank. They will also dry the foot on land before bringing it forward to insert it under the feathers. This drying of the foot has also been seen with adult trumpeter swans (Banko, p. 121), but is seldom indulged in, other than by mute and black swans (Delacour, p. 66).

9. The birds are sociable to man and tame very readily. They are less friendly during their breeding season, occasionally becoming

aggressive toward man, but more frequently toward other waterfowl, although not necessarily all of the time. It was observed that there are aggressive days and aggressive times, the latter being usually between 10 A.M. and 12 noon, or between 3 P.M. and 6 P.M. Sometimes, aggressive periods would go on and off for a whole day, with, oddly enough, a break between 1 and 2 P.M. as though the swan "went to lunch." It is suggested, however, that this behavior may be peculiar to the particular cob and that aggression and time need not necessarily be linked.

10. There appear to be two tones of hissing: the first, hard and flat and coming from the back of the beak over a raised tongue; the second, rather softer, more like a gentle letting out of air. The first kind of hiss is usually accompanied by a display of aggression with the neck feathers ruffled and the wings slightly arched, the whole suggesting a warning to keep away. However, I have never seen this display followed up by a positive act that would indicate intention to attack, but rather by a shying away and a ducking of the head and neck, which are more indicative of fear or uncertainty than of anger. The second, gentler tone is more conversational and quite friendly, being mostly accompanied by a very brief ruffling of the neck feathers and a slight raising of the elbows which lasts only a second or so.

11. Young mute swans have two color phases, gray or white, which are evident in the chick from the time of hatching. The white phase is less common than the gray one, but becomes more frequent as one moves eastward across Europe. Adults of the white phase are characterized by their fleshy gray legs and feet, while the legs of the gray phase are black. The same color phases are noted among trumpeter swans in Yellowstone National Park, where over a period of four years, from 1937 to 1940, 13 per cent of the cygnets were those of the white phase. There is one other record of the phase occurring in the wild, outside of Yellowstone Park, on the Icehouse Reservoir, Idaho, in 1956 (Banko, p. 70). According to Hilprecht, the mute swan's white phase is only reported in captive birds, apparently as a result of inbreeding (pp. 107–8). This is possibly doubtful. The white phase also occurs among feral birds, as, for example, a flock in Rhode Island (Munro, Smith and Kupa, pp. 504–5), and among the feral birds that are the subject of this book. Munro et al., in the summary of their study, indicate that the gray and white color phase segregating the Rhode Island population studied was due to a single sex-linked

gene. The gray was dominant and the gene frequency of the recessive allele (white) was estimated to be .293. Delacour states that mixed broods sometimes occur (p. 65). In the case of Hans and Leda, mixed broods occurred invariably.

12. I am reasonably sure that the six birds that came flying were birds in passage, and that if we had not seduced them into staying by means of heavy feeding, they would never have remained of their own accord. It is more than probable that they were going to join some wintering flock, probably that on the river Lippe, and that the old birds would have disposed of their young there. In fact the whole of their lives was changed by being captured, pinioned, stabled and kept together for a whole winter. By the time they were let out again, they had experienced conditions that disturbed the natural rhythm of their lives. Firstly, the enforced holding together of the family unit under unnatural circumstances in the stable was the whole reason why the breeding pair had not driven off the brood of the previous year at the right time. Secondly, because one brood of the previous year was incapable of flight, and always would be, meant that after their release into the open, they were constrained to remain on what was to become the breeding territory—an intolerable situation as far as the breeding pair was concerned. Thirdly, because they were pinioned and therefore rendered temporarily flightless, they could not return to their old breeding territory, wherever that may have been, at the time that they normally would have. They had no choice but to adopt the new territory or not to breed at all. It was precisely this set of conditions that forced the breeding pair to act as they did. They had to dispose of the previous year's brood, and as soon as possible, by every and any means, even if it meant killing them, which they also tried to do in a half-hearted kind of way. The old birds were right up to a new breeding season at the time of their release, and at that time, we had thrown the whole course of their natural life sequence out of gear. It was not until the end of that breeding season that they were able to become normal again with the renewal of their power of flight. By that time they had accepted and adopted the new territory. The old one was forgotten.

13. Hans never was a significant killer. His technique was to frighten off by bold and sweeping dashes across the water. However, he has killed a number of other waterfowl, as a result of which all

unexplained deaths on the water tend to be laid at Hans' door; he has also tried to kill the original cygnets that came with him. The cob would partially launch himself into the air and catch the subject of his attack by the neck, just behind the skull, while attempting to mount on the victim's back. He would then attempt to press the head of the other swan under the surface of the water, and drown it. H. M. Swan Keeper, Mr. F. J. Turk, confirms this method of attack, but adds that the stronger cob "uses the wings as a lock" when on the opponent's back (1967, correspondence). I have never seen this since the cob was unable to get on the back of any of his strong children. I have seen Hans attacked in this way by a very strong Canada gander who caught the cob in a vice-like grip on the back and attempted to climb up. Ogilvie writes that "small numbers of birds are killed or severely injured in fighting other swans, usually during territorial disputes," and adds that a male swan is physically capable of killing another swan but that this is unlikely unless the attacked swan is unable to escape (p. 72).

14. Constant references are made to aggression and attack. Forms of defensive or offensive attack can be categorized under four headings. First: attack from the air when flying low over the water, or partially flying, where the beak is used in conjunction with the swan's momentum to deliver a killing punch at the back of the neck or spine, as described in this chapter. Second: attack on the water or partly above the water, with beak and wings; here the beak is the main offensive weapon but aided by the wings. There is an excellent example of this form of attack, given by Banko, of a trumpeter swan on a muskrat (pp. 105–6). Third: attack on land with the beak, and where that fails, with the wings which are used to deliver blows. This is defensive, the beak is used to stave off the attacker and when that fails the wings come into play (see the next chapter). Fourth: attempted drowning as detailed in note 13.

15. The swans were at too great a distance to observe accurately if the cob actually *fed* the pen, but she came down from her nest and joined in eating the leaves which he had carried up to the nest. Whether he had brought the leaves specifically for the pen or for himself is not known. Certainly no trace of fresh leaves was to be found in the nest or its vicinity when I subsequently went over to investigate some ten minutes later. I am therefore convinced that the leaves were meant as food rather than as additional nesting mate-

rial, especially since the local nests are always made of twigs and sticks.

16. On the subject of ménage-à-trois, Banko reports on one observation of his own involving three adult trumpeter swans with a brood of three cygnets. He also cites three others who mention this phenomenon: Low's two cases among mute swans, and one among trumpeters at Woburn Abbey; Dewar, who cites six cases from the literature and who personally observed a seventh; and Ellis' one, or possibly two instances among mute swans in English parks (p. 98). All of these birds were in captivity. The term "ménage-à-trois" was applied by Dr. Dewar, who defined its meaning thus: "As a label, ménage-à-trois is preferred to its synonym, bigamy, because ménage-à-trois means setting up an establishment, which bigamy does not necessarily do . . ." (Banko quoting Dewar, p. 98).

17. In his seven-year study of the pairing and breeding of mute swans, Minton deals with the subject in detail, and his findings give us cause to feel that the swan's reputation of mating fidelity is, on the whole, quite justified. Among his findings was "that 85% of paired breeders retained the same mate from year to year, if it was still alive." Nonbreeding pairs were less stable in their bond. Divorce was 3 per cent among breeding birds and 9 per cent among nonbreeders. Our cob, Hans, divorced the third mate that he brought back to the breeding territory after the presumed death of the original pen. During the month of April, after this pen had failed to accept any of the nests that he had partly built and offered to her and had consequently failed to lay any eggs, he slipped quietly away and abandoned the territory to her. She remained until late November, alone but for the company of the Canada geese with whom she kept company, ultimately flying off for good. The cob appeared the following season with a new pen.

18. The annual return of the swans depends upon the general weather conditions prevailing during the first quarter of a new year. Usually the more severe the weather, the longer the postponement of the return. Contradicting this is the fact that they have been known to return when there is still ice on the water, making it fairly reasonable to assume that their movement is influenced by some local condition, either shortage of food or bad weather, prevailing at the winter habitat, rather than by an expectation of better conditions with us.

19. A motion picture taken of the cob landing, although short and unsatisfactory, is worth mentioning because it shows the final act of landing in some detail, even though the detail may only be an isolated instance. Only many shots of a similar nature would show if what follows is a rule rather than an exception. At normal running speed, the film shows the bird drawing its wings to their normal position shortly after tobogganing begins after a flight. Projected at the slowest possible speed, the action changes. The bird lays its spread wings on the surface of the water on either side of it and appears to use them as a final brake or stabilizer, it is hard to tell which, after which it raises the wings and folds them into the normal position.

20. Perrins and Reynolds remind us that Heinroth states that about 25 per cent of the young mute swan's weight at hatching is made up from yolk sac: this is retained in the body cavity, and Heinroth records that the young swans can live off this for several days. They also mention a brood which Dr. Kear observed, and which for some reason could not be induced to feed, that survived until they were ten or eleven days old. Reynolds, in a study of swans around Oxfordshire, calculated the death rate in each week of life. This was highest in the second week (p. 80). It is noteworthy that of the large broods which we have had, we have only lost three cygnets as long as the broods were with us and that all of these losses may be accounted for by accidents.

21. It seems deserving of more than passing notice that rejected nests which have been offered by the cob to the pen are never more than partially complete and are abandoned relatively quickly. Responsible for my theory that these nests are begun with the intention of *exciting* the pen to nest, is the consistency with which this procedure has taken place year after year, before the establishment of, and building on, the final nesting site. Not only did this form of nest-building and rejection take place with the original Leda, but with two subsequent pens of that name, and was especially pronounced with the second Leda, who proved to be infertile. Only once in my experience was a suggested nest accepted by the pen as the ultimate nesting site, on a site often previously rejected by her although offered by the cob every year. In this nest, she laid her record clutch and had her record brood; a 100 per cent success. Subsequent troubles connected with the getting of the chicks up and down

the steep and slippery banks to the islet point to her superior instinct in nest site selection and nest management. Although it might
seem logical that the ultimate nesting site would be returned to in
the first place, it was always held in reserve until it was time for the
ultimate nest to be built, first partly by the cob to the stage at
which other nests were offered and rejected. However, the suggested
nest on the ultimate site was never rejected and the pen would
immediately join the cob in finishing it. What determined the moment of the cob's move to this site in order to build the ultimate
nest was impossible to establish. The cob followed the normal procedure with the second pen, repairing the nest on the islet, making
four excitation nests in a row, each about ten yards from the next,
and finally repairing the old ultimate nest. The pen proved to be
incapable of breeding. The third Leda accepted the third nest
offered, this being part-built on the islet on the carp pond and
resulting in the establishment of a totally different territory for the
1970 breeding season.

22. Availability of material determines the shape and size of the
nest. The Abbotsbury swans, also mute swans, breed colonially and
make a nest which appears to be smaller in circumference and deeper
at the center than that made by our breeding pair. Since ours nest
under trees and surrounded in part by bushes, there is always a
lavish supply of material from which to build the nest. The outside
is fortified with large, heavy sticks or pieces of driftwood found in
the immediate vicinity, or transported to the site by the cob. These
are laid on top of each other so that they roughly interlock, after
which the nest is complete. Nests measured seem to average 160
centimeters in diameter, about 20 centimeters at the central point of
depth where the eggs are laid, and are roughly 30 centimeters high
at the perimeter. Nests cut in half after the brood had finished with
them showed a central depth of 15 centimeters to the ground, the
material having been compressed and partly become a kind of soft
compost.

23. Our swans were a highly successful breeding pair. Clutch sizes
increased after the first two years from seven to eight and eleven has
been the highest. Perrins and Reynolds, in their study of birds in
the Oxford area, give a figure of 6.0 as the mean clutch size, citing
Eltringham and Campbell, who also give figures of 6.0 respectively.
In table 11 they give clutch sizes varying from 1 to 11 for individuals,

with the largest clutch sizes—over a period of three years—of 9, 10 and 11 all laid by the same female, who raised 5, 8 and 8 respectively in the brood stage (p. 80). Our female laid 48 eggs in a period of six breeding seasons, of which 5 were fertile but did not hatch, and 4 were lost by human predation, the broken eggs and downy young being found near the river as the eggs were robbed a day or two before hatching. She raised the balance of 39 successfully, with one exception—a four-week-old chick found dead and bloodied on the second preening site. Leda's large clutches and her success in rearing were probably due to her ideal nesting sites, which were above flood level, plentiful in natural food and had no animal predation.

24. Back-carrying by the temperate-breeding swans, all of which may carry their young when swimming, partly replaces brooding which takes place entirely on land in the northern, mostly arctic-breeding species, *C. cygnus* (including *buccinator*) and *C. columbianus* (including *bewickii*) (Johnsgard and Kear, p. 94). Back-carrying is engaged in during the first two weeks of life, but apparently varies, F. J. Turk having observed swans on the Thames carrying their young in this way up to six weeks of age. The number carried may vary from three to four, according to Turk, though I have seen up to five (correspondence, 1967). Both parents may engage in carrying, but I have never observed it.

25. Foot-warming seems to be as essential as foot-drying (see note 8), and frequently takes place immediately after the latter, the swan tucking away the dried foot into the plumage of the flank. The body position on the water is the same as that adopted when foot-drying. When resting on land, the swan leans over on its flank and draws the foot into the plumage of the flank that is held uppermost. The photograph referred to in the text, of a flying trumpeter swan warming its feet in flight, may be found in Banko's book on that species (p. 74).

26. Johnsgard and Kear, Figure 8, pp. 97–8.

27. *All* feathers of the wing are important in flight. However, in order to make the explanation simpler for the nonexpert, I have confined my remarks to the flight feathers and, also for the sake of simplicity, have avoided mention of the coverts, their classification and disposition. I have retained the term "tertiaries" for those who may refer to older textbooks, and have described them as exten-

sions of the secondaries, instead of modified secondaries. Those who wish to go more deeply into the disposition of wing feathers are advised to refer to textbooks.

28. Although this photograph is of trumpeter, not mute swans, it was chosen not alone because of its beauty, but also because it best explains the text. It was taken at the Red Rocks National Wildlife Refuge, Montana, by Winston E. Banko.

29. "Photographs show a peculiar path followed by a bird's wings through the air amounting almost to a complete figure of eight, with wings swept *forward* at the bottom of the downstroke. . . . The swept-forward position at the end of the downstroke is caused by the 'propellering' tips dragging the wings forward and ahead of the body. As the wings are raised they therefore travel somewhat backward as well as upward to get to the up position" (Gibbs-Smith). What happens here is that the emarginated primaries twist as the force of the air presses on the rear vane—with the downbeat of the wing—and become little propellers that produce thrust.

30. The use of a "training whip" as an extension of the hand in the dressage of young dogs to the lead is independent of the Baroness Beck's book or of her methods, and is therefore not included in the text of her book. Her system was, and still is, used by us in the training of the dogs to the gun. It was we who devised the method of training with the whip and found it especially useful in communicating with the young dog, wordlessly but by light pressures, when leading it on crowded town pavements and training it to traffic. In such situations it becomes an extension of the hand and obviates the need of jerking on the lead or of giving vocal commands.

31. Minton lists "flying into objects" as the "major cause of death" among mute swans, and mentions that man places "an ever increasing number of obstacles such as electricity wires (so frequently sited in river valleys) in the way of flying birds" (p. 49). Dealing with causes of death in the same species, Ogilvie gives a table of causes of death, in which death by flying into wires accounts for by far the greatest number in the table: 464 deaths of swans of all ages from a total of 1,051 deaths from all causes given in his study. He writes that "the evidence suggests that there is no learning by Mute Swans to avoid wires as they get older. . . . The deaths from hitting overhead wires

and other obstacles, show no decline with increasing age" (p. 70). Since different sets of high pylons carrying mult-wires cut through this estate and take a northwest to southeast direction, and since other, lower wire complexes cover the industrial neighborhood within our swans' flying range, it is not beyond probability that the original pen met her death from this cause.

32. Delacour, p. 67.

33. Johnsgard, p. 25.

34. Mute swans stretch frequently and with great relish. At some-time or other during the preening session, they enjoy a good stretch of wings, legs and neck. The stretching downward and outward of one wing and leg is frequently simultaneous. The birds also stretch when in prone positions. They have been observed to stretch neck and legs at the same time, the bird resting on its belly all the while; both legs are stretched back toward the tail at the same moment while the neck is stretched parallel to the ground, but with a slight crook in it. Another favorite moment to stretch is when the swan is on its side, warming a foot as described in note 25, with a foot buried in the flank plumage. A leg and foot will suddenly be stretched out and quickly covered by a stretching wing. Often the birds will roll over onto the other side and repeat the same stretch. A thorough wagging of the tail follows most of these stretching operations. Standing really erect, with the beak pointing to the sky, the bird feather-shakes and flaps its wings vigorously at the end of most preening sessions.

35. Waterfowl don't like being caught by the beam from a flash-light, and most of the ducks, including the wild mallard which will take flight on being illuminated, are much troubled by it. It is differ-ent when a stretch of water is illuminated at night. The Bewick swans at Slimbridge do not appear to be troubled by the illumina-tion of Swan Lake there, but of course the light covers the whole of the water area, and it is this that makes the difference.

36. Two things emerged from this particular study. First, all move-ments appeared to be fairly closely linked to time. If one wished to find the swans at a particular *time,* all that one had to do was to go to a specific *place.* Only on very rare occasions did this prove diffi-cult. Even their association with humans—if they were not called over during the day, which was not done during the experiment—

was time-linked and conditioned by habit. The second thing that emerged was that the movements were habitual in the consistency of their direction. The twenty-four hour movement began southwest then south, east, north, east and north again, and then north, west, south, west to southwest, after daylight. The situation where the nocturnal movement might have been reversed, that is, beginning north, west, etc., never did arise. Why the movement pattern took the direction that it did was probably more due to noise and disturbance than to feeding. It has to be remembered that the public road runs southwest and east of the chapel pond and that the moat is surrounded by meadow on the east side once the chapel pond has been left, while the fishponds and the north side of the moat are completely free of traffic noise disturbance. After midnight the road is relatively quiet with only the occasional car passing, and most of the wild mallard will drop in to spend the night there in the company of the few semi-wild ducks that are always there—whose territory it is. It is conceivable that noise played a role in the formation of the habit. It might be argued that if this is the case, the selection of the nesting site on the chapel pond–mill pond dike is an odd one since it is only thirty yards or so from the road, but it has to be remembered that topographically it is one of the best sites available because of the all round vision point of view.

A Bibliography

Aymar, G. C. *Bird Flight.* Garden City, N.Y.: Garden City Publishing Co., Inc., 1938.

Banko, Winston E. *The Trumpeter Swan.* North American Fauna, No. 63: United States Fish and Wildlife Service, April 1963.

Beck, Baroness Elizabeth. *Train Your Own Labrador.* London: Country Life Ltd., 1965.

Delacour, Jean. *The Waterfowl of the World.* Vol. 1. London: Country Life Ltd., 1954.

———— *Ducks and Geese.* Ministry of Agriculture, Fisheries and Food, Bulletin No. 70: Her Majesty's Stationery Office, 1967.

Gibbs-Smith, C. H. *Aviation.* London Science Museum: Her Majesty's Stationery Office, 1967.

Hilprecht, Alfred. *Hockerschwan, Singschwan, Zwergschwan.* Wittenberg Lutherstadt: A. Zimmsen Verlag, 1956.

Johnsgard, Paul A. *Handbook of Waterfowl Behavior.* Ithaca, New York: Cornell University Press, 1965.

Johnsgard, Paul A.; and Kear, Janet. "A Review of Parental Carrying of Young by Waterfowl." *The Living Bird,* Vol. VII, October 1968.

Minton, C. D. T. *Pairing and Breeding of Mute Swans.* Wildfowl, No. 19. Slimbridge, England: Wildfowl Trust, 1968.

Munro, R. E.; Smith, L. T.; and Kupa, J. J. "The Genetic Basis of Colour Difference Observed in the Mute Swan (*Cygnus olor*)." *Auk,* Vol. 85, July 1968.

A Bibliography

O'Connor, Ulick. *The Times I've Seen, Oliver St. John Gogarty.* New York: Ivan Obolensky, 1963.

Ogilvie, M. A. *Population Changes and Mortality of the Mute Swan in Britain.* Wildfowl, 18th Annual Report. Slimbridge, England: Wildfowl Trust, 1965–6.

Perrins, C. M.; and Reynolds, C. M. *A Preliminary Study of the Mute Swan ("Cygnus olor").* Wildfowl, 18th Annual Report. Slimbridge, England: Wildfowl Trust, 1965–6.

Witherby, Harry Forbes; Jourdain, Francis Charles Robert; Ticehurst, N. E.; Tucker, B. W. *The Handbook of British Birds.* London: F. H. & G. Witherby, 1939.

A NOTE ON THE TYPE

The text of this book has been set on the Linotype in a type-face called "Baskerville." The face is a facsimile reproduction of types cast from molds made for John Baskerville (1706–1775) from his designs. The punches for the revived Linotype Baskerville were cut under the supervision of the English printer George W. Jones. John Baskerville's original face was one of the forerunners of the type-style known as "modern face" to printers: a "modern" of the period A.D. 1800.

The typography and the binding design are by Christine Aulicino. The book was composed, printed, and bound by H. Wolff Book Mfg. Co., New York, N.Y.